English Fiction of the Early Modern Period 1890–1940

Longman Literature in English Series

**General Editors: David Carroll and Michael Wheeler
University of Lancaster**

For a complete list of titles see pages viii and ix

English Fiction
of the Early
Modern Period
1890–1940

Douglas Hewitt

Longman

London and New York

Longman Group UK Limited,
Longman House, Burnt Mill, Harlow,
Essex CM20 2JE, England
and Associated Companies throughout the world.

*Published in the United States of America
by Longman Inc., New York*

© Longman Group UK Limited 1988

First published 1988

BRITISH LIBRARY CATALOGUING IN PUBLICATION DATA
Hewitt, Douglas
   English fiction of the early modern period,
   1890–1940. — (Longman Literature in English
   series).
   1. English fiction — 20th century — History and
   criticism
   I. Title
   823'.912'09   PR881
ISBN 0-582-49285-8 CSD
ISBN 0-582-49284-X PPR

LIBRARY OF CONGRESS CATALOGING IN PUBLICATION DATA
Hewitt, Douglas John, 1920–
   English fiction of the early modern period
1890–1940/Douglas Hewitt.
   p.   cm. – (Longman literature in English series)
   Bibliography: p.
   Includes index.
   ISBN 0-582-49285-8.   ISBN 0-582-49284-X
   (pbk.)
   1. English fiction – 20th century – History and
criticism. 2. Modernism (Literature) – Great Britain.
3. English fiction – 20th century – History and
criticism.   I. Title.   II. Series.
PR888.M63H48 1988
823'.8'091 – dc 19   87-32996
                                          CIP

Set in Linotron 202 9½/11pt Bembo

Produced by Longman Singapore Publishers (Pte) Ltd.
Printed in Singapore

Contents

Editors' Preface

The multi-volume Longman Literature in English Series provides students of literature with a critical introduction to the major genres in their historical and cultural context. Each volume gives a coherent account of a clearly defined area, and the series, when complete, will offer a practical and comprehensive guide to literature written in English from Anglo-Saxon times to the present. The aim of the series as a whole is to show that the most valuable and stimulating approach to literature is that based upon an awareness of the relations between literary forms and their historical context. Thus the areas covered by most of the separate volumes are defined by period and genre. Each volume offers new informed ways of reading literary works, and provides guidance to further reading in an extensive reference section.

As well as studies on all periods of English and American literature, the series includes books on criticism and literary theory, and on the intellectual and cultural context. A comprehensive series of this kind must of course include other literature written in English, and therefore a group of volumes deals with Irish and Scottish literature, and the literatures of India, Africa, the Caribbean, Australia, and Canada. The forty-seven volumes of the series cover the following areas: pre-Renaissance English Literature, English Poetry, English Drama, English Fiction, English Prose, Criticism and Literary Theory, Intellectual and Cultural Context, American Literature, Other Literatures in English.

David Carroll
Michael Wheeler

Longman Literature in English Series
General Editors: David Carroll and Michael Wheeler
University of Lancaster

Pre-Renaissance English Literature

* ★ English Literature before Chaucer *Michael Swanton*
* English Literature in the Age of Chaucer
* ★ English Medieval Romance *W. R. J. Barron*

English Poetry

* ★ English Poetry of the Sixteenth Century *Gary Waller*
* ★ English Poetry of the Seventeenth Century *George Parfitt*
* English Poetry of the Eighteenth Century 1700–1789
* ★ English Poetry of the Romantic Period 1789–1830 *J. R. Watson*
* ★ English Poetry of the Victorian Period 1830–1890 *Bernard Richards*
* English Poetry of the Early Modern Period 1890–1940
* English Poetry since 1940

English Drama

English Drama before Shakespeare
* ★ English Drama: Shakespeare to the Restoration, 1590–1660
  Alexander Leggatt
* ★ English Drama: Restoration and Eighteenth Century, 1660–1789
  Richard W. Bevis
  English Drama: Romantic and Victorian, 1789–1890
  English Drama of the Early Modern Period, 1890–1940
  English Drama since 1940

English Fiction

* ★ English Fiction of the Eighteenth Century 1700–1789 *Clive T. Probyn*
* ★ English Fiction of the Romantic Period 1789–1830 *Gary Kelly*
* ★ English Fiction of the Victorian Period 1830–1890 *Michael Wheeler*
* ★ English Fiction of the Early Modern Period 1890–1940 *Douglas Hewitt*
  English Fiction since 1940

English Prose

English Prose of the Renaissance 1550–1700
English Prose of the Eighteenth Century
English Prose of the Nineteenth Century

Criticism and Literary Theory

Criticism and Literary Theory from Sidney to Johnson
Criticism and Literary Theory from Wordsworth to Arnold
Criticism and Literary Theory from 1890 to the Present

The Intellectual and Cultural Context

The Sixteenth Century
★ The Seventeenth Century, 1603–1700 *Graham Parry*
★ The Eighteenth Century, 1700–1789 *James Sambrook*
The Romantic Period, 1789–1830
The Victorian Period, 1830–1890
The Twentieth Century: 1890 to the Present

American Literature

American Literature before 1880
American Poetry of the Twentieth Century
American Drama of the Twentieth Century
★ American Fiction 1865–1940 *Brian Lee*
American Fiction since 1940
Twentieth-Century America

Other Literatures

Irish Literature since 1800
Scottish Literature since 1700

Australian Literature
Indian Literature in English
African Literature in English: East and West
Southern African Literature in English
Caribbean Literature in English
★ Canadian Literature in English *W. J. Keith*

★ *Already published*

Author's Preface

The period from 1890 to 1940 saw the publication of a very large number of good novels, including some of the greatest in the language. The period since then has seen the publication of immense quantities of criticism directed towards those novels. A comprehensive study of even one of the major novelists – Conrad, say, or Joyce or Lawrence – must be the work of years. What, then, do I hope to do in one study of the fiction of those fifty years? The answer is obvious enough: provide an introduction. What is not so obvious is what sort of introduction. This book is not offered as a survey of fiction; if it mentioned every novel which is still worth reading it would become a slimly annotated bibliography, of which there are a number, some of which I recommend on pages 243–44. It is not an attempt to classify novelists into schools or groups; there are obviously writers whom it is sensible to compare with one another, but one of the few generalizations which I would make about fiction of this period is that it was extraordinarily varied and cannot be fitted into categories. It is not a digest of critical thinking about the period; though I discuss different critical opinions about, say, Joyce and Bennett, I am sure that our starting point must be a close engagement with specific texts. What I do offer, then, is detailed discussion of individual novels and, on the basis of this, some account of the novelists' work in general and an introduction to certain general issues which emerge from the books. Most of the chapters concentrate on individual novelists; chapters 6, 9 and 11 tackle the general matters.

The book is not arranged chronologically because I do not believe that – except in some very obvious ways – writers as astonishingly different from one another as Hardy, Conrad and Joyce (not to mention Kipling, Lawrence and Compton-Burnett) can usefully be considered as parts of a developing tradition. I have chosen instead to deal with major works by a number of writers who seem to have some preoccupations in common and to compare and contrast them. Thus, for example, Conrad, Kipling and Forster were all preoccupied by questions of power and dominance; I discuss them one after another and follow this with a chapter which ruminates about how politics has been treated in this period by various writers and in various modes. Arnold Bennett and Virginia Woolf argued about how the novel could do justice to modern consciousness and this has become a famous set-piece battle in the war about 'Modernism'. Accordingly I follow discussions of their works with a chapter on this general issue. A consideration of Joyce leads naturally to thoughts about changes in the reading public and the critical tradition, and to this I devote a chapter.

I particularly wish to draw attention to the Bibliographies. There are a number of writers whom I have not found room to discuss but whom others would wish included. The Author Bibliographies are not confined to the novelists whom I have chosen and each gives summary information about the writer's life and works and suggests useful scholarly and critical studies. There are also six general bibliographies concerned with (i) historical and political background; (ii) cultural background; (iii) general studies of fiction; (iv) general studies of literature, 1890–1940; (v) studies of fiction in this period; (vi) bibliographies and editions. From time to time in the text I draw attention to some of these works, but I would recommend readers to refer to them throughout. They include numerous works which take a different line from my own and should continue the arguments which this book is intended to start.

Who are these readers of whom I speak? Primarily I think of them as the common readers with whom Dr. Johnson rejoiced to concur, but a large number of them now will be students in higher education, in universities, polytechnics, extra-mural classes. Since I have formed many of my ideas in the process of teaching and discussing with them I have obviously had them in mind.

The dates given for books in the text, footnotes and bibliographies are, unless specifically stated otherwise, for first publication in volume form. Place of publication, except for periodicals, is, unless otherwise stated, London. References to specific passages in novels are by chapter numbers in parentheses, e.g. (14), or, where appropriate by book and chapter number, e.g. (iv. 7). Raised numerals in the text refer to the notes at the end of each chapter.

I began writing this book during a period of sabbatical leave, for which I would like to thank the Department for External Studies of Oxford University. For the rest of the time that I was working on it I was teaching students of that Department, undergraduates of Pembroke College and various graduate students at Oxford. To them all I owe a debt. Like all critical studies this is a work of co-operation. I have learned from discussions with my students, with friends and with colleagues and I thank them all for what they have contributed. There are also a few more specific debts for which I wish to give thanks: to my editor, Michael Wheeler, for his patience; to my colleague, Lawrence Goldman, for historical advice; to Angie Sandham for typing and good humour and frequent exhortations to relax; above all to my wife for all those arguments about early modern literature, at the end of which, I think, she agrees with much of what is in this book. To her it is rightly dedicated.

D. H.
December 1987

For Karen

Chapter 1
Introduction

In 1890 Queen Victoria still had a decade to reign and Gladstone had not yet formed his last administration; the internal combustion engine was a novelty and the aeroplane was not to be invented for another thirteen years. In 1940 Winston Churchill formed his National Government, British forces were evacuated from Dunkirk, and London was heavily bombed; penicillin was developed and work started on the giant cyclotron at Berkeley. In 1890 Thomas Hardy, who had been born ten years before Wordsworth's death, had not yet published *Tess of the d'Urbervilles*; in 1940 Graham Greene, who is still writing, published *The Power and the Glory*.

All ages doubtless seem to be moving fast to those who are living in them but the transformation in this half-century from the late Victorian world to one recognizably like our own was vertiginous.[1] We ask, inevitably, whether and in what ways these immense changes were reflected in the literature of the period. Can we detect a new literary era akin to that brought about by the technological and political change? Epochs are normally named retrospectively; only in parodies of Hollywood epics do we hear such stirring cries as 'Forward, Men of the Middle Ages!', but in the early years of this century various writers were sure that they were 'Modernists' and a great deal of criticism has been directed towards the question of what is the nature of modern literature, with the tacit assumption that some generalizations will be possible.

It is natural to seek to relate literary works to the society in and for which they are written and to do so in a way which suggests a coherent line of development. This has seemed particularly important for some writers and critics over the last century, understandably enough in the case of Marxist critics, for a method of analysis which claims omnicompetence must of necessity include the arts in its explanations. But this tendency has not been confined to Marxists; T. S. Eliot's description of *Ulysses* as based upon a myth so as to give some shape to 'the panorama of futility which is the modern world', Virginia Woolf's statement that 'in 1910 human nature changed' and that the writer's task was to do justice to this change, do not merely suggest that individual works may illuminate some aspect of the life of a community or deal with social changes which we can all observe; they postulate a *Zeitgeist* which infuses a whole society and to which great works of literature bear witness.

There are a number of reasons for such a belief. Apart from those who accept Marxism it seems likely that the possibility of such a comprehensive conceptual framework has attracted even those who oppose this particular system. The great expansion of literary studies as an academic discipline inevitably leads to a desire on the part of those who practise it to elevate their subject-matter to an index of social change or, in some cases, the moral health of a society. Moreover, despite the attacks on Romanticism which accompanied the proclamations of such influential theorists as T. S. Eliot, the assumptions of Romanticism have remained strong and these take much more kindly than do, say, the assumptions of the eighteenth century, to the concept of great writers as, in Shelley's noble words, 'the unacknowledged legislators of mankind'. Pope might have thought of himself as speaking for the wits or Fielding as being the voice of the sound country party; only with the rise of Romanticism could a writer think that he was speaking for Man.

There has been no shortage of socio-literary accounts of the development of modern literature and Modernism in general, and there are a number of well-established schools of thought. I would refer readers to the Bibliography and I discuss the matter further in Chapter 9. But some of the assumptions are so pervasive that it seems necessary to refer briefly to them in this Introduction.

The most prevalent line of thought goes roughly thus. Between 1890 and 1940 there were immense and often catastrophic shifts of power, both between countries and within them, and these were accompanied not only by much physical suffering but also by a breakdown of assumptions about continuity and stability. For some this represented new hope but for many it was profoundly distressing. The speed of technological change was so great as sometimes to suggest that it had a life of its own, beyond human control (though to others it suggested rather that control over nature by man which Bacon had preached 300 years before). In the sphere of ideas such revolutionary theories as those of Freud changed our conceptions of human nature and of the assumed rationality and knowableness of the human personality. In the arts, the argument goes on, this was reflected in works which broke sharply with the conventions, both of technique and subject-matter, of the past; much of the art of the period was marked by disjunction, fragmentariness, the denial of logic, and the breaking of previously assumed patterns of response. Only such an age could have produced Picasso, Joyce, the Surrealists, Eliot, the Expressionists, and serial music. This Modernist movement is, as the names suggest, to be found in all the arts and it is international in scope.

Such generalizations are inevitably made in large terms, jump about a good deal in time and space, and are most convincing when viewed from a distance. To say this is not to imply that they are necessarily false or shallow. It is the nature of generalizations to be general. The problems arise when we try to fit a number of highly individualistic writers within them, or when we try to answer such questions as whether they have distorted our judgement of some novelists, or why, from about 1930 onwards, the influences seem to have ceased to operate within most English fiction. I shall revert to these specific points in later chapters.

For the moment I wish to consider a few factors which ought to be in our minds when we think about the relationship between literature and society. Mostly we have to mediate between extremes. It is not difficult to achieve an eye-catching *tour d'horizon* which makes enough connections to impress us with its plausibility but which ignores all those parts of the literary and historical scene which do not fit; one incidental effect of this is that English fiction in this period seems to be rather peripheral, even at times provincial. It is equally easy to make generalizations impossible by demanding such proofs of causality as cannot be given so that we end with the conclusion that, each book being unique, no general statements can be valid. In an attempt to make possible some middle position I set out here some reflections which bear upon the criteria of relevance for any generalizations which we may want to make.

Any choice of a starting-point for a development is arbitrary; in particular we must resist any suggestion that there existed a stable situation which was broken by 'modern' developments. Individual countries may have periods of relative stability, but if Modernism is taken as an international movement, we have to remember that famine, wars, revolutions, pogroms, broke out in various places in Europe throughout the nineteenth century and, indeed, earlier; a conception of a period of order rudely disrupted is fallacious. The same is true of ideas; Freud is certainly of importance in helping to change conceptions of personality and responsibility, but the impact of Darwin's *Origin of Species* (1859) was very quickly felt and we can, if we wish, trace much earlier assaults on orthodoxy – Schopenhauer's *The World as Will and Idea*, for example, appeared in 1819.

But to say that an influence was quickly felt can mean only that it was felt by some. The permeation of ideas is a very complex matter, moving very fast in some places and very slowly in others. Moreover people, including writers, do not always acquire their ideas directly from their originators. Ideas, often partial and distorted, filter down through many channels. The influence of Schopenhauer on Conrad has been much discussed, but Zdzisław Najder, in his *Joseph Conrad: A Chronicle*, shows beyond doubt that many of Conrad's most Schopenhauerian utterances can actually be traced to Anatole France. If we note that Hardy was at the suggestible age of nineteen when Darwin's great work was published it should not necessarily be because we think that he read it (though he claimed to have done so) but because some of the basic ideas in it were likely to have filtered down, diluted and contaminated and possibly misunderstood, to Hardy and those with whom he talked. Not all Marxists have read Marx and an actual reading of Freud might inhibit Freudian generalizations.

In mentioning Hardy's formative youth I am suggesting that most people form their ideas and attitudes fairly early in life. They may not ossify thereafter but their general outlook and assumptions are usually set. This means that for the writers with whom I shall be concerned in this study the currents of thought most likely to have influenced them were those which were circulating long before their major works were published. This is well shown in *D. H. Lawrence: A Personal Record* by E. T. (Jessie Chambers). She gives an account of what books excited Lawrence when he was a young man, sometimes to agreement and sometimes to resistance, and we observe him arguing about and annotating not only such recent works as Haeckel's *The Riddle of the Universe* (1899) and William James's *The Varieties of Religious Experience* (1902) but also Thoreau's *Walden* (1854), Carlyle's *Sartor Resartus* (1833), and Locke's *Essay Concerning Human Understanding* (1690), together with large numbers of ephemeral works from which he took what he wanted at the time.

We should also beware of producing a canon which allows tendentious circular arguing. In choosing which writers to discuss we are all, of course, engaged in producing a canon. I am well aware that there are many minor interesting writers whom I shall not have time to discuss in this book (Richard Aldington's *Death of a Hero*, 1929, and Antonia White's *Frost in May*, 1933, come to mind at once) but the kind of canon which I have in mind is that which is created by the adoption of a theory. If, for example, we become convinced from our reading of both serious writers and best sellers that there is an appalling gap between the two and if we relate this to the rise of the popular press and popular magazines in response to the coming of universal elementary education in this country we may come to believe that there has been a catastrophic lowering of general human standards. One effect of this is to make us overvalue the evidential significance of certain writers who fit in with the generalization and to play down those who do not; the obstinate fact, for example, that Bennett's *Old*

Wives' Tale was immensely popular is dismissed because Bennett is not taken with the seriousness which he deserves, while some of D. H. Lawrence's more dubious utterances about the spiritual state of modern man are taken as self-evident truths. The selective choice of works is then fed back into the argument via the assumption that our literary tastes are an adequate guide to our moral and emotional lives to demonstrate the impoverishment of feeling among the mass of the golden age. I discuss this tendency in Chapter 11.

But though such factors as these convince me that any overarching scheme which achieves a tidy fit between literature and society is bound to be dubious yet obviously the writers were affected by the great changes of the half-century, though they responded to them in different ways.

Inevitably they were influenced by the political forces and, more strikingly, they were aware of this influence. Our lives have always been largely controlled by economic and political realities, and this is true whether we realize it or not. The structure of village society of which Jane Austen wrote was determined by Great Britain's position as a trading nation and by continuing conflicts between different groups within society. But it was possible to be an intelligent and sensitive observer and not to show any awareness of this. By the period with which I am dealing this unawareness was no longer possible except for the stupid or the deliberately blinkered.

The shifts of power within society were of a kind which could not be ignored, though attempts to come to terms with them in fiction often seem inadequate. Forster's Leonard Bast, whom he sees as the progenitor of those who will inherit the country, is far from convincing and it is hard not to feel that Virginia Woolf's Charles Tansley is seen by her as a Jude the Obscure who has been let in. One of the most sustained attempts in fiction to diagnose the effects of industrial change is in the works of Lawrence, though it is, in my opinion, the weakest part of his work.

The one catastrophic happening from which few escaped was, of course, the Great War (as it was called until after the end of the period of this study), though we should remember that James Joyce, a refugee in Zurich, shows little sign of having been affected by the disaster. There are no war novelists of the same significance as some of the poets, though Richard Aldington's *Death of a Hero* (1929), R. H. Mottram's *The Spanish Farm* (1924), Frederic Manning's *Her Privates We* (1930) and Ford Madox Ford's Tietjens tetralogy (1924–28) are not negligible. Moreover an awareness of the recent bloodletting lies behind much of Lawrence's later work and Virginia Woolf's *Mrs. Dalloway* (1925).

But, partly because of the chances of birthplace and job, the political aspect which is most treated by the great novelists is the impact of imperialism. By 1890 Great Britain was at the height of its imperial power and the arguments for and against imperialism were widespread; hardly a year passed between 1890 and 1910 without either the annexation of territory or a colonial war, though the Boer War of 1899–1902 was the only one which much affected the general public. Conrad, Kipling, and Forster all see the imperial situation and colonialism as central political facts, as do, a little later, George Orwell and Joyce Cary. In discussing their works I shall not only deal with their approach to imperialism as such but also the implications about class and national identity which are inherent in it.

Changes in fundamental belief are as important as political changes and it is generally agreed that belief in orthodox Christianity was declining, especially among the educated.[2] The causes of this were manifold. The specific assault of science on what were thought of as necessary doctrines was perhaps the most obvious and here the most powerful cause of scandal was the effect of the ideas of Darwin and other biologists on the concept of man as a special creation. Such anthropological studies as those of J. G. Fraser, whose *The Golden Bough* appeared from 1890 onwards, encouraged a relativist attitude towards the claims of one unique religion. The general diffusion of the concepts of positivism and other philosophies hostile to Christianity made a large effect, though no doubt often at second and third hand.

In our period some writers, such as Joyce, record the struggle for emancipation from orthodoxy; some, like Bennett, take the decline of religion for granted; some search angrily or, in Forster's phrase, 'wistfully' for something to take its place. Of these last the most striking is Lawrence, though I hope to show that Virginia Woolf as well as Forster is a sceptic with a sense of loss.

Linked with this loss of religious certainty goes a feeling that social, familial stability has been weakened, not merely in such obvious matters as changes in sexual mores and standards of decorum and in relationships between parents and children, but in larger and more impalpable ways. This is at the heart of some of the large generalizations which I have previously mentioned and of which I am dubious. But it is clear that during this period the novel shows in the hands of many of its practitioners a tendency to move away from supposedly objective representations of social life towards the inner experiences of the characters, and there is an increasing tendency for the novel to be left in suspense at its conclusion as if to assert the impossibility of the stable resolution which is normal in earlier fiction. We find novels in this period of which this is not true, just as we find earlier works which have some of these 'modern' characteristics, but there are enough which fit the generalization to suggest that the point is worth exploring. There is one very obvious correlation – that between theories of the mind which reach their culmination in the work of Freud and his associates and the attempt on the part of some writers to do justice to irrational and unconscious elements of personality by means of the technique which is commonly called the 'stream of consciousness'.

Concern with this large and impalpable area of modern consciousness will not be confined to discussion of any one writer or group, but some of its implications for the doctrines of 'Modernism' are explored in Chapter 9 on Virginia Woolf's contest with Arnold Bennett, since this has so often been taken as a *locus classicus* of Modernist criticism and so much used by those who have held that modern consciousness is in some ways strikingly different from earlier ways of looking at the world and that new forms alone can represent it.

Though the chief literary influences on most of the novelists of this period were doubtless earlier English writers, when they proclaim their loyalties they just as frequently name novelists from other languages. This is not, perhaps, surprising when we consider the diversity of their backgrounds. Henry James was an expatriate American who had been given a deliberately cosmopolitan education; Joyce, Jesuit-educated, lived most of his adult life in Trieste, Zurich, and Paris; Conrad, born in Russian-occupied Poland, did not even learn English until he was twenty-one. But cosmopolitan sympathies were not merely the result of upbringing; Bennett, born in the Midlands and the most obviously regional novelist after Hardy, lived in France for nine years, married a Frenchwoman, proclaimed himself a disciple of the de Goncourt brothers and was on familiar terms with many French painters, musicians, and writers. This period was one in which national and linguistic boundaries were crossed far more than previously and more than has happened in the last half-century. This was particularly true of the poets and critics who thought of themselves as being in the forefront of change – Pound, Eliot, T. E. Hulme, Wyndham Lewis; their points of reference are as often Mallarmé, Rimbaud, de Gourmont, and Laforgue as their English forebears. The novelists have much less sense of being part of a movement or of wishing to create one, but they, too, in their letters and essays pay their debts to Zola, Maupassant, Flaubert, Turgenev, and Dostoevsky.

It remains to say that the response of authors to the happenings, the ideas, the beliefs, the changes which they experienced manifest themselves in different and often contradictory ways. Increasing democratization, the sense that men and women should be treated equally, and the increasing power of the enfranchised population can be seen in Forster as a sense that Leonard Bast's child ought to inherit Howards End and that the Indians should not be excluded from the club. In

Virginia Woolf it shows itself as a withdrawal from the public world of issues and the cultivation of private sensations. In Waugh, a generation on, it displays itself as a rampant yearning for county families and in Ivy Compton-Burnett as a feeling that she cannot write about anything after 1910. The decline of religion is aided and abetted by Hardy and Joyce; its lack is felt by Lawrence as a central absence of meaning. Kipling is obsessed by a fear of anarchy and the need for rules and control; Conrad is unable to believe in the legitimacy of any government.

This book is not organized on a chronological basis because I do not detect any important line of chronological development. The writers who contributed most to the art of fiction in this period were extraordinarily different from one another. They could not possibly see themselves as part of a developing tradition. This is obvious if we think of the following sequence of novels, one from each of the major novelists of this period, and reflect on their astonishing variety: *Tess of the d'Urbervilles* (1891), *What Maisie Knew* (1897), *Nostromo* (1904), *The Old Wives' Tale* (1908), *The Rainbow* (1915), *Ulysses* (1922), *A Passage to India* (1924), *To the Lighthouse* (1927). It is, of course, possible to find links between them. Lawrence had some admiration for that other Midlands novelist, Bennett; Virginia Woolf asserted some similarity of aim with Joyce, though she repudiated it almost as much; Conrad had a slightly wary respect for the old master, James. But to pursue these links in the hope of distinguishing a general line of development or even the existence of a number of schools is a waste of time. I have chosen instead to include a number of chapters which suggest connections – and contrasts – between various writers, and which consider their relationship to social and other developments. Thus, for example, a discussion of political issues follows chapters on Conrad, Kipling, and Forster and a chapter on changes in the reading public follows my discussion of James Joyce. But it must not be forgotten that these are only some of the issues raised by the writers. Conrad, Kipling, and Forster all grappled with crucial political issues of their age and in ways very different from one another; but Conrad can also be discussed as an example of a writer who operated in terms of symbolic patterns and in this has resemblances to some aspects of the work of Lawrence; Forster has often been discussed as an associate member of the Bloomsbury Group and as such has links with Virginia Woolf.

Nor have I followed a systematic procedure in discussing the writers with whom I deal because it seems to me that what is needed varies from one author to another. I have confined discussion of Bennett largely to one book, *The Old Wives' Tale*. This is because, although he is not as disregarded as he was twenty years ago, he is still frequently underrated or praised in ways which suggest that he belongs to a different kind of literature from D. H. Lawrence, say, or Virginia Woolf. It seems important, therefore, to treat one of his books with the thoroughness and rigour which we reserve for great novels. If I convince my readers of his value they can be trusted to move on to such other major works as *Clayhanger* and *Riceyman Steps*. Forster, by contrast, has received a great deal of critical attention and there is no need to argue that *A Passage to India* should be taken with full seriousness; but a proper understanding of his work demands a recognition of the similarity of theme in all his books, combined with a consideration of why only one of them is a major success and one a major failure. Consequently I discuss his whole *œuvre*. Kipling gets, perhaps, more space than he deserves in terms of quality because his work raises so acutely questions about how we come to terms with outdated attitudes of mind and because it seems necessary to disentangle what is good in his work from what is not merely bad but atrocious. I have concentrated in my chapter on Joyce on the question of how to read him – how much attention to give to arcane and cryptographic elements – because this issue is perhaps the most important with which readers are now faced, though the form in which it presents itself may have changed somewhat.

I shall disappoint some readers – to some extent I disappoint myself – by not discussing a whole host of minor but not valueless writers. Shortage of space would only allow a cursory and hence superficial account of them. They should be read and not read about, so I have included many in the Bibliographies and hope that my readers will turn to them. The Bibliographies are intended to supplement what I have to say and the books cited will often be found to put counterarguments to mine.

Finally, I must emphasize that I do not present a clear and logical picture of literary development because I do not believe that it exists. The more I read in this period and think about it the harder I find it to make generalizations or trace patterns of development. This is perhaps true for all periods of literature, but I am convinced that it is particularly true of fiction in this period. I detect some patterns and I hope that readers will detect some of their own, but they are always limited ones and can only be made comprehensive by Procrustean exercises.

Notes

1. See Chronology and historical works recommended in Bibliography.

2. Figures given in A. D. Gilbert, *Religion and Society in Industrial England* (1976) suggest that the decline in religion among the population as a whole was less than is sometimes thought. He gives a table of the percentage of the population over the age of fifteen attending Easter Day communion: for 1801 it is 9.9 per cent and for 1891 is 8.4 per cent; the lowest figure is 7.2 per cent for 1831. These figures also suggest that churchgoing was lower throughout the nineteenth century than is usually suggested.

Chapter 2
Surviving Giants: Hardy and James

In 1890 the two writers who had perhaps the highest reputations among serious critics and their fellow novelists were Hardy and James. Both appeared to be in mid-career, though Hardy was only to write two more major novels before abandoning fiction for an exclusive concentration on poetry; both were controversial, though the nature of the controversy was totally different: Hardy had already scandalized many with his subject-matter and he was often reproached for clumsiness, while James's technical method, especially his prose style, raised problems for many readers by its complexity. They appeared, indeed, to be polar opposites and the passage of time has not diminished this impression. A careless reading still sometimes allows readers to believe that Hardy is essentially a naive writer whose interest lies only in his subject-matter, and there is still plenty of room for argument as to the effects of James's choice of, as he once put it, doing things in such a way that they undergo most doing. It is entertaining to note their comments on one another. James's judgement in a letter to R. L. Stevenson is the better known: 'The good little Thomas Hardy has scored a great success with *Tess of the d'Urbervilles*, which is chock-full of faults and falsity and yet had a singular beauty and charm.' Hardy's entry in his journal is no less feline: 'After this kind of work one feels inclined to be purposely careless in detail. . . . James's subjects are those one could be interested in at moments when there is nothing larger to think of.'[1]

Hardy was born ten years before the death of Wordsworth and was a young man at the time of the publication of *The Origin of Species* (1859), *Great Expectations* (1861), and *Adam Bede* (1859); he died two years before D. H. Lawrence and six years after the publication in 1922 of *The Waste Land* and *Ulysses*. He appears in many ways as the last of a line of nineteenth-century novelists writing with confident authorial presence of an England that has virtually disappeared, living on into an age of experiment and Modernism. Yet he felt very acutely that he was living in an age of change and his choice of rural Wessex as subject-matter in no way implies an idea of stability or certainty. Indeed, in *Tess of the d'Urbervilles* (1891), Angel Clare sees Tess as an example of the 'ache of Modernism' (19) and even though he reflects that her melancholy is akin to that 'which men and women have vaguely grasped for centuries', it is a curious phrase to use of her since at first glance her plight is timeless, that of the betrayed maiden of folk-story and romance.

It is fitting, however, for the novel as a whole has a strangely dual-istic vision. This is seen in its most superficial way, as in virtually all his novels, in his construction of a Wessex which is simultaneously factual and fictional. The giving of a fictitious name to a place which for many readers is clearly real is not uncommon, but the re-creation of a whole region is a characteristic shared, among major novelists, only by William Faulkner. The purpose, presumably, is that of combining the sense of authenticity which comes from the actual (as Jane Austen asserts, by implication, that when we are told that her characters go to Bath or Lyme Regis we can remember what the place is like or, if we choose, visit it) with a degree of freedom which dis-entangles them from unwanted associations (we need to forget, perhaps, that we have an aunt who lives in Casterbridge/Dorchester and that there is no room in the fictional town for her, just as Faulkner removes the University of Mississippi from his Jefferson/Oxford). But this hovering between the actual and the fictional effects a transformation of several counties of England into 'Hardy's Wessex'. Moreover, as I have said, this corresponds to his whole habit of mind and he performs the same kind of feat with time. *Tess* can be located not only in a version of a real place but also in an actual historical time. His commentary in Chapter 51 on rural depopulation, the description of Sandbourne with its piers and promenades on the edge of Egdon Waste, the highly topical choice of Brazil for Angel's emigration, all these allow of little temporal leeway. Yet there are moments when we feel that any date must be irrelevant. There are, for example, two striking passages where the tense changes to the present with the paradoxical distancing effect which such changes often produce. Chapter 18 begins: 'Angel Clare rises out of the past not altogether as a distinct figure, but as an appreciative voice, a long regard of fixed, abstracted eyes' and we are suddenly in a world in which old men tell stories of things long ago. Even more striking is the description of Tess as she walks towards Flintcombe Ash in Chapter 42:

> Thus Tess walks on; a figure which is part of the landscape;
> a field-woman pure and simple, in winter guise; a gray
> serge cape, a red woollen cravat, a stuff skirt covered by a
> whitey-brown rough wrapper, and buff-leather gloves.

The clothing may be of a period but the effect of the change to the present tense is to fix Tess as a permanent figure in a landscape, an exemplar not only of the field-woman but also of the betrayed maiden.

It is this double vision, this coexistence of the historic and the legendary, which allows Hardy to show Tess's two lovers as a disguised man stirring a fire with a fork and a man called Angel who plays a harp, of whom the latter may be thought the more damaging. Similarly, the extreme coincidences have their justification. For a farm worker of the late nineteenth century to take her last sleep as a free woman on what was thought to be the sacrifice stone at Stonehenge would be too gross a contrivance, but for the heroine of the timeless folk-tale it is what is appropriate.

It has often been suggested that Hardy's view is a nostalgic one in which an apparently timeless rural past is contrasted with the impact of those modern changes which were destroying it. There are certainly moments when the modern is regretted; Tess's ordeal on the mechanized threshing machine is an obvious example, though the un-mechanized labour in the turnip field hardly suggests an idyllic rural past. But the truth is rather that Hardy is showing the coexistence of the temporary with the unchanging.

There is, however, a far more significant way in which he treats processes and developments. His characters are typically caught between two viable worlds in a transitional situation where they can do most harm to themselves and to others. In the preface to *Late Lyrics and Earlier* (1922), Hardy proclaimed his continuing belief in 'evolutionary meliorism', but what most concerns him in his novels, and especially in the later ones, is the plight of those who seem to be the victims of a social-evolutionary process, inevitable victims in that struggle for survival in which the fittest may not be the ones who most engage our sympathies.[2]

The education which Tess has received has taken her away from the way of life of her parents with all its crudeness but also its resilience, a durability akin to that of dark Car and the other farm hands with whom she is contrasted, 'these children of the open air, whom even excess of alcohol could scare injure permanently' (10). It has given her aspirations towards culture and elegance, has even made her bilingual in dialect and 'good' English, and has given her those marks of refine-ment without which she could not attract Angel Clare. This devel-opment has, in short, removed her from a 'lower' but safer way of life to a 'higher' but more perilous one, without taking her far enough to make her as self-confident and self-reliant as her vulnerability demands. The man with whom she falls in love is equally caught between two ways in a developing social process. He is emancipated enough to reject family beliefs and to marry a farm girl but not emancipated enough to reject the dual standard of sexual morality traditional in his society. He wants the sexual mores and experience of Mercy Chant in Tess's body. Both Tess and Angel are caught up in a process which is evolving towards situations with which Hardy would have expected us to sympathize away from ones which, in retrospect, appear static. I do not think that Hardy wants us to believe that such a transitional vulnerability is unique to the late nineteenth century, for *The Mayor of Casterbridge* (1886) shows that even before the repeal of the Corn Laws change was both inevitable and destructive to his hero, but his choice of social issues and the increase, especially in *Jude the Obscure* (1896), of overt didacticism suggests that this is a particularly critical time.

Jude displays this theme of the vulnerability of a man caught between two worlds with almost schematic clarity. Earlier generations would not have conceived of wanting to go to Oxford; later generations as intelligent and industrious as Jude will succeed.[3] Hardy's despairing hero is at that point at which desire has been aroused but fulfilment is denied. This was his last novel, for though *The Well-Beloved* was published in volume form two years later it had appeared as a serial some years earlier. Hardy gave the hostile reception of *Jude* as his reason for abandoning fiction, though we may suspect that denunciations of immorality from the pulpit would not have deterred him if he had not come to the conclusion that he had come to the end of what he could achieve in novels. Henceforward he devoted himself to poetry and though, unlike Henry James, he is rarely cited as an influence on later fiction, his significance in the tradition of English poetry is increasingly emphasized.

James had set out in 1884 in his essay, 'The Art of Fiction', his ideas about the claims which could be made for that art; the novel of the age of Dickens, he says, was 'naïf', but recently more attention is being paid to fiction as an art which involves the writer in aiming at concentration of effect; there are two very celebrated passages in the essay – the injunction 'Try to be one of the people on whom nothing is lost!' and the proclamation of unity and consistence:

> I cannot imagine composition existing in a series of
> blocks, nor conceive, in any novel worth discussing at all,
> of a passage of description that is not in its intention
> narrative, a passage of dialogue that is not in its intention
> descriptive, a touch of truth of any sort that does not
> partake of the nature of incident, or an incident that
> derives its interest from any other source of the success of
> a work of art – that of being illustrative.

The essay is a proclamation of faith, not least in its emphasis on the seriousness with which the art of fiction should be considered, and James's influence on other writers has probably been less a matter of technical procedures or choices of subject-matter than of this sense of dedication.

By the 1890s he had thoroughly entered what it is common to call his middle period, marked by tightly organized plots, the exclusion of inessentials (and a definition of inessential which went very far), and his beloved 'indirect method' of appearing to remain neutral, even non-existent, so that everything seems to be presented through the consciousnesses of his characters and all interpretations appear to be theirs, leaving to the reader the task of assessing reliability and making moral judgements. It has often been suggested that his unavailing and disheartening attempts to achieve success as a dramatist encouraged him to tighten up the structures of his novels and to deal with his material by a succession of scenes, but this had been his tendency from the start. He had always been, in Conrad's phrase, the 'historian of fine consciousnesses', probing the shifts of feeling and subtleties of response of characters who were conscious of their plights. The praise of his admirers and the doubts of others were alike founded on an awareness of this. The reviewer in the *Nation* of *The Tragic Muse* (1890), in saying 'Mr James is, in fact, guilty of selecting complex creatures – creatures who are centuries away from savage simplicity – and of devoting his greatest energy to the exhibition of the storehouse of their complexities, the mind' is noting the same quality as does Mrs Henry Adams when she writes to her father with the confidence of the American intellectual aristocracy, 'he chaws more than he bites off'.[4]

Increasingly he deals with those who can share with their creator an awareness of the situation in which they find themselves, an almost aesthetic appreciation of their roles within an intrigue. I choose the word 'intrigue' deliberately, for the elements of contriving, acting, and hoodwinking play an extraordinarily large part in his works. There is a strange paradox in James's approach to the civilization which he chose in reaction against what he saw as the barbarism of the United States. In the life of Hawthorne which he wrote for the *English Men of Letters* series in 1879 he waxes eloquent about the varied forms of life which abounded in England but which were not to be found in America and he proclaims that 'the flower of art blooms only where the soil is deep, that it takes a great deal of history to produce a little literature, that it needs a complex social machinery to set a writer in motion'. Yet, with the exception of *The Princess Casamassima* (1886), he confines himself to a very small area of English life, the personality types which he chooses are restricted and, by and large, he does not appear to like what he has chosen. One sometimes feels that what he actually means is that the corrupt in England are corrupt in a more self-conscious and a more interesting, even elegant, way. Hardy was reproached for the immorality of his characters and themes, but they appear ingenuously virtuous by comparison with James's. His favoured subject is the ravages committed on the innocent by the predatory, by those who regard others as objects – often *objets* to be collected – by greedy hypocrites and connoisseurs of relationships. In the earlier novels this often appears, as it was to do in the last three major novels, as a contrast between American innocence and European corruption, though matters are a good deal less straightforward than this formulation suggests. In *The Portrait of a Lady* (1881), for example, though Gilbert Osmond entraps Isabel Archer with all the lures of European fineness, he is himself American, and the more one thinks of Isabel herself the more ambiguous does her innocence seem; is she the epitome of betrayed nobility which many critics have thought her or is she, in words applied to her early in the book, one who keeps the flag flying after the citadel has surrendered and so connives at the evil done to the indubitably innocent Pansy?

In the novels of the 1890s the American theme disappears for a time; of these books none exemplifies more completely the theme of innocence and corruption than *What Maisie Knew* (1897) and it seems to me to suffer less than some of the others, such as *The Spoils of Poynton* (1897) and *The Awkward Age* (1899), from those ambiguities of judgement which lead one at times to feel that we are invited to attend less to richness of registration than uncertainty of viewpoint.

In the preface to the New York edition of this novel James discusses the technical opportunities and the concomitant problems presented by the theme. This is one of the most interesting of the prefaces and, besides giving an unusually clear account of the story itself, indicates the general aim of James in his fiction, not least the manner in which questions of technical choice are what lead him to his meanings. Here he describes being told of the child of divorced parents who divided its time between them, each parent at first trying to keep the child beyond the time allotted while blackguarding the other, but, when one of them remarried, trying to abandon it to the other. He observes that 'the ideal of the situation' requires the second parent, too, to remarry and he speculates as to how the situation might be turned to the child's advantage, especially in its relation to the step-parents, and the possibility that it might bring together people 'who would be at least more correctly separate' and also keep some virtue alive 'by sowing on barren strands, through the mere fact of presence, the seed of the moral life'. At this point, he says, he decided that the child must be a little girl, since girls have more developed sensibilities than boys, and from this realized that his design, 'dignified by the most delightful difficulty', must be to present his story through the child's consciousness. This difficulty and the opportunities which it presents have the great virtue of being 'a plan of absolutely definite and measurable application – that in itself always a mark of beauty'.

There remains the problem of choosing the appropriate language and, deciding that 'small children have many more perceptions than they have terms to translate them', he resolves to present the child's perceptions in his own developed prose and thus to imply what she cannot understand.

After a short introductory account of Maisie's parents and their divorce, this is largely what he does, though there are moments where his commentary does go somewhat beyond Maisie's perceptions. The introduction is in a tone of high farce: Beale Farange obtains his divorce from Ida not because he is less 'bespattered' but because

> it was not so much that the mother's character had been
> more absolutely damaged as that the brilliancy of a lady's
> complexion (and this lady's in court, was immensely
> remarked) might be more regarded as showing the spots.

We are thus given the clearest possible indication that, despite the possibilities for pathos latent in the theme, James will not appeal directly to our pity for Maisie. The book is not lacking in a sense of the deprivation of parental affection, the bewilderment of divided loyalties, and simple loneliness, but they are approached obliquely in such images as 'life was like a long, long corridor with rows of closed doors. She had learned that at these doors it was wise not to knock – this seemed to produce from within such sounds of derision' (5) or by implications of previous experiences, as when, talking to the Captain, 'she became on the spot indifferent to her usual fear of showing what in children was notoriously most offensive – presented to her companion, soundlessly but hideously, her wet distorted face' (16).

James's choice of his own prose for rendering Maisie's perceptions obviously involves the risk of making her seem implausibly precocious and there are times when she does, indeed, seem a very knowing little girl, though reflection usually convinces me that circumstances have nurtured certain specific kinds of knowingness while leaving her in other ways unaware. In the earlier parts of the book we are frequently put in a position to understand situations which she can only accept at their face value and to make judgements which she could not understand. Here the discrepancy of language is very telling. When she is collected from her mother's house by Beale and her governess, Miss Overmore,

she put to Miss Overmore, after another immense and
talkative squeeze, a question of which the motive was a
desire for information as to the continuity of a certain
sentiment. 'Did Papa like you just the same while I was
gone?' she enquired – full of the sense of how markedly
his favour had been established in her presence. (5)

We soon realize that Miss Overmore is now Beale's mistress as she and
Beale hurl jocular raillery at one another over the child's head, culminating in Miss Overmore's instructing 'her little charge that she was
not to listen to his bad jokes: she was to understand that a lady couldn't
stay with a gentleman that way without some awfully proper reason'.
We are in no doubt that, with sickening vulgarity, they are making
use of Maisie as a pretext and as an opportunity for innuendo, but
Maisie sees only gaiety and a jolly reunion. One of the reasons why
we can make these judgements and why we can pick up the different
significances for Maisie and for her two step-parents when, for
example, she says 'I've brought you and her together!' is, of course,
that we have a clear idea of how the adults ought to behave to Maisie
(a clarity which is often in question in relation to characters in some
of James's other books) and because we know what might be meant
here by innocence; at the early stages of the book, at least, it means
ignorance.

By the time that Maisie is beginning to lose that ignorance, she has
also begun to make judgements of her own. But they are not judgements of the kind which her elders might expect. Mrs Wix, the frum-
pish governess, originally employed by Ida and later, after Ida has
'bolted', kept on by Sir Claude, whom she adores, exhorts Maisie to
have a 'moral sense', speaking of the acquisition or loss of this as if
it were a discrete object. But Maisie begins to judge before she can
have any sense, for example, of the traditional wickedness of adultery;
one of her most devastating verdicts comes rather early in the book.
She plays with her doll Lisette, imitating with her the entertainment
which she herself has provided for some of Ida's friends:

> She was enlightened by Lisette's questions, which
> reproduced the effect of her own upon those for whom
> she sat in the very darkness of Lisette. Was she not herself
> convulsed by such innocence? In the presence of it she
> often imitated the shrieking ladies. . . . There were, for
> instance, days when, after prolonged absence, Lisette,
> watching her take off her things, tried hard to discover
> where she had been. Well, she discovered a little, but
> never discovered all. There was an occasion when, on her

being particularly indiscreet, Maisie replied to her – and
precisely about the motive of a disappearance – as she,
Maisie, had once been replied to by Mrs Farange: 'Find
out for yourself!' She mimicked her mother's sharpness,
but she was rather ashamed afterwards, though as to
whether of the sharpness or of the mimicry was not quite
clear.   (5)

Maisie never shows any sign of being interested in orthodox moral or
social rules; her judgements are effectively about kindness and love and
whether people can be trusted. A subtle limiting judgement about one
of her favourites, Sir Claude, is made when, having previously given
Mrs Wix the present of an umbrella with a malachite knob, he

came back from Paris – came bringing her a splendid
apparatus for painting in water-colours and bringing Mrs
Wix, by a lapse of memory that would have been droll if
it had not been a trifle disconcerting, a second and even
more elegant umbrella.   (11)

The plot – in effect the judging by Maisie of each of the adults in
turn – is, as James noted in his preface, very symmetrical. It is possible,
as so often in James's novels, to draw the plot, to produce a diagram,
which in this case places Maisie at the centre of four points, her parents
and step-parents, all connected, with further symmetrically arranged
points which represent the successive liaisons of her mother and father,
plus Mrs Wix who might be described as eccentric, the only personage
who does not fit neatly within the pattern of adultery and deception.
There are a number of scenes which closely parallel one another, of
which the most striking are those in which Maisie is abandoned, set
adrift in turn by her father and her mother, each of whom she still
wants to admire and even to love but, even more, wants to please and
therefore, circumstances being what they are in the Farange way of life,
wants to allow to depart with some rags of self-respect. It is in the
second of these partings, that from her mother, that James breaks for
the first time the comic surface.

Some time before, Maisie, walking with Sir Claude in Kensington
Gardens, has met her mother with her new lover, 'the Captain'; after
an embrace from her mother in which 'amid a wilderness of trinkets,
she felt as if she had suddenly been thrust, with a smash of glass, into
a jeweller's shop-front' (15), she is sent off to talk to the Captain while
Ida confronts Sir Claude. It is here, as much as anywhere in the book,
that James, still working in the comic mode, makes us see the deprivation of Maisie's feelings; we recognize the Captain as an amiable

booby who has succumbed to Ida's picture of herself as a much maligned woman, but Maisie is overjoyed at hearing 'the first real kindness' in someone talking about her mother; she presses the Captain to proclaim his love for Ida and, swept away by a longing for what she has never had, cries 'So do *I* then. I do, I do, I do!'

When, therefore, her mother comes to her some time later to announce that she is leaving England, probably for South Africa, Maisie, though she recognizes desertion, nevertheless hopes that her mother's companion will be the Captain. The whole scene is finely orchestrated with Maisie aware of her mother's posturings and also that she is extracting a coin, her farewell tip, from the purse which she keeps in 'the rustling covert at her rear', while trying to please her mother and let her know that she hopes that the Captain who had spoken so admiringly of her will be with her. But Maisie never gets the money; Ida's response is 'Him! – the biggest cad in London!' and her purse clicks shut. For the first time Maisie's powers of judgement rise above her desire to please and James brings out a rhetoric which he has held back so long:

> there rose in her a fear, a pain, a vision ominous,
> precocious, of what it might mean for her mother's fate to
> have forfeited such a loyalty as that. There was literally an
> instant in which Maisie fully saw – saw madness and
> desolation, saw ruin and darkness and death.   (21)

It is appropriate that after this scene Sir Claude jocularly treats her as a young woman and escorts her in to dinner with 'Will Miss Farange do me the honour to accept my arm?', for she is now well on the way to what James in his preface calls 'the death of her childhood, properly speaking'. It is with an almost adult eye that she now judges Sir Claude as a man who will always be weak with women and will be afraid of his weakness and so she leaves him to her stepmother and takes herself off with Mrs Wix. He knows this, too, for at parting 'their eyes met as the eyes of those who have done for each other what they can' (31).

James produces the title of his novel in its last three words: 'Mrs Wix gave her a sidelong look. She still had room for wonder at what Maisie knew.' The reader does not wonder because he has watched her acquire her knowledge by what is described at one point as learning 'to read the unspoken into the spoken'. This is a peculiarly satisfactory method for this novel because there are by definition certain things which will not be spoken in the circumstances in which Maisie finds herself; the reader, older than Maisie and knowing more of the adult world, will be in a position to distinguish between those things which are not said because one does not say them before little girls, those which one does not say because they are understood already, and those which would shame even oneself if spoken, and to appreciate the double focus which is achieved by placing his interpretation against Maisie's. This often approaches a *tour de force* but it is far more; it is inherent in the process of Maisie's learning to discriminate that the reader should be surprised by the little girl and, indeed, undergo some revelations as to how moral judgements may be made.

James's last three major novels, *The Wings of the Dove* (1902), *The Ambassadors* (1903), and *The Golden Bowl* (1904), are sustained exercises in reading the unspoken into the spoken but without the enforcing presence of a child as register.

The Golden Bowl is as geometrically structured as *What Maisie Knew*. The American Maggie Verver is devoted to her father, Adam, a fabulously rich connoisseur and collector; she marries Prince Amerigo, an impoverished Italian whose ancestry and family history are as glamorous as any of the paintings which Adam Verver is collecting for his museum in America; Amerigo has, unknown to Maggie, been in love with her old friend Charlotte Stant, also impoverished and therefore impossible as a wife. Adam, to prevent Maggie's unease at the sense that she is abandoning him, marries Charlotte. The Prince and Charlotte become lovers. All this is watched by old friends, Bob and Fanny Assingham, who both discuss the action and act in various ways as informants and go-betweens. Maggie discovers the situation and resolves to separate her husband and his mistress without ever breaking the surface of civilized relationships. Regarded as naïve by the lovers, she nevertheless plays her cards so skilfully as to attain her end; Adam takes Charlotte back to America – 'the dreadful great country', viewed by Charlotte as akin to hell – and Maggie is left with her Prince who has been brought to abandon his mistress without letting her know what has been happening and to admire his wife.

Clearly, though for rather different reasons from those obtaining in *What Maisie Knew*, much will be unspoken and much will depend upon hints, and it would, I think, be generally agreed that the prose of this novel is as elaborately 'Jamesian' as any. From the earliest reviews it was this idiosyncratic complexity which formed the grounds for unfavourable criticism, the suspicion that the complexity was adopted less as a way of expressing subtleties of relationship or perception and more for its own sake or, more speculatively, because of some inhibiting obliquity in James's view of the world. That the prose is idiosyncratic could hardly be denied, but in *What Maisie Knew*, in which much that we think of as typical of his style is already well developed, what seem to some readers to be mannerisms can be shown to contribute to a concentration of meaning. The baroque luxuriance of imagery is highly informative as well as decorative, as, for example, when Ida turns to the Captain 'the face that was like an illuminated garden, turnstile and all, for the frequentation of which he had his season-ticket' (15); the implications of the turnstile alone and the implication that some who passed through it might only pay for one admission range very widely. The seemingly coy introduction of a colloquialism – 'Mrs Wix 'stood up' to her in a manner that the child herself felt at the time to be astonishing', for instance – implies the kind of language in which matters are discussed around Maisie. The apparently pedantic and convoluted syntax repays in meaning the labour which goes to its unfolding, as in the comment on Maisie's meeting with her father when she knows that he intends to abandon her without losing too much face: 'there was an extraordinary mute passage between her vision of this vision of his, his vision of her vision, and her vision of his vision of her vision' (19).

In *The Golden Bowl*, however, not only are the idiosyncratic elements more extreme but they do not seem to deepen the meaning. What – to take a slight example – is the reason for the awkward inversion in the description of Amerigo's feelings: 'Foolish in public beyond a certain point he was scarce the man to brook his wife's being thought to be'? The Prince is not a subtle man; indeed, if it were not for the glamour of his lineage he would surely stand revealed as a rather uninteresting one; a more natural word order would convey his sentiments at least as convincingly and the effect of the inversion's pedantic archness is more akin to that of mock heroic. Certainly there is a frolicsome, slightly distancing air about much of the prose, with a little consciousness shared between the writer and the reader, as in the Prince's sense of the opportunity for intrigue at a house party:

> What with the noble fairness of the place, meanwhile, the
> generous mood of the sunny gusty lusty English April, all
> panting and heaving with impatience or even at moments
> kicking and crying like some infant Hercules who
> wouldn't be dressed; what with these things and the
> bravery of youth and beauty, the insolence of fortune and
> appetite so diffused among his fellow guests that the poor
> Assinghams, in their comparatively marked maturity and
> their comparatively small splendour, were the only
> approach to a false note in the concert, the stir of the air
> was such, for going, in a degree, to one's head, that, as a
> mere matter of exposure, almost grotesque in its flagrancy,
> his situation resembled some elaborate practical joke
> carried out at his expense.   (III. 7)

But the extreme convolution of syntax often has a more significant function than this; the effort which we expend in following the twists and turns prevents us from pursuing some of the more natural lines of thought which the social and emotional situation provokes. I have already suggested that there is a radical ambiguity of evaluation at the centre of many of James's most admired works. Increasingly, and in the last three novels in particular, this appears as a demand that we should often respond in a manner which seems hardly compatible with psychological plausibility or moral sense. It is hardly too much to say that the effect of the prose is intimidatory; it forbids us to challenge James's statements on pain of being convicted of obtuseness. A clear example of this, and one which leads close to the heart of what seems to me to be perverse in the novel, is the way in which Adam Verver is presented to us at the opening of the second part. We find him, positively taking refuge from the predatory Mrs Rance, in his billiard-room, and we are told that he is a man who 'had fatally stamped himself – it was his own fault – a man who could be interrupted with impunity' (II.1) because he finds it hard to refuse any appeal, so that when he wants to be alone he must adopt 'the innocent trick of occasionally making-believe that he had no conscience, or at least that blankness, in the field of duty, did reign for an hour'. Yet some account must be given of his acquisition of that immense fortune which now allows him to consider only how he may best 'rifle the Golden Isles' for his museum in American City. James can hardly have been unaware that his readers would find it surprising that one of the financial giants of the Gilded Age should be characterized by excessive sensitivity to the feelings of others, yet the role of Adam demands both that he should be immensely rich, though without distinguished lineage, and also intensely private, self-effacing, and vulnerable.

The account of his success in accumulating his fortune is presented in terms of a 'spark of fire' which 'the stiff American breeze of example and opportunity' had fanned into a flame in the forge of his brain. It continues:

> The essential pulse of the flame, the very action of the cerebral temperature, brought to the highest point, yet extraordinarily contained – these facts themselves *were* the immensity of the result; they were one with perfection of machinery, they had constituted the kind of acquisitive power engendered and applied, the necessary triumph of all operations. A dim explanation of phenomena once vivid must at all events for the moment suffice us; it being obviously no account of the matter to throw on our friend's amiability alone the weight of the demonstration of his economic history. Amiability, of a truth, is an aid

> to success; it has even been known to be the principle of
> large accumulations; but the link, for the mind, is none
> the less fatally missing between proof, on such a scale, of
> continuity, if of nothing more insolent, in one field, and
> accessibility to distraction in every other.   (II. 1)

The first clause appears to claim that the cause is the effect; the last
sentence starts with an implausible account of how large accumulations
are made and then seems to me to turn a corner and lose itself. This
is not a complexity which aims at greater precision but one which
confuses. Its aim seems to be to bluff the reader into believing that he
is offered a subtlety which will make his rational doubts appear irrelevant or simple-minded.

If this stratagem works we can more easily accept the relationship
between Maggie and her father as within the bounds of normality and
the acquisition of Amerigo and Charlotte as other than purchases. We
can then agree that Maggie, learning of her husband's adultery and
knowing that she must confront the situation, is faced, as Fanny
Assingham puts it, with 'what's called Evil'. We can, in fact, do what
most readers seem to take for granted as the right way to read the
book, appreciating and applauding the way in which Maggie regains
her husband at the price of losing her father to America, whither,
attached by a 'silken rope', he takes Charlotte.[5] Such a reading requires
that we should not take our directions from the numerous occasions
when Amerigo is likened to a *morceau de musée* which Adam's wealth
has allowed him to buy for his daughter nor jib at the Ververs' plan
to add Charlotte to the family for the sake of the relationship between
father and daughter. Yet if we did so – and the idea of purchase is
repeated often enough, even in the very last chapter where Amerigo
and Charlotte are described as 'concrete attestations of a rare power
of purchase' – we should be tempted to turn the novel on its head;
Maggie and her father then become monsters, Charlotte a victim and
Amerigo a bought coward quite unworthy of the mistress whom he
is abandoning for the sake of continued supplies. But there are large
sections of the book which forbid this view. We are obliged to
sympathize too much with Maggie who, like Maisie, is not in the
know and has to learn, and the conclusion in particular forbids any
interpretation but the triumph of marital love achieved through, and
not by repudiating, the power of purchase.

What we are thus presented with is total ambiguity, not the kind
of fruitful ambiguity, akin to that encountered in life, in which we
know that matters can be looked at from more than one point of view,
but a clash between two incompatible sets of judgements. The split is
deep within James's temperament and is certainly related to his fasci-

nation with shape, form, perfection, the ideal of a situation, with the element of connoisseurship in his appreciation of situations and people. There is a conversation in the first chapter between Maggie and the Prince in which she tells him that he is 'a rarity, an object of beauty, an object of price' and they fence amiably about what he may have cost and whether she would pay rather than lose him. It is hard to conceive of a more blatant exhibition of vulgarity, but I do not think that James sees it thus because for him, at this stage in his writing, he is himself very close to appreciating people as collectors' items.

If we say that the relationships in this novel are perverse we are saying, I think, that they are very theoretical. When James writes in the preface to *What Maisie Knew* that 'the ideal of the situation' demands that both her parents remarry we can accept the symmetry because it is also emotionally plausible. To effect a similar symmetry in *The Golden Bowl* demands in Adam a view of Charlotte which, if we allow ourselves to consider it, can hardly be other than inhuman; I do not think that James wants us to think Adam wicked but he is more interested in symmetrical conjugations than in the untidiness of feeling. This, of course, tends to make his characters also appear to see matters in terms of awareness. There is a passage towards the end of the book where Maggie imagines what Charlotte must be thinking as she knows that she is losing Amerigo and she produces a phrase which sums up the point that I am making: 'Ours was everything a relationship could be, filled to the brim with the wine of consciousness' (VI. I). Consciousness, the quality necessary to the creator, is here, as so often elsewhere, transferred to the created character, just as 'the ideal of the situation', so necessary for James as a novelist, often seems to be possessed also by the characters.

Notes

1. James: letter to R. L. Stevenson, 19 March 1892, cited in *Thomas Hardy: The Critical Heritage*, edited by R. G. Cox (1970). Hardy: *Journal*, July 1888, cited in *Henry James: The Critical Heritage*, edited by Roger Gard (1968).

2. This subject is discussed most interestingly from a somewhat different point of view in Roy Morrell, *Thomas Hardy: The Will and the Way* (Kuala Lumpur and Singapore, 1965).

3. To be fair to the Oxford Extension Lectures Committee, for whose successor, the Department for External Studies, I have worked for many years, it should be said that Jude would have stood a better chance than Hardy allows him.

4. Both cited in *Henry James: The Critical Heritage*.

5. Though this seems the usual way of seeing the book a number of critics, notably F. R. Leavis in *The Great Tradition* (1948), have taken a different view.

Chapter 3
Joseph Conrad and the Politics of Power

With the publication in 1895 of his first novel, *Almayer's Folly*, Joseph Conrad was hailed, understandably enough, as a trafficker in the exotic. Matters did not change much with his second novel. Reviewers seize upon what comes readily to hand and the title – *An Outcast of the Islands* (1896) – might have been chosen to direct attention towards local colour, romance, savages, half-castes, and, in the more serious reviews, questions about whether white men degenerate in the East. With his third novel, *The Nigger of the 'Narcissus'* (1897), Conrad was in danger of being classified as someone who had widened out from the Malayan Archipelago and Borneo to the high seas and joined the category of 'marine story-tellers'.

Conrad criticism for the next half-century or so was often concerned to controvert this – often at Conrad's own bidding. He complained on a number of occasions about the 'sea stuff' with which his name was associated; in the well-known letter to Henry S. Canby written in the last year of his life he is still concerned to argue that the problem which faces the crew of the *Narcissus* is not a problem of the sea but one which happens to arise on board a ship where it stands out with particular force.

There is now little danger that he will be discussed as a genre novelist or a romantic novelist of exotic passions, so that it may be useful to comment that it is actually time that his subject-matter, the range of feelings with which he is concerned and the circumstances under which his characters operate, are somewhat specialized. He writes little about love, marriage, and family life and, with a few notable exceptions, when he does so he is not very successful; the exceptions tend to be such unhappy or suppressed families as the Goulds and the Verlocs. Most of his stories are set outside what for most of his readers is normal life, the professions of his characters are unusual ones, and the opportunities and problems which confront them are unlike those which face most of us. We can of course note that the plights of his characters are often extreme forms of our own. The narrator of 'The Secret Sharer' (1909) is not unusual in having doubts about his competence in a new job and Marlow in 'Heart of Darkness' (1899) is not the first man to tell a lie to save the feelings of a survivor.[1] We may go on emphasizing that he deals with moral problems against a background of shipwreck, revolution, conspiracy, and exploration and not with these unusually exciting happenings for their own sake, but we are aware that the material of his stories now occurs most often in such specialized forms as the thriller, the genres which we associate with Graham Greene's entertainments and the books of Eric Ambler. I discuss in Chapter 6 how some of the material which we take for granted in much nineteenth-century fiction has now been hived off into special forms.

But if his work was once trivialized by labelling it exotic and maritime there may now be a danger of not paying enough attention to his primary themes. These, particularly because they are presented allusively and indirectly and with a high rhetoric, may seem so alien to many readers that they are assimilated to more general concerns. I have the impression that, more than other novelists of this century, Conrad has too often been talked about in the large phrases of generalization about twentieth-century man and his existential dilemmas. Quite often in endeavouring to establish some relationship with Conrad's themes critics have reinterpreted them so as to bring them closer to their own situations and preoccupations and to some supposedly shared problems. This is the effect, if not the intention, for example, of J. Hillis Miller's comment in the Casebook Series study of The Secret Agent (1973):

> The theme of The Secret Agent seems to be the disjunction
> between matter and spirit. . . . Man is the meeting place
> of matter and spirit, and he is riven apart by their
> contradictions.

I would also include among examples of this tendency the line of thought which emphasizes the self-referential nature of the novels (basing this on the choice of a teacher of languages to narrate Under Western Eyes and Conrad's frequent comments on the difficulty of conveying information in the unreliable medium of words), many of the psychoanalytical interpretations, and those which, noting that Conrad's characters often have many names (Charles Gould, Charlie, El Rey de Sulaco, the Señor Administrador, Don Carlos) recruit him into the camp of those with identity crises.

There are, of course, elements of all these matters in his work; Nostromo is unsure of his role, Marlow does emphasize the impossibility of making his listeners see Kurtz as he saw him, Winnie Verloc certainly thinks of Stevie as both matter and spirit. But the effect of claiming that these are the central themes is to deny that Conrad is writing about betrayal and treachery and doubts about courage and the realization that your masters who have praised you have also used you and given you a special, slightly patronizing, name in the process. Conrad writes about these subjects partly because, when he came to writing, these were what he knew in a way that very few writers have known them and partly because he thought that the English needed to be told them. For Conrad certainly thought of himself as in some ways an exotic. He may have been glad in later life to play the part of the retired sea-dog, but he often made it clear that – to take a minor example – he did not really understand the English sense of humour; the English, it may be added, often did not understand his and, on occasions, found it offensive. His outlook is alien and it is rooted in politics.

Conrad is often described as having a 'political' phase in his career and to an extent this is true. Three novels written within a few years of one another stand out as overtly political in theme and they are generally judged to be among his best – *Nostromo* (1904), *The Secret Agent* (1907), and *Under Western Eyes* (1911). But the preoccupations of his earlier works are not different in kind. From the beginning, though not dealing with specifically political themes, he nevertheless displays interests which underlie the political novels. It has often been commented that he is preoccupied by the essential loneliness of each one of us and this is emphasized because his characters tend to be wanderers and exiles, seeking adventure or acceptance. One of the ways in which he shows this isolation is in the contrast between private experience and public appearance. This is, of course, true of all novelists – Bennett in *The Old Wives' Tale* makes it clear that only the draper's wife, Constance Povey, knows what her experience is; Forster in *A Passage to India* shows that only the chaperone, Mrs Moore, can reckon with what happens to her in the Marabar caves – but Conrad so designs his stories that we are made particularly aware of multiplicity of roles and of the extent to which the public ones are as real as the others and cannot be denied by their possessors. The very title of *Lord Jim* (1900), for example, underlines this. It names the central character in the form in which others would speak of him and in so doing directs attention to what is central in Jim's plight. Put at its simplest we may say that, as an officer in the merchant navy, Jim's situation is irredeemable; no later courage, no devotion to duty can ever wipe away the professional failure; nobody, knowing the facts, would ever give him the only job which could satisfy his urge to link his dreams of success with daily life. Indeed, it would be illegal for them to do so; his certificate has been cancelled. Yet as a private man he cannot accept this. All the ruminations of Marlow and the other reflectors take place within the area of this contradiction. Whether we believe that there can be no appeal against the dismissive verdict of the French lieutenant or whether we believe that the fixed code of professional duty is inhuman, we know that all Jim's efforts are quixotic, sometimes heroic, always romantic delusions. Jim is not willing to lead a purely private life; his early romantic daydreams centre round the exercise of his profession and his career in Patusan is an attempt to expunge a failed public life by the creation of a new triumphant one. In this it is akin to Charles Gould's desire in *Nostromo* to transform his father's failure with the silver mine into his own success as a power for good in the land.

One concomitant of this concern for the public life is an awareness of power, not simply economic or institutionalized authority – though there is a good deal of this in the hierarchy of command in many of his early works – but what in his letter to Canby he called 'the psychology of a group of men', the way in which one man imposes his will upon another by emotional or moral suasion, the way in which groups can be moved to follow or to resist. In particular he is fascinated by those kinds of appeal which rest not upon institutions but upon psychological ascendancy. Wait in *The Nigger of the 'Narcissus'* (1897) and Gentleman Brown in *Lord Jim* have often been instanced as examples, as has, of course, the most striking example, Mr Kurtz. Lord Jim's own appeal to Marlow is similar, though complicated by their sharing of a profession and the feelings of loyalty, responsibility, and shame which this brings to the older man.

Relationships of this kind, dealing so much with unacknowledged feelings and normally unexplored recesses of the personality, could not be presented in any cut-and-dried way. They seem to demand indirect methods which hint and suggest rather than state – methods which we may loosely call impressionistic or symbolic without implying that Conrad was deliberately allying himself with any fictional doctrines. Related to this is his use of sharp contrasts of viewpoint and sudden disjunctions in time which force us to keep revaluing our judgements. No sooner do we receive an acceptable view of a character's actions and motives than we are given a very different account from within a different framework of reference. Ford Madox Ford's account of this in his discussion of Conrad's work attributes it to their shared ideas of the *progression d'effet* but, quite apart from the question of Ford's reliability, this does not adequately explain the relationship between the technique and the outlook. My suggestion is that the strange paradox of the coexistence of sharp, often brutal contrasts produced by shift of viewpoint with an apparently vague and free-floating description of psychological states – the mingling of hints which will not become statements on the one hand and sardonic summings-up on the other – corresponds to Conrad's basic conception of men as living in a world which imposes many judgements on them and in which no integration of the whole man is possible. It would be too simple to suggest that the floating states correspond to the more private aspects of personality and the sudden reversals of judgement to the public, professional, political aspects, because Conrad does not make the mistake of taking the public as merely external; he knows that we are made privately of what we are made publicly; but it is apparent that he often makes his sharpest political judgements by a juxtaposition of two viewpoints.

The combination of dogmatic statements, hints, and the eloquence of the prose. which has often been commented upon in terms of its orotundity, leads inevitably to the suspicion that Conrad is asserting that he is dealing with the most fundamental issues while retreating into vagueness when we most hope for a statement. This objection was most forcefully put by E. M. Forster in 1920. Though initially writing here about *Notes on Life and Letters*, the criticism extends beyond this volume to what Forster calls 'half a dozen great books': 'These essays do suggest that he is misty in the middle as well as at the edges, that the secret casket of his genius contains a vapour rather than a jewel.'[2] It is interesting that Forster goes on to suggest that the obscurity is due to a kind of double vision; 'there are constant discrepancies between his nearer and his further vision, and here would seem to be the cause of his central obscurity'. This is surely the criticism which must be met, and if there is one story against which it could most reasonably be made it is that one in which we are specifically told at the outset that the meaning of the narrator's stories lies not 'inside like a kernel but outside, enveloping the tale which brought it out only as a glow brings out a haze' – 'Heart of Darkness'.

'Heart of Darkness' has probably had more critical attention per word than any other modern prose work, with the possible exception of *Ulysses*, whose greater length may be thought to dilute the criticism a little. The obvious reason for this is that it resists simple readings and demands an effort of interpretation. Some of the critical accounts have been excellent but in many ingenuity takes over rather early from sense. The question arises: has it attracted so many divergent interpretations because Forster was right? Have critics been forced to wilder and wilder excesses of interpretation not only because the story is a favourite text in Eng. Lit. courses but because at its heart there is a hollow waiting to be filled up?

It is around Mr Kurtz that uncertainties are bound to accumulate because it is in the relationship between him and Marlow that the book centres. Since Marlow narrates the story and is coming to terms as he tells it with an experience from his past, it is a part of the effect of the story that he should find some difficulty in telling it and, indeed, that at times he should seem overwhelmed by what he is remembering.

Much of this sense of being overwhelmed is given by the dynamics of narration, the hints, foreshadowings, speedings up, slowings down, and it is for this reason regrettable that we do not usually discuss 'Heart of Darkness' until we have forgotten what it is like to read it as distinct from what it is like to have read it: that is, when the sense of the novel as a temporal activity has been virtually entirely expunged from our minds by the sense of it as a spatial quasi-object.

A very simple example of the importance of temporal progression is the way in which Conrad often achieves vividness of description; the most obvious example in this story is the account of the stabbing of the helmsman, which is first registered as his pulling a stick out of someone's hand and overbalancing and is then reinterpreted as his being stabbed in the side and falling over, clutching the spear. Moreover if this is true of such localized effects as the stabbing of the helmsman it is also seen in the larger sweep of the story where we are presented with a sequence of happenings, many of them bewildering and fragmentary, and only subsequently comprehend them. But the effect is not merely one of vividness; more significantly the narrative method is the form in which Marlow's fascination with Kurtz is dramatized. Our sense of the effect of Kurtz on Marlow is not produced primarily by statements about him but rather by the dynamic way in which we see Marlow being overwhelmed.

The form of retrospective narration gives great freedom for the narrator's mind to range backwards and forwards; for example, in the middle of explaining that he got the job because his predecessor had been killed, Marlow leaps forward to say 'when an opportunity offered at last to meet my predecessor, the grass growing through his ribs was tall enough to hide his bones'. But for a considerable stretch up to the attack on the boat, the narrative settles down to a forward chronological movement: the passage round the coast, the arrival at the station, the overland journey to the Central Station, delay, then the journey up-river and then the attack by what Marlow assumes to be Kurtz's enemies but, by the time he is telling the story, knows to be his devotees. The helmsman is killed, the attack is beaten off and then the steady forward movement is broken and memories of Kurtz come flooding hardly comprehensibly into Marlow's narrative – 'the deceitful flow from the heart of an inpenetrable darkness' . . . 'I have heard more than enough' . . . 'I laid the ghost of his gifts at last with a lie'. The effect is as if, having described the defeat of the last obstacle to his encounter with Kurtz, Marlow can no longer maintain control over his memories.

But what, we must ask, is the nature of this power which Kurtz has to impose himself upon Marlow to the extent that he chooses to allow the other officials to lump him in with Kurtz as a member of the party of 'unsound method'? The answer, it seems to me, is implied in those two words. Kurtz is not a hypocrite; he is not to be moved by euphemistic labels. Nor – and this point is often blurred – is he significantly worse than the others. He has killed for his pleasure but those he kills are no more dead than those worked to death or condemned to death by the others for their economic and professional advancement. Kurtz is not so much a new figure, transcending the rapacity of colonization, as its logical culmination gifted with self-knowledge. He does not speculate about what the head office will think of his activities and he does not attempt to justify what he is doing in terms of sound trading methods. This makes him more compelling than the respectable chief accountant who makes 'correct entries of perfectly correct transactions' within sight of those whom these strictly legal dealings, recorded with arithmetical accuracy, have killed; but it only makes him more wicked if we judge individual evil as worse than communal evil.

Much of the puzzlement which has been felt about this story has come about as a result of dividing it into two parts – the picture of colonialism in the first half and an explanation of the second half in terms of a rather vague conception of metaphysical evil. I think that this has happened because it has often been felt that the overwhelming sense of horror and evil of the later parts in some ways transcends the sphere of politics. This may be understandable if we think of political choices as having to do with slightly theoretical matters of administration. But that was not a mistake which was likely to be made by someone with Conrad's background and if we consider the wider hints given in the story, especially those related to what we may loosely call the framework of narration, we are less likely to make this mistake.

It has often been pointed out that the end of the story contains a precise verbal echo of a passage near the beginning:

> The offing was barred by a black bank of clouds, and the tranquil waterway leading to the uttermost ends of the earth flowed sombre under an overcast sky – seemed to lead into the heart of an immense darkness.

This harks back to the paragraph which describes how

> The old river in its broad reach rested unruffled at the decline of day, after ages of good service done to the race that peopled its banks, spread out in the tranquil dignity of a waterway leading to the uttermost ends of the earth.

The effect is to return us at the end to the same waterway that has, at the beginning, seemed to invite admiration for the explorers and imperialists who have sailed from it and to show, with the echo of that word 'darkness' on which so many changes have been rung, that those voyages have led out to actions not unlike those of Mr Kurtz. More generally, the awareness of darkness which the story has generated is brought back home; not only the centre of Africa is dark.

The story was written for *Blackwood's Magazine* and the introduction of a narrator within an appropriate setting for the spinning of a yarn is a very familiar way of opening a magazine story; *Blackwood's* specialized in adventurous stories and the original readers must have felt quite at home with the first page or two. But they would have received something of a shock towards the end of the paragraph of which I have been speaking when they came across mention of 'the *Erebus* and *Terror*, bound on other conquests – and that never returned'. The men of Sir John Franklin's expedition in search of the North-west Passage did not merely fail to return; they were sought for a long time and in 1854 John Rae reported to the Admiralty, on the basis of Eskimo accounts, that some of them appeared to have prolonged their lives by cannibalism. This suggestion was opposed at once in *Household Words* on the basis that Eskimos were unreliable and British seamen would not have done such a thing, but thereafter the scandalous story rose to the surface from time to time, often provoking denials of its possibility. In October 1880, for example, Admiral Richards wrote to *The Times*, blaming Eskimos for cutting up some of the bodies, in reply to the account of the American expedition to the Arctic led by Lieutenant Schwatka. At the beginning of 'Heart of Darkness', in short, the readers of *Blackwood's* (though not, so far as I have been able to discover, modern critics) were reminded of a well-known scandal about an activity popularly supposed to be practised in the heart of the dark continent (and which is associated when we come to the middle of the tale with surprising restraint) but which may actually have been committed by their own countrymen.[3]

I am emphasizing these original readers because it seems clear that Conrad is taking into account certain of their likely expectations and playing ironically against them, most strikingly in his dealing with the concept of 'going native'. He arouses expectations about this supposed activity in speculations about how the Romans felt when they arrived among the British 'savages', but he soon checks any simple assumption not only by his descriptions of the farcical brutality of white men by contrast with the black men who 'wanted no excuse for being there' but also by likening the local people's abandoning of the countryside over which the white men travel to the probable behaviour of the English if they were subjected to forced labour by a lot of men who were 'travelling on the road between Deal and Gravesend'. There are inconsistencies in the attitudes to colonization expressed, especially at the beginning of the story; Marlow, for example, sees with approval those parts of Africa coloured red on the map, he speaks of efficiency as the only quality which saves 'us' (presumably the English) and shows with contempt the inefficiency of the traders of the story, yet the efficient accountant is perhaps the most chilling of them all. These, and other, inconsistencies may be the result of uncertainties in Conrad's own mind; he is not a systematic and theoretical thinker and his works gain much of their force from the sense that he is exploring his own contradictions.[4] He was certainly a paradoxical man who often claimed impeccably respectable and rather conservative views while writing corrosively subversive novels. But the inconsistencies may be intentional and designed to prevent his readers from being alienated too soon and we may assume that Marlow, in telling his story, is re-creating the frame of mind of that part of it which he is narrating at the time. The easy way out for the English reader of the time was presumably to disapprove of King Leopold's notorious exploitation of the Congo without drawing any general conclusions about colonization.

It is with the account of Kurtz's report to the International Society for the Suppression of Savage Customs that the inadequacy of the concept of 'going native' is made clear. This society is clearly based upon the International Association for the Suppression of Slavery and the Opening Up of Central Africa which had been formed by Leopold II in 1876 and its rhetoric is reminiscent of the common European account of relations between Europeans and Africans.[5] Of this report Marlow says:

> The opening paragraph, however, in the light of later
> information, strikes me now as ominous. He began with
> the argument that we whites, from the point of
> development we had arrived at, 'must necessarily appear to
> them [savages] in the nature of supernatural beings – we
> approach them with the might as of a deity,' and so on,
> and so on. 'By the simple exercise of our will we can
> exert a power for good practically unbounded,' &c., &c.

After a parody of the hollow rhetoric – the peroration gives him 'the notion of an exotic Immensity ruled by an august Benevolence' – he quotes the note at the foot of the last page, 'Exterminate all the brutes!' The opening paragraph is, indeed, ominous, for it makes perfectly clear that Kurtz, of whom we are told 'all Europe contributed to the making of Kurtz', took with him from Europe this conception of the superior race which alone justified colonial activity and which led to vast slaughter in the Congo. Conrad makes it quite clear that Kurtz has not 'gone native', except in the sense that some of his indulgences are peculiar to Africa. What he has manifested is not a succumbing to the more primitive but oppression by the advanced European.

But Conrad is not only writing about the evils of colonization; he makes perfectly clear towards the end of the story that he regards it as an index of what men may come to do in Europe. The other 'pilgrims' of trade are held back by timidity or hypocrisy from following Kurtz's logic, just as Marlow tells his listeners that they are themselves kept in order by social forces, 'the holy terror of scandal and gallows and lunatic asylums', but once someone arrives to whom you can appeal in the name of nothing but himself there will be little to stop him. Nor need he be a 'great' man, if by 'great' we mean possessed of striking originality of mind or intellectual powers. Kurtz is a hollow man, he is 'avid of lying fame, of sham distinction, of all the appearance of success and power'. The combination of burning eloquence and mean ambition must have seemed, when the story was written, puzzling, for the obvious type of the eloquent and charismatic leader must for most people have been Napoleon; we, the better part of a century later, should not be surprised at the combination of demagogic leadership with banality.

The implication that colonization is merely a special case of domination is stated without ambiguity when Marlow returns to Europe:

> They [the inhabitants of the capital] were intruders whose knowledge of life was to me an irritating pretence, because I felt so sure they could not possibly know the things I knew. Their bearing, which was simply the bearing of commonplace individuals going about their business in the assurance of perfect safety, was offensive to me like the outrageous flauntings of folly in the face of a danger it is unable to comprehend.

The journalist, who knew Kurtz before he went to Africa, defines Kurtz's potentialities very clearly:

> 'but heavens! how that man could talk! He electrified large meetings. He had faith – don't you see? – he had the faith. He could get himself to believe anything – anything. He would have been a splendid leader of an extreme party.'
> 'What party' I asked. 'Any party,' answered the other. 'He was an – an – extremist.'

Even the not very successful interview with the Intended, a passage in which Conrad's tendency to idealize young women in a manner which also diminishes their reality is seen at its worst, is more effective if we do not try to relate Kurtz to a vague metaphysical sense of evil but rather to that evil which is done under the sun and which we can see, the evil which Conrad saw as lying at the heart of colonial exploitation and potentially in other oppressions. The Intended then takes her place with the other inhabitants of the European capital and also harks back to Marlow's aunt who, living in the middle of 'all that humbug', saw him as 'Something like an emissary of light' and who talks about 'weaning those ignorant millions from their horrid ways'.

The sense of confusion and at times of vagueness and muddle in the story is not, I think, at the heart of it. Indeed, the heart of the darkness is very precise and if Conrad's only intention had been to alert us to the evils committed by others, if, that is, he had wanted to be one more denouncer of the behaviour of Leopold in the Congo, he could have performed the task very expeditiously. But the essence of the story is that Marlow, in his alternations of contempt and revulsion and fascination, should take us with him; I have suggested that in one very simple way he was meant to take with him the original *Blackwood's* readers; within the story he takes not only the listener who reports his story but also the other listeners, the Accountant, the Director of Companies and the Lawyer (well may one of them interject 'Try to be civil, Marlow' when he seems to disparage their work). Marlow is struggling with his memories, trying to make sense of his reactions; in returning us at the end to a Thames which leads out to 'the heart of an immense darkness' the story may be taking a step beyond what Marlow could know.

But there is one very simple question which is not asked in 'Heart of Darkness' and it is, in this, like several of the early works. Why, if he is convinced near the beginning of his journey of the inherent evil of the colonizing process, does Marlow continue to work for the colonizers? Why does not Conrad raise this issue? Why, similarly, we may ask, does Conrad exclude from 'Youth' any question of the morality of shipping men in a coffin ship; a merchant seaman would have been well aware of everything that led up to the Plimsoll Merchant Shipping Act of 1875; but the only hint we have is a jocular one about saving as much as possible from the burning ship for the underwriters. To such questions there are a number of answers; the simplest is that Conrad himself had done what he describes and he writes of what he knows. We can add to this that there is no room in the stories for such concerns; we must have a Marlow to observe Kurtz and the colonizers and he has enough to digest without worrying about the morality of his own employment. More generally, this delimitation is a manifestation of a framework within which short-term efficiency and the doing of one's duty are accepted virtues. Captain Beard is allowed to have certain aims untarnished and so is Marlow, though it is worth noting that he comes back down the river not as a captain but as a passenger. The questions would not even occur to one were it not that in the overtly political novels these are often the kinds of issues with which Conrad does deal; in them he seems to take nothing for granted. The policeman who is mentioned in 'Heart of Darkness' is a traditional figure of order; in *The Secret Agent* when Stevie asks what the police are for, his sister, avoiding the word 'steal' which upsets her feeble-minded brother, formulates her answer in terms which could hardly be improved upon by the anarchist Professor: 'They are there so as them as have nothing shouldn't take anything away from those who have' (8).

The three novels which we call political – *Nostromo*, *The Secret Agent*, and *Under Western Eyes* – widen the scope of Conrad's presentation of human dilemmas and represent the summit of his achievement before a marked decline. But they are not fundamentally different in outlook from the earlier works. Conrad does not conceive of a separate sphere of life, an optional extra, called politics. An Englishman of his generation might have thought that politics was an activity into which he was free to dip or not. The son of Apollo and Evelina Korzeniowski could not and this was not merely because of any specifically familial situation, though it must have been that, too, but because anyone born into the educated classes in what had once been Poland but was now a part of the Tsarist Empire would have known that every significant detail of social life was political. The plight of Razumov in *Under Western Eyes* can stand as a parable of this: he does not wish to involve himself in politics and positively isolates himself from the political concerns of his fellow students; therefore he is the man to whom Haldin goes for shelter after he has assassinated the Minister of State. He cannot be neutral; he must connive at assassination and risk Siberia or he must betray Haldin and, as he discovers, work for the secret police.

The specifically political nature of the first, the largest and the best, of the three political novels, *Nostromo*, published in 1904, is made abundantly clear from the start. It is often found confusing and unwelcoming by readers coming to it for the first time and this is because its form throughout asserts its meaning – the subordination of individuals to the social and political situation. The apparently rebarbative presentation, the going backwards and forwards in time, the introduction of characters in asides or as if we already know about them, the effect of muddle, are part of the meaning. Much of what we see in the second, third and fourth chapters in a series of sharply presented but often incomprehensible actions is described clearly and sequentially much later in Decoud's letter to his sister, just as the past history of Costaguana with all its oppression, civil warfare, and suffering is doubtless made easily comprehensible in Don José Avallanos's famous *Fifty Years of Misrule*. Individuals experience and suffer in a confused situation which can later be seen as part of a process of which other people can make sense. People are less important and less free than they think. It is typical of this irony that the removal of the silver in the lighter by Decoud and Nostromo is intended as a desperate measure to retain the support of the financiers upon whom Gould and the Blancos depend; the silver is lost but this has no effect whatever upon those financiers and nobody even mentions this apparently surprising miscalculation.

What we acquire in the first fifty pages or so is not a feeling that we are getting to know individual characters, though a number of them are introduced to us in sharp, usually visual, detail, but a sense of the economic and political situation in which they are involved. The unifying factor of the presentation is the emphasis upon manipulation and the exercise of power. The first mention of the politics of Costaguana is typical; Mitchell asserts his priorities, which are the priorities of all those who have invested time and money in this underdeveloped republic, when he says that 'he accounted as most unfavourable to the orderly working of his Company the frequent changes of government brought about by revolutions of the military type' (I. 2). It is no surprise that the chairman of the railway company knows that the acquisition of land for the line is a matter of 'the judicious influencing' of those in power; 'it was only a matter of price'. The rhetoric and the realities of Costaguanan politics are summed up well in the reflection about the President-Dictator: 'After all he was their own creature – that Don Vincente. He was the embodied triumph of the best elements in the State' (I. 5). The effect which Conrad achieves by his fragmented and allusive presentation is of a situation which is taken for granted; there is no moment at which we feel that a moral stance should be taken, no moment of shocked revelation. When, much later, in Part III, Chapter 7, we are specifically informed that 'Every Minister of the Interior drew a salary from the San Tomé mine. It was natural' it does not surprise us; the best elements in the State, the allies of the honourable Avellanos, the opponents of the mob, are not less greedy than Sotillo or Montero, merely more discreet and more respectable.

One of the most striking ways in which Conrad asserts the immersion of his characters in a political situation and the consequent attrition of their individual freedom is the manner in which their roles are defined by titles, sobriquets, simplifying descriptions: Gould is the

Senõr Administrador, the Inglese, el Rey de Sulaco, Don Carlos as well as Charlie; often the titles are piled up in one description; Decoud is 'The brilliant "Son Decoud", the spoiled darling of the family, the lover of Antonia and journalist of Sulaco', Viola is 'sailor, champion of oppressed humanity, enemy of kings, and, by the grace of Mrs Gould, hotel-keeper of the Sulaco harbour'; Nostromo is 'Gian' Battista Fidanza, Capataz de Cargadores, the incorruptible and faithful Nostromo'. This last example is particularly striking for it occurs at the moment when he decides to steal the treasure, but the effect of such descriptions is always mockingly diminishing.

The progress of many of the characters is towards an understanding of what roles they are forced to play and how small is the area within which they are free. This effect of determinism is announced by the introduction on the second page of the story told by the local people, 'associating by an obscure instinct of consolation the ideas of evil and wealth', of the treasure seekers who died on the desolate promontory of Azuera and haunt the treasure from which they cannot tear themselves away. Nostromo repeatedly likens himself, and Sotillo, to the legendary guardians of treasure, but the image reverberates throughout the book as appropriate to so many of them. Their fate is determined by the chosen symbol even before we meet them.

The most thoroughly developed study of a man who is devoted to the silver of the mine is that of Charles Gould, whose ancestry, courtship, marriage, and subsequent career as administrator of the mine is the first lengthy sequential section of the book after the setting out of the scene and the political assumptions in the first five chapters.

I have suggested that Conrad assumes in 'Heart of Darkness' that his expected reader will have certain assumptions about the colonial enterprise which it is his intention to undermine. It is equally true here that Gould is initially presented as the personage with whom the English reader may most readily be expected to feel at home and to sympathize. He has, indeed, a very good claim on our sympathies. The story of the atrocious exploitation of his father by a succession of corrupt governments is told us in Part I, Chapter 6, in a tone of gentle but implacable irony ('It was an ordinary Costaguana Government – the fourth in six years – but it judged of its opportunities sanely') and we cannot but sympathize with Charles Gould's determination to make a practical success of that which had virtually killed his father; the first suggestion of his ability to idealize, even to anthropomorphize, material things, a tendency of which he is accused so effectively later by Decoud, is attractive:

He visited mines in Germany, in Spain, in Cornwall.
Abandoned workings had for him strong fascination. Their

desolation appealed to him like the sight of human misery, whose causes are varied and profound. They might have been worthless, but also they might have been misunderstood.

He knows that, given the nature of South American politics, he will have to bribe and he knows that he needs the backing of Holroyd and his associates who talk in terms of economic domination: 'On the other hand, Europe must be kept out of this continent, and for proper interference on our part the time is not yet ripe' or 'we will go with you as long as the thing runs straight. But we won't be drawn into any large trouble.' But his accounts of his aims are far removed from ignoble acquisitiveness:

I pin my faith to material interests. Only let the material interests get a firm footing, and they are bound to impose the conditions on which alone they can continue to exist. That's how your money-making is justified in the face of lawlessness and disorder. It is justified because the security which it demands must be shared with an oppressed people. A better justice will come afterwards.

For Gould politics is a dirty activity; of his uncle Harry who became President of Costaguana he says:

He made use of the political cry of his time. It was Federation. But he was no politician. He simply stood up for social order out of pure love for rational liberty and from his hate of oppression.

But politics is not, despite Gould's wishes, a separate sphere and the man who can present his uncle as a non-political President finds that he is himself a President-maker, for 'the Ribierist party in Costaguana took a practical shape under the eye of the administrator of the San Tomé mine', and in time the Separationist proclamation will be written upon San Tomé paper. The government which is formed to defend that order which the mine requires and which Gould trusts will lead to a better justice makes its appeal in the expected impeccable terms. One of the most effective methods by which Conrad enforces judgements is by shifts of tone. At times the effect of a series of rapid shifts is to induce a sense of insecurity as one apparently secure response is suddenly shown by a change to be unreliable. At other times, as here, Conrad enshrines within a general texture of sub-ironic prose a series of clichés which simultaneously report with accuracy what is being recounted and imply a sardonic comment on it. The effect is of undermining farce. Even if we had not seen the débâcle of the regime with poor Ribiera fleeing for his life we would find fatuous the description of the terms of the government appointment:

> It was a specific mandate to establish the prosperity of the
> people on the basis of firm peace at home, and to redeem
> the national credit by the satisfaction of all just claims
> abroad.   (II. 1)

Few passages in Conrad's novels convey so forcefully his sardonic contempt as such unexceptionable sentiments. Gould says of the Monterists who call themselves Liberals that the words he knows well have a nightmarish meaning in Costaguana, but do we not feel the same about the reassuring platitudes of Westminster-style political rhetoric?

Inevitably, with the failure of the Ribierist government, Gould becomes disillusioned with the cause which he has espoused; the attempts of the President of the Provincial Assembly, Don Juste Lopez, to 'save the last shred of parliamentary institutions (on the English model)' (III. 7) by leading a deputation to hand over power to Montero fill him with a mixture of contempt, compassion, and despair. The parliamentarians themselves feel that, in not using the mine as a bargaining card on their behalf, he is abandoning them. But Gould is now committed to nothing but the continuance of the mine under his own direction or its destruction. Bearing in mind the frequent sincere praise of Gould by the likes of honest men such as Hernandez the bandit (later to be created a general in the last flurries of the Blancoist cause) and the small-scale welfare state created by Mrs Gould among the mineworkers, we may well feel that his trust in the civilizing effects of material interests is not totally misplaced, but Conrad's comments on his manipulation of the politics of the country and his ultimate lack of commitment to the regime he has created are harsh. 'To him, as to all of us,' Conrad says pitilessly, 'the compromises with his conscience appeared uglier than ever in the light of failure' (III. 4), and he is likened to an adventurer and a buccaneer 'throwing a lighted match into the magazine rather than surrender his ship'. And he is described as finding himself unable to speak to the Blancos in defeat because he 'suffered from his fellowship in evil with them too much' (III. 7).

We may better understand this harshness if we pay attention to many underplayed moments in the story which elucidate the society with which he has allied himself and for which, like any investor who manipulates the local politicos, he must share responsibility. The

Blancos, once known as the Oligarchy, are not so very different in their effect upon the people of the country from the vulgar revolutionists. One of the first signs that Montero is disloyal to the Blancos, for example, is that

> notorious democrats, who had been living till then in
> constant fear of arrest, leg irons, and even floggings, could
> be observed going in and out at the great door of the
> Commandacia.   (II. 8)

Loyalty to Gould's nominee for the Presidency would presumably have entailed a continuation of those leg irons and floggings. The apparent superiority of the Blancos rests to a large extent upon their more elegant style of life and much play is made with the vulgarity of the revolutionaries and the mob whom they use. One of the more entertaining examples of this is that the railway engineer points out that Fuentes is 'a man of birth and education' (III. 2) who appears miserable at being linked with the vulgar Gamacho and fears him; seventy pages later we discover that birth will tell as Fuentes ingratiates himself with Montero and with a few well-chosen words sees to it that Gamacho will be ousted.

Conrad frequently gives to the revolutionists crude outbursts which ask for denial and then obliges us to recognize the amount of truth in them. Montero's toast 'I drink to the health of the man who brings us a million and a half of pounds' (I. 8) is not to the taste of Sir John to whom it is addressed but it is a true account of the function of the 'financier of railways'. The Monterist press attacks the 'sinister land-grabbing designs of the European powers' and Ribiera who 'plotted to deliver his country, bound hand and foot, for a prey to foreign speculators' (II. 2). We already know that the railway has bribed the Commissioners to let them have the land and the point has been driven home when Gould, after the reception for Sir John, looks at the populace enjoying themselves eating and drinking and dancing and says: 'All this piece of land belongs now to the Railway Company. There will be no more popular feasts held here' (I. 8).

Nowhere is the tactless expression of the aims of foreign investment and commerce more strikingly expressed than in the scene in which Barrios and his troops are seen off at the port. This section – the fourth chapter of Part II – brings together most of the central characters of the novel and brings to mind most of the main themes; it ends with the often quoted image of the triumph of material forces; as the crowd disperses a train passes and 'a series of hard, battering shocks, mingled with the clanking of chain-couplings, made a tumult of blows and shaken fetters under the vault of the gate'. Earlier the telegraph wire has been likened to 'a slender, vibrating feeler of that progress waiting outside for a moment of peace to enter and twine itself about the weary heart of the land'. Barrios, upon whose mission the fate of the Europeans and the Blancos seems to rest, is a man of acknowledged honesty and courage, though it is believed that he has obtained the 'reputedly lucrative Oriental command' through the efforts of his creditors. His reassurance to those seeing him off is expressed in terms which are not too dissimilar from the Monterist rhetoric:

> Señores, have no apprehension. Go on quietly making
> your Ferro Carril – your railways, your telegraphs. Your –
> There's enough wealth in Costaguana to pay for
> everything – or else you would not be here. Ha! ha! . . .
> 'Fear nothing, develop the country, work, work!

He is thought to have had too much to drink and most of the listeners do not respond to what is described as 'his interpretation of Senor Avellanos's ideals', but one of them, Young Scarfe, caught up in the enthusiasm of the moment, puts matters in his own words:

> In a loud and youthful tone he hoped that this Montero
> was going to be licked once for all and done with. There
> was no saying what would happen to the railway if the
> revolution got the upper hand . . . it had been an immense
> piece of luck for him at his age to get appointed on the
> staff of 'a big thing like that – don't you know.' It would
> give him the pull over a lot of chaps all through life he
> asserted. 'Therefore – down with Montero!'

Mrs Gould defends him on the grounds of his youth against Decoud's ironic praise of him as 'an enlightened well-wisher' but when the party has returned to the Casa Gould Decoud leaves no doubt that he does not believe deeply in the cause that he has espoused; to Avellanos's insistence that they must reassure their financial backers in Europe and the United States he replies, 'Oh, yes, we must comfort our friends, the speculators.'

Conrad is peculiarly harsh to Decoud. He is far and away the most clear-sighted of the characters and his analysis of Gould's self-deception, in particular, is unanswerable. Yet he is placed in a situation of total solitude, cracks under the strain, and is summed up as the 'victim of the disillusioned weariness which is the retribution meted out to intellectual audacity' (III. 10). It could be held against him that he takes part in political action, the separation of Sulaco from Costaguana, not because he believes in it but because it gives him some hope of marriage with Antonia. But this is not mentioned in the chapter which describes his last days and in which a number of specific statements, amounting to a judgement, are given as reasons for his suicide. All tend towards the conclusion that, in solitude, his death is inevitable because he shares his view of life with his creator.

A scepticism equal to Decoud's has certainly been established in the most unexpected and inventive section of the book: Chapter 10 of Part III. We have been prepared for a grand climax: Sotillo, Montero, Gamacho, and Fuentes occupy the town; the Blancos have fled; Monygham is planning to buy time by deceiving Sotillo about the whereabouts of the silver; Gould is fencing with Montero while Don Pépé and Father Román are preparing to blow up the mine if Gould so orders; Nostromo, back from disposing of the silver, is about to leave on the railway engine to fetch Barrios's men back. Chapter 10 begins, promising further action and a resolution of the suspense:

> The next day was quiet in the morning, except for the
> faint sound of firing to the northward, in the direction of
> Los Hatos.

The second sentence, slipping into the pluperfect, announces that the suspense is over and that the climax lies in the past: 'Captain Mitchell had listened to it from his balcony anxiously.' For the next sixteen pages we are given the disjointed retrospective account which Mitchell was in the habit of inflicting on uncomprehending and often bored visitors. All the actions and all the participants in them are reduced to stock phrases while his listeners wonder who these people can be. Each description of the fighting resembles a stock adventure story; each cliché diminishes the individuality of the person it describes and assimilates him or her to the retrospective praise of the status quo.

The effect is initially one of disappointment, of total narrative anticlimax, but this reaction is transformed as we go on reading about the improved streets, the Sulaco National Bank, the monument to Avellanos ('worn out with his life-long struggle for Right and Justice at the dawn of the New Era') the Parliamentary party with Don Juste Lopez at its head, the recognition of the Occidental Republic by the United States and the repeated quotation from the *The Times's* description of Sulaco as 'The Treasure House of the World'. The anticlimax of narration is replaced by a climax of realization as the basic theme of the novel comes uncompromisingly to the fore – the realization that all these individuals with whom we have been concerned are, in the development of Sulaco as 'The Treasure House of the World', dispensable. Their functions have mattered but not their individuality. For the 'distinguished bird of passage' who is listening they are figures in history who have served their turn in bringing about the present situation. Monygham is given the specific statement – the often quoted:

> There is no peace and no rest in the development of
> material interests . . . the time approaches when all that
> the Gould Concession stands for shall weigh as heavily
> upon the people as the barbarism, cruelty, and misrule of
> a few years back.   (III. 11)

But all that he says is more brilliantly implied in Joe Mitchell's retrospect and its brusque rejection of our expectations.

Apart from a little tidying up, all that remains after this is in effect a coda. I have suggested that the verdict of Monygham and the consequent despair of Mrs Gould have already been established. But they must be seen to be worked out. Similarly, Nostromo's fate must be shown. The ending is, in terms of the legend of the treasure seekers of Azuera and Nostromo's own frequent mention of it, allegorically right, but it leads Conrad into the somewhat over-picturesque or operatic mode into which the person of Nostromo tempts him. Nostromo has, indeed, often been criticized as a creation and Conrad himself felt that he was in need of some defence. The silver of the mine was, he said, the true hero of the book and the eponymous hero is described by him in a letter to Cunninghame Graham as a 'romantic mouthpiece of the people'.[6] But, though he may be conceived in romantic terms, there is surely something more than this to be said about him. Perhaps he can be seen as a central figure in the novel because he does represent so clearly the fate of the enterprising and reliable man who, in most societies, can fill an honourable place and enjoy the respect of his own people. His fate in this society is described, albeit with the anger of irritated love, by Teresa Viola:

> 'That is all he cares for. To be first somewhere –
> somehow – to be the first with these English. They will
> be showing him to everybody. This is our Nostromo!'
> She laughed ominously. 'What a name! What is that?
> Nostromo? He would take a name that is properly no
> word from them.'   (I. 4)

Another clear-sighted observer, Monygham, wonders at his fidelity – 'I don't know why the devil he should be faithful to you, Gould, Mitchell, or anybody else' (III. 1) and expresses most brutally the degree to which Nostromo is used when he answers his suspicion that he might be betrayed by saying: 'You are safe because you are needed. I would not give you away for any conceivable reason, because I want

you.' (III. 9) There is no wonder, then, that at the time when, seeing
the mine 'lording it by its vast wealth over the valour, the toil, the
fidelity of the poor', he resolves to grow rich slowly by stealing the
treasure, he is named ironically with his titles – 'There was no-one in
the world but Gian' Battista Fidanza, Capataz de Cargadores, the
incorruptible and faithful Nostromo, to pay such a price'. (III. 10)

Notes

1. I give the dates of first publications of Conrad's short stories. Collections in
   volume form usually came a few years later.

2. The review is reprinted in *Abinger Harvest* (1936).

3. For a fuller account of this long-running scandal see D. Hewitt, '"Heart of
   Darkness" and Some "Old and Unpleasant Reports"', *Review of English Studies*
   Vol. XXXVIII, Number 151, August 1987, pp. 374–76. Since writing this I
   have discovered that Peter Knox-Shaw, in his excellent book *The Explorer in
   English Fiction* (1987), makes the same point.

4. I use the concept of authorial intention (and would be more than prepared to
   make that author as near anonymous as possible, i.e. not taking into account
   anything but what is contained within the story) and come to the conclusion
   that there may here be something of a muddle. I don't think it matters much
   whether we admit that the author seems to have been slightly muddled (i.e.
   that he hadn't applied to this part of the story some judgements which are
   implied elsewhere) or whether we think that he wants to show Marlow as a
   little muddled without making a muddled Marlow a significant and consistent
   part of the story's effect. In either case there is an inconsistency. It is not a
   major matter and is best dealt with by accepting it as a minor flaw. If we are
   not prepared to do this, either because we cannot accept the existence of an
   unfulfilled intention which nevertheless allows itself to be decoded or (more
   likely) because we can't admit a flaw in a great work, we will be led to
   speculate about Marlow as an unreliable narrator. This will vastly increase the
   effect of the flaw and disintegrate some sections of the story. There is no end
   to this line of thought and it is essentially destructive. If the weaknesses of any
   work of art cannot be recognized as such but have to be considered as subtle
   successes the whole work is distorted.

5. Norman Sherry in *Conrad's Western World* (1971) quotes, p. 120, a speech by
   H. M. Stanley which draws a parallel between the European gift of civilization
   to 'these unhappy Africans' and the Roman colonization of Britain.

6. See *Joseph Conrad's Letters to Cunninghame Graham*, edited by C. T. Watts
   (1969), p. 157. Conrad owed a good deal in the way of South American
   history and local colour to this aristocratic Scottish socialist. Their friendship is
   a very interesting one in terms of what they shared and what they did not.

Chapter 4
Rudyard Kipling: Imperial Responsibility and Literary Escape

When the anonymous reviewer in the *Spectator* of *Almayer's Folly* suggested that Conrad might become the Kipling of the Malay Archipelago he was, no doubt, clutching at a straw of likeness. But the comparison stuck and was used several times thereafter. It is well to remember, though, that the Kipling that the reviewer had in mind was still, though less radically than Conrad, an outsider. Looking back, we see him as so thoroughly an established figure – the friend of Rhodes, the cousin of Stanley Baldwin, the man chosen to decide on the wording on war graves, the man whose ashes were conveyed to Westminster Abbey by, among others, a Prime Minister, an admiral, a general, and the Master of a Cambridge college. He first burst on the literary scene, however, as a visitor from India, bringing demotic stories of often disreputable people and news of a far-away and exotic world.

From the start he inspired strong and mixed feelings; the reviewers of his first volume applauded his energy and the novelty of his tales, but they were bothered by lapses of tone, vulgarity, and the lack of what one called a 'sustaining philosophy'; much of the later development of Kipling's reputation has about it the air of a rather outraged acceptance that he has brought it off, together with outright hostility by some. His work still rouses strong feelings.

The variation of quality in his work and the fact that some of it aims (successfully) at popular success is hardly enough reason; we have learnt to distinguish between Bennett's good novels and his bad ones. But Kipling, unlike other writers, tends to make us feel that in admiring or disliking him we are taking up a position and there are, I think, two reasons for this. The less important one is that he has written himself into the national consciousness as a children's storyteller. He is still a part of many people's childhoods and this leads to kinds of rejection or possessiveness which are not dangers for writers whom we encounter later in life. What would be the effect on us if someone unearthed a number of stories about the struggles of small farmers against bureaucracy by Beatrix Potter or a study of senior common-room intrigues by Lewis Carroll?

The more important reason for our sense of taking up a position is that his relationship to political ideas is basically different from, say, that of Yeats, who expresses opinions which might be expected to prove unacceptable to those who dislike Kipling's imperialism. But Yeats treats his politics frivolously; he starts a poem, as he tells us in *The Cat and the Moon and Certain Poems*, with a belief that democracy is worn out and we need a new, violent annunciation but as he writes the politics disappears, bird and lady take possession, and he ends up with 'Leda and the Swan'. Kipling seems to believe that political matters are more important than his stories; a direct didactic purpose is obvious in many of these – 'The Army of a Dream', for example, and 'The Mother Hive' – and throughout his writing there recur appeals which give the impression that the writer is happy to take instruction from the practical man. Certainly those who greatly admired Kipling in his lifetime, as well as those who disliked him, were in no doubt that he was a teacher; nor did Kipling himself show any sign of wishing to dissociate himself from such praise.

But the particular quality in Kipling which rouses such immediate feelings of liking or disliking is more widespread than a number of didactic stories. His dominant beliefs are more basic than his imperial faith and they are not merely declared but embodied in his narrative structures.

What is fundamental to Kipling's view is that, like Conrad but unlike (as I hope to show) Forster, he sees men as inextricably parts of society and he agrees in seeing society as often harsh. He differs from Conrad in believing that society has the right, even the duty, to make great demands because what at bottom he fears is anarchy and disorder. Conrad's distrust of organized states is congenial to our late-twentieth-century view of the matter, for we have observed that the worst atrocities of our century have been committed by men obeying orders and doing their duty with clear consciences. The forces of anarchy and disorder have had remarkably little to their discredit by comparison with, say, the camps set up in the Third Reich and Stalinist Russia. It was easier to believe, when Kipling began writing in the late 1880s, that the danger came either from an alien and more primitive society (Picts or, as in 'The Man Who Was', Cossacks) or from disorderly forces within. There has, in recent years, been a good deal of discussion of Kipling's beliefs in terms of the sociologists of the later nineteenth century and it may be true that his ideas can be assimilated to the concepts of Pareto and others, but this hardly seems necessary, though one can gain a good deal of innocent amusement from speculating as to what Kipling would have made of having his faith in the civilizing power of Rome or the British Empire likened to those of foreign theoreticians.

A contrast with Conrad's narrative method is a useful way of making clear the essence of Kipling's attitude. Conrad's technique is a distancing one. This distance may be achieved by his interposing narrators – Marlow, for example, in 'Heart of Darkness' and various personages in *Nostromo*: Mitchell, Decoud, and the authorial persona who opens the book with a historical survey and maintains, throughout, a detached observing position. It may also be achieved by a tone, as in *The Secret Agent*, which seems to hold his characters at a distance and present them for our inspection (paradoxically this proves to be the one method which could in such a scene as the cab drive across London make us feel intensely both the pathos of the poor in general and the rightness of Stevie in particular). Kipling's tone, by contrast, endeavours to bring us as close as possible, sometimes to the extent of being positively buttonholing. He constantly asserts shared experience and shared standards. Conrad's aim is often to disorientate the implied reader; we think that we can in *Under Western Eyes* take the teacher of languages as a reliable guide and are then obliged to reconsider this when Natalie Haldin speaks with such disdain of those who are secure because they have made a bargain with fate. Kipling never to any significant extent throws us off balance; when he uses irony he signals it too clearly to be missed. Security is too valuable to be put at risk.

The circumstances of Kipling's first publication favoured his method. Writing for the *Civil and Military Gazette* of Lahore, he had a specific public with whom to identify and he took full advantage of this. We see it in 'Thrown Away', a simple and sad story of a young man, spoiled from childhood, who makes stupid mistakes when he is stationed in India, has none of the sense of proportion which a more rough-and-tumble life would have given him, and kills himself in the belief that he has wasted his life and committed unforgivable offences. To achieve the effect of pathos and inevitability Kipling insistently implies our joint membership of a group or class or caste which is uniquely in a position to understand what is happening. The tone is that of one man of the world speaking to another and the effect is reinforced by a multiplicity of references to supposedly shared judgements and experiences. He says:

> Now India is a place beyond all others where one must
> not take things too seriously. . . . Nothing matters except
> Home-furlough and acting allowances and these only
> because they are scarce.

The boy, by contrast,

> took his losses seriously, and wasted as much energy and
> interest over a two-goldmohur race for maiden *ekka*-ponies
> with their manes hogged, as if it had been the Derby.

Presumably the original readers, or most of them, would have known
about *ekka*-ponies and the scarcity of Home-furlough, but the appeal
is the same for English readers of the English publication. They are
invited to feel that they are being addressed as members of a society
in which these references come naturally. It is often, and correctly, said
that Kipling makes great play with his status as a man who knows the
passwords and the technical terms and the finer points of private
rituals, and that this can grow tedious; but it is equally true that he
is asserting that we know them, too, and name-dropping can be effectively indulged in with some people even when they are not certain
to whom the names refer.

This urge to assert the solidarity of the reader with the writer and
their society continues throughout his writing and towards the end of
his life even increases. There are stories in which it seems more
important than anything else, so that they become predominantly acts
of mutual self-identification and the assertion of community of judgement. The frame of the tale is more important than the tale itself.

It is an inevitable consequence of this narrative method that
Kipling's beliefs and social attitudes should become an issue for his
readers; a technique which seeks to incorporate the reader in a group
whose judgements enforce a belief in the paramount importance of
society over the individual does not allow us any room for aesthetic
detachment. This is reinforced by the nature of many of the stories,
which are based upon an opposition between groups and beliefs.
Kipling is not very often concerned to show complexities or contradictions of feeling within one person. Apart from his simpler anecdotes
he usually puts us in a position where we are called upon to take sides.
His famous comment about needing both sides of his head may imply
not only greater variety of attitude than is sometimes thought but also
a tendency to see matters in terms of bipolar oppositions.[1]

Thus those who in general agree with his political and social views
find no problem, except that sometimes the fellow is a bit ingratiating.
Those who do not agree with him are likely to feel that they want to
extricate themselves from the implied relationship in which they find
themselves.

Moreover, as has constantly been said, very many of the stories are
concerned with those issues which have been most controversial in this
century – war, inter-racial encounters, class and group conflicts, certain

views about the continuity of historical experience – and many of those which do not specifically tackle these themes have settings in which the issues figure largely. And there can be no doubt that in most cases he demands that we accept what will go against the grain of most of us – cowardly Babus, straightforward Pathans who respect our firm rule, treacherous Boers, pitied young men who have married beneath them, outspoken old rustics who yet know their place and accept it; there is hardly a reactionary cliché which we will not find.

His treatment of war provides the best example of the problems which his narrative method presents for readers. A comparison with a short-story writer who greatly admired Kipling makes the problem very clear. Isaac Babel's stories in *Red Cavalry*[2] show every bit as much awareness of blood and wounds and pain and death as Kipling's and, like Kipling, Babel appears to believe that the war he is recording is necessary and that his Cossacks are the men to do the job (he had also, which Kipling had not, taken part in the campaign). But his cold, clear presentation, his astonishing images ('Into the cool of evening dripped the smell of yesterday's blood, of slaughtered horses') come from a distance; we are not asked, as we are by Kipling, to enjoy the slaughter. The problem with Kipling is not that we cannot accept that violent cruelty happens, that it may for those performing it be necessary and even an enjoyable release, but that we cannot join in the enjoyment. It comes as a shock, now, to find Henry James, for one, expressing such admiration for 'The Drums of the Fore and Aft' with its vicarious pleasure in combat ('The red lances dipped by twos and threes, and with a shriek, up rose the lance-butt, like a spar on a stormy sea, as the trooper cantering forward cleared his point'). Since about 1915 it has not been possible for a decent civilian, sitting at his ease, so to relish warfare; this inhibition is one of the legacies of Loos and Ypres and the Somme. But there *were*, as he said, two sides to Kipling's head, even though to a striking extent they seem normally to have operated separately. In 'Kidnapped', from *Plain Tales from the Hills* (1888), we are asked to applaud a jaunty tale of how Miss Castries is cheated of her lover because he is a white man and she is a half-caste. 'Without Benefit of Clergy', in *Life's Handicap* (1891), is a sad and touching story of the love between an Englishman and an Indian woman and the question of race arises only because the reader knows that even if death had not separated them the rules of their society would eventually have found them out.[3] There are numerous stories, often employing the metaphor of the breaking-in of a horse, about the training, often brutal, of young men for their job where we are asked to applaud the necessary harshness; but there are also stories, particularly in the later volumes, about those who have been tried too hard.

But the two kinds of attitude do not mingle; they are kept in separate stories.

One story in which the two sides do coexist proves to be the clearest sign that they cannot blend. 'The Brushwood Boy', in *The Day's Work* (1898), is the story of George Cottar, a dazzlingly successful army officer, adored by his men and respected by his superiors, who has a series of repeated dreams, sometimes frightening and sometimes inexplicably happy. Returning on leave, having just won the DSO for rescuing wounded under fire, he is introduced to a young woman who reveals, by a song which she has composed and sings, that she is the companion whom he meets in his dreams. He declares himself, and we leave the youngest major in the army to a future which seems to be a daytime life of military success and public virtues and a night-time life of enchantment and terrors shared, while they are asleep, with his soul mate. Neither half of the life means anything in terms of the other half, nor is there any suggestion that the split is even potentially upsetting or dangerous.

Kipling lavishes on Cottar more success than, perhaps, any other of his characters. He is to inherit a large and beautiful house with a superb estate where the servants from butler to under-keeper worship him; he is very attractive to women but does not realize it; his success at school ('head of the school, *ex officio* captain of the games; head of his house') is equalled by his success first at Sandhurst and then in his regiment ('Cottar nearly wept with joy as the campaign went forward'); and he has a relationship with his mother which is summed up, on his return from India, in the statement that 'they talked for a long hour, as mother and son should, if there is to be any future for our Empire'. The prose in which he is presented alternates between two of Kipling's most favoured tones: the gruff colloquial ('he kept his pores open and his mouth shut') and the biblical ('he bore with him from school and college a character worth much fine gold'). The almost parodic presentation of the officer and gentleman is surely so extreme because there is a bit of Cottar, albeit an unconscious bit, which is out of bounds and Kipling has to strain to show that it has done him no harm. In his dreams he may flee from terrors to sanctuary but in real life he commands men who, serving as a rearguard 'covered themselves with great glory in the eyes of fellow-professionals'.

Kipling can write brisk and entertaining and sometimes macabre anecdotes about the ruling group – his initial reputation was founded on these plain tales from the hills – but if he goes any deeper into their characters he tends towards the idealized and stereotypical as if afraid that he might weaken the moral and political imperatives which are central to his outlook. His best work – apart from some of the anecdotes, the only work on which any significant claim for him can be based – is done when he escapes from the power of these imperatives and writes about those who are not called upon to carry the burden of responsibility. There are three groups who are sometimes able to fulfil this requirement – children, other ranks, and (despite George Cottar's mother) women.

He wrote a good deal for children – the *Just So Stories*, the *Jungle Books*, *Puck of Pook's Hill*, and *Rewards and Fairies* – and it is certainly true that in some of these he is concerned with his imperatives, concerned to teach the need for the law and obedience and the duty to defend the wall, but one book stands out as totally different from the others. He lavished most time upon *Kim* – it was seven years in the writing, interspersed with other work – and it is the work which has most unquestionably established itself as a classic. It has often, and rightly, been compared with Mark Twain's *Huckleberry Finn* (1884), another story of a boy from the supposedly higher race but on the margin of society, travelling with a member of a supposedly lower race whom he comes to love along a great highway and coming to face the conflict between this love and the demands of society. Both books raise the question of how far they are addressed to boys and how far to adults.

What is the nature of the appeal of *Kim* to the grown-up reader? Is it for most of us the affection that comes from reading it, in Lionel Trilling's words, 'fixed deep in childhood feeling'?[4] There are certainly many parts which the adult, even if he did not read it first as a child, has to read as if through the eyes of a child; the exchange of passwords on the train and the disguising of the hunted Mahratta, for example, demand a straightforward relish for excitement without too much worry about plausibility. Yet we often find that we are involved in conflicts of feeling which demand some complexity of response. We are, in fact, asked to read in that special frame of mind which is appropriate to fables and legends and the modulations of tone insist on this.

The prose of the very first paragraph enforces a double focus:

> He sat, in defiance of municipal orders, astride the gun
> Zam-Zammah on her brick platform opposite the old
> Ajaib-Gher – the Wonder House, as the natives call the
> Lahore Museum. Who hold Zam-Zammah, that 'fire-
> breathing dragon,' hold the Punjab; for the great green-
> bronze piece is always first the conqueror's loot.

The move between the two sentences from the brisk realism of 'municipal orders' to the incantatory archaic 'Who hold . . .' prepares

us for a tale which will hover between different appeals and different
plausibilities or, as Kipling might have wished us to put it, between
two racial outlooks which join in the boy. The second paragraph reinforces the effect. It begins:

> There was some justification for Kim, – he had kicked
> Lala Dinanath's boy off the trunnions, – since the English
> held the Punjab and Kim was English.

and ends:

> So it came about after his [Kim's father's] death that the
> woman sewed parchment, paper, and birth-certificate into
> a leather amulet-case which she strung round Kim's neck.

The effect is inevitably a precarious one but it succeeds because the
choice as protagonist and observer of a boy, and, moreover a boy who
is initially in effect an honorary Indian, appears to release in Kipling
a variety of feelings which elsewhere are so often stopped short by his
sense of responsibility. Kipling himself said that the story was 'nakedly
picaresque and plotless' and, though this minimizes the theme of Kim's
conflicting love of the Lama and of the Great Game, one of the
strongest effects of the book is sheer delight in variety of people and
places and the energetic and irresponsible curiosity of Kim about them.
Kipling put into this novel many of the fruits of his observation of
India which did not altogether fit into the framework of assumptions
of, say, the *Plain Tales*. It is but rarely outside *Kim* that he presents
the life of the inhabitants of the sub-continent except in relation to the
British. Here there are hints of the British presence on the road –
mention of police stations and so forth and the somewhat stereotyped
figure of the Ressaldar who remained loyal in the days of the Mutiny
(a Nostromo of the Raj, as it were) – but there is much which seems
quite untouched by the British and one effect of this is naturally to
enlarge the scope of India. One of the functions of seeing Indians
largely in relation to their rulers is to reduce the size and variety to
order; it is not only a framework of administration that is imposed
upon a country but also a conceptual framework. In *Kim*, drawing one
supposes upon his childhood memories and, as we know, aided by his
father, who had worked with Indians a great deal, Kipling reveals an
India which is large and varied beyond categorization.

In giving such a panoramic view Kipling set himself the substantial
problem of finding a language, or set of languages, in which to render
the variety; and he did not make matters easier by having at the centre
of the book a holy man who talks with the solemnity and formality

appropriate to holy men. For the vernacular he adopts an archaic style, with second personal singular usages, interspersed with apparently proverbial phrases to add pungency – 'That North country is full of horse-dealers as an old coat of lice.' This runs the risk of making his cultivators and prostitutes sound like old-fashioned Quakers or notional medieval peasants, but in so far as the latter effect is achieved it is not altogether inappropriate for his purpose. There are times when it may seem unintentionally comic and I have no idea how close it may or may not approximate to a literal translation from Urdu or Punjabi or any of the other languages which we must imagine spoken, but one of the purposes which it serves is to suggest an immemorial quality about India which goes about its business away from the Europeans who speak normal colloquial English.

The intermittent formality and archaism of the narrator's prose, too, reinforce this sense of the continuity and decorum of Indian life which is contrasted with the crude and graceless manners of the chaplain, Bennett, say, or the drummer boy who is set to keep Kim away from the bazaar. 'At noon they turned aside to eat,' we are told, 'and the meal was good, plentiful, and well-served on plates of clean leaves, in decency, out of drift of the dust. They gave the scraps to certain beggars, that all requirements might be fulfilled, and sat down to a long, luxurious smoke' (4).

Because Kim is a boy and we share his experiences, Kipling is able to make good use of what is so often elsewhere one of his most damaging habits – the knowingness which, I have suggested, is part of his desire to involve us in a group but which becomes a veritable tic. When Kim learns the truth of the pedigree of the white stallion or stops the railway clerk from cheating the lama and cheats the railway instead or, dressed in a white boy's suit, astonishes a sweeper by fluent Urdu abuse, we do not feel the laboured knowingness of the narrator of so many of the stories, but the pleasure of a clever child who likes Creighton because he 'was a man after his own heart – a tortuous and indirect person playing a hidden game', a boy far more at home (and making us more at home) with the country-bred and half-caste boys at St Xavier's than with the white men with their 'dull fat eyes'.

We are not, however, merely released into the safety of pre-adolescent fantasy; from Kim's viewpoint we see many harsh matters which Kipling's adult characters are not allowed to recognize. He is strikingly successful, through the boy's perceptions and his delight in intrigue, at showing the disingenuousness within one's own side. It is not perhaps surprising that, when Kim teasingly asks Mahbub Ali what would have happened if he had betrayed him, the horse dealer replies: 'Then thou wouldst have drunk water twice – perhaps thrice, afterwards. I do not think more than thrice.' What does surprise us is the admission of the ruthlessness of the English side in the Great Game when Kim, going back to school from Lurgan Sahib's, reflects that he could tell stories which would astonish his schoolmates about his adventures on the road, and then realizes that this would cause Creighton to 'cast him off – and he would be left to the wrath of Lurgan Sahib and Mahbub Ali – for the short space of life that would remain to him'. He is already committed to the game and if he is indiscreet he will be killed by the British Intelligence Service. The Brushwood Boy's daytime mind, one feels, would hardly come to terms with murdering schoolboys. But boys grow up; Kipling fudges the issue of Kim's age; we can work out that he is thirteen at the beginning of the novel and sixteen at the end but he is kept for as long as possible in that limbo in which he can frolic on Zam-Zammah and also be one step ahead in calculations about men who come to murder Mahbub Ali. We feel, despite chronology, that he spends some years at school and yet remains the same age; but by the end of the book he is almost a man and the episode with the woman of Shamlegh points this up.

Open talk about sex has played quite a large part in the book; Kim is accustomed from his earliest years to carrying messages for prostitutes; the woman who drugs Mahbub Ali so that his belongings can be ransacked rolls his head off her lap, recalling her customers, with the comment 'I earn my money'; Kim knows that the place to go to be disguised is a brothel where he chats gaily with the girls; the Sahiba enjoys nothing so much as joking innuendoes about strong-backed men. Nevertheless, despite his knowledge and the compliments often paid him, Kim is pre-sexual in his feelings to an extent which, though hardly plausible in the reality of sixteen-year-olds, is acceptable within the framework of this story. The same could be said of Huck Finn, and Twain knew as well as Kipling that the particular balance of feelings which is needed to anchor the book to its quasi-fabulous childhood response could not coexist with the presence of sexual feelings in his protagonist.

The appeal of the woman of Shamlegh to Kim, however, is openly sexual and our recollection of her earlier appearance in the *Plain Tales* adds to her sexual reality. Though Kim promises her 'payment' and 'reward' after she has helped him (and there cannot be any doubt of the nature of the payment nor of her offer to him when she puts out 'a hard brown hand all covered with turquoise set in silver') the need to take the lama down to the plains removes Kim from Shamlegh before he can pay it. His virginity is saved by a hair's breadth, though not before we have been reminded, as the woman tells him the story of her early life as Christian Lispeth, of her grief and anger at the white man's triviality and betrayal of love. They kiss, European fashion, and Kim, looking back as they go down to the plains, reflects 'she did not treat me like a child'. Indeed, he no longer is a child and one sign of this is that he ceases to be infinitely resourceful and energetic and lively. He has said, when telling the woman of Shamlegh that he would like to stay, that he is very weary, and on the journey back to the plains this weariness increases and becomes something more than mere physical tiredness. He feels the burden of obligations and responsibility – 'Kim's shoulders bore all the weight of it – the burden of an old man, the burden of the heavy food-bag with the locked books, the load of the writings on his heart, and the details of the daily routine.' He breaks down and cries at the lama's feet because the burden is too great for his years and only gains some relief when the books and letters are stored in a locked box under his bed. The Sahiba restores him to health with drugs and massage and when Hurree collects the documents he feels that he has got rid of 'a burden incommunicable'.

The exhaustion, the massage, the convalescence, and the sleep on the earth after the moment when 'with an almost audible click he felt the wheels of his being lock up anew on the world without' are in the nature of a *rite de passage* which take him from childhood to manhood. What this means is that he must now choose and take responsibility. So far there has been for him no conflict between his love of the lama and his love of playing the Great Game and this has prevented us, the readers, from dwelling on the contradiction. Logically, he has in his journey into the hills to use the lama as a stalking horse for the purpose of spying on the foreign spies, though the framework of childhood's lack of reflection keeps this very much at the back of our minds. But the conflict has told on him and exhausted him at the end and now his choice is, so it seems, made for him by his nature. When, walking into the open after rising from his convalescent bed, he sees that

> Roads were meant to be walked upon, houses to be lived
> in, cattle to be driven, fields to be tilled and men and
> women to be talked to. They were all real and true –
> solidly planted upon the feet – perfectly comprehensible –
> clay of his clay, neither more nor less.   (15)

His nature is choosing a path which is not that of the lama, for whom the visible world is an illusion and who, having found his River, smiles 'as a man who has won salvation for himself and his beloved' and whom we are surely meant to feel has come to the end of his life. But Kim, of whom Mahbub Ali says to the Lama, 'the boy, sure of Paradise, can yet enter Government service', will indeed take up as a man that government service which has so far been a play.

It is at this point that the book must end. Mahbub Ali may say that the conflict between the two ways of life can be reconciled, but the reader, as soon as he begins to think in those adult terms to which Kim is being brought, knows that they cannot. They could only coexist in one man as they do in 'The Brushwood Boy'; the exhaustion and illness of Kim and his recovery are Kipling's acceptance of the end of childhood.

The army's other ranks are cut off from the imperatives of power even more thoroughly than Kim. He grows up and has to answer the question 'What is Kim?', but Kipling's most famous and successful portrayal of those who do society's dirty work – the Soldiers Three – is of men who by circumstances of birth and, to a lesser extent, of temperament, will never determine their own fates. The eighteen stories in which they appear are of varying types and quality.[5] Some, such as 'Black Jack' and 'On Greenhow Hill' are among his best works, while others, like 'The God from the Machine' and 'The Incarnation of Krishna Mulvaney', are more in the nature of elaborated anecdotes or exaggerated tall tales; but the whole is far greater than the sum of the parts. The three soldiers start in 'The Three Musketeers' as stock types: the blarneying Irishman, the slow Yorkshireman, and the sharp Cockney. By the time we have read all the stories, though they still retain marked elements of blarneydom, stolidity, and sparrowdom, they have been individualized as men who endure a weight of frustration, resentment, and despair quite outside the comprehension of those who make the decisions which govern their lives.

This is conveyed to us partly by the stories which they tell but even more by the framework of shared experience, gossip, and relationship within which the stories are set. This interrelationship of frame and tale can be shown very clearly in the story which has probably attracted more critical attention than any other, 'On Greenhow Hill'. As they lie in wait on a Himalayan spur for a deserter from a native corps, Learoyd tells his two comrades the story of how he came to enlist. This account of how he thought that his chance of marrying Liza Roantree was being frustrated by a Primitive Methodist minister, how he nearly killed the man in revenge and then found that he alone has not realized that she is ill and his real rival is death is akin to Hardy in its sense of the irony of circumstances and its lack of patronage of the illiterate and the inarticulate. It has flashes of the comic which keep the pathos from slipping into sentimentality: when the young Learoyd is refused admission to the house where the girl is dying, her father embodies his Methodist rejection of the supposedly wild young man in the phrase 'and long as thou lives thou'll never play the big fiddle'. At the end of the story Learoyd enters the army and the lack of forgetfulness:

Th' recruiting-sergeant were waitin' for me at th' corner public-house. 'Yo've seen your sweet-heart?' says he. 'Yes, I've seen her,' says I. 'Well, we'll have a quart now, and you'll do your best to forget her,' says he, bein' one o' them smart, bustlin' chaps. 'Ay, sergeant,' says I. 'Forget her.' And I've been forgettin' her ever since.

At this point the deserter whom they have been ambushing crawls into view and Ortheris shoots him. They have speculated before that perhaps there is a woman behind the desertion and Mulvaney has said that women make most men enlist and they've no right to make them desert, too, and it is this indeed which has started Learoyd telling the story. Now, with the man dead by a red rock with his face in a clump of blue gentians, we reflect that Learoyd has been brought here by the bunch of ribbons, pinned on his hat as a sign of enlistment and put straight and admired by Liza on her death-bed.

But the framework is doubly effective if we know the three soldiers already and know, among other things, that Learoyd is no talker. Mulvaney tells eleven of the stories and Learoyd has only narrated one previously, a slight anecdote of a stolen dog.[6] We have gained the sense of Learoyd as a taciturn, slow presence and have waited to understand him better; now that he does speak it is with the effect of the lumbering, silent man at last finding words for what has been in his mind all the time. The insight given into Ortheris is greater and more disturbing. He never tells a full story; in 'The Madness of Private Ortheris' we see him hysterically homesick for a London which includes such memories as going with a girl to see 'the Humaners practisin' a-hooking dead corpses out of the Serpentine o' Sundays', though there are plenty of hints that his childhood was harsh. He can only reveal himself by fits and starts and the effect which he often makes of cold viciousness is related to these spasmodic utterances. That effect is at its strongest in this story. The three men have been encouraged by a subaltern to hunt the deserter, but there is something chilling about Ortheris's pleasure in 'a 'evinly clear drop for a bullet' across the valley and in his mockery of Learoyd's conversion to Methodism under the influence of Liza and in the calculated blasphemy with which he takes out the cartridge from his rifle and greets it as his chaplain, making 'the venomous black-headed bullet bow like a marionette'. But we do not only see him as a callous man who enjoys killing. When, in the last words of the story, 'He was staring across the valley, with the smile of the artist who looks on the completed work', we do not only relate this to the present story and wonder what it is that he so much enjoys destroying; our response is also connected with a sense of the Ortheris whom we have got to know as one of the three friends and we are shocked to find that he is in as bad a way as this.

The dominant effect of the series of stories is, indeed, that all three are in a bad way. About half the stories are of triumphs in war, in stratagems, in rivalries, but their cumulative effect is extraordinarily sad. The three soldiers are conventionally patriotic, admiring good officers, and devoted to efficiency in their profession of arms, but through all the stories comes a sense of loss, not only because of the passage of time and the ravages of the bad climate and disease but also a sense of potentialities unfulfilled and feelings thwarted. Mulvaney regrets his seductions or near-seductions and speaks repeatedly of how drink has ruined his chances of promotion and his self-respect and yet he cannot stop boasting not only of his prowess as a fighter in the old days but as a lover and a drinker, too. They live through the hot weather in squalid cantonments or barracks, their refuge is drink, and they must endure being men who cheat or wheedle or steal to get it. They are loyal to that service which degrades them and their concep-tion of a gentleman-ranker is as plain a statement as can be that the fortunate ones of this world would not lead their lives unless they were blackguards.

Kim escapes the limitations of what Kipling could usually envisage by the irresponsibility of childhood and Mulvaney and his friends by their membership of the class which is denied the responsibility of power. Kipling's view of women also liberates him in some of his stories, though here success is more unpredictable. His view of women is often the conventional one of the society about which he writes: the eponymous heroine of 'William the Conqueror' is the tomboy and staunch comrade, Mrs Hauksbee the flirtatious older woman (an unpassionate *Marschallin* as it were) and the mother of 'The Brushwood Boy', the ideal of imperial womanhood. But since his world is one which is dominated by men who are responsible for its ordering and where women gain their ends and play their part most often by exer-cising their influence upon men, they are inevitably under less disci-pline. They are often seen as lonelier than men, living more in their impulses and with more of the primitive and there are a number of stories, such as 'The Wish House' and 'A Madonna of the Trenches', both from the volume *Debits and Credits* (1926), where he seems to feel that women are closer to quasi-supernatural powers. There are also two most striking stories about the Great War in which he deals with states of emotional deprivation in women who have lived with their feelings shut away from public view and with no possibility of admitting them socially. One, 'The Gardener', from *Debits and Credits*, is the story of a woman's concealing, even after his death in action, that her supposed nephew is really her illegitimate son; it has great force but is ruined by a sudden twist at the end. The attendant at the war cemetery directs her to the grave, using the word 'son', and the story ends 'and she went away, supposing him to be the gardener'. The biblical echo is either totally gratuitous and the man has merely made an accurate guess as to the relationship or else (and surely this must be Kipling's intention) we are to take him as Jesus Christ, a demand that we should adjust ourselves to a supernatural element totally unrelated to anything that has gone before and come to terms with ideas about resurrection and forgiveness which are therefore inert.

The other story of the Great War and a woman's feelings about it is 'Mary Postgate', which he wrote in 1915 and which appeared in *A Diversity of Creatures* (1917). All commentators have emphasized its horror and many seem to have regretted it. Whatever interpretation we give to it is likely to raise feelings of outrage but what gives it a resonance unusual in Kipling is the complexity and contradiction of feeling which prevent an easy reading. The simplest reading, apparently underwritten by the appending to it of the poem 'The Beginnings' which proclaims how 'the English began to hate', is as a straight revenge story. Mary Postgate, the mousey and ladylike companion of Miss Fowler, has adored Miss Fowler's nephew, Wynn, who has treated her as a bit of a joke, gone off to the war as an airman, and been killed in an accident while training. As she is disposing of his effects, lighting the fire 'that would burn her heart to ashes', she hears a groan from a German airman who, after dropping a bomb on the village and killing a child, has crashed. He cries out for help, but Mary Postgate refuses to get help and watches him die. Love for our own side makes us hate the other side and Mary Postgate reflects that if she tells anyone else the German airman will be saved. Any man would be a 'sportsman' and it is woman's work to see that the German dies in pain. Kipling, it has often been pointed out, is interested in revenge and certainly seems to have enjoyed the thought of its being taken with a good conscience. Several of the comic extravaganzas, notably 'The Village that Voted the Earth was Flat', are acts of revenge and, more seriously, the theme is followed through in the context of the Boer War in 'A Sahib's War' and in 'The Sea Constables', written at about the same time as 'Mary Postgate'. But in these stories and in others where the revengers are men there is always the sense of communal action and consequently of a reinforcement of solidarity by the sharing of revenge by the group. Mary Postgate's revenge is secret and the more closely we look at the story the more we find that her feelings must be kept secret for reasons more significant than the simple fear that a good sportsman would take the German off to the nearest hospital.

Throughout the story we – not, apparently, Mary Postgate herself – have been aware how abominably Wynn has behaved to her. The

disrespectful jocularity of the young to the old may be taken as callow-
ness concealing affection, and if we were merely told that she was
'always his butt and his slave' this might be so here; but Kipling gives
plenty of evidence that Wynn is stupidly callous. When she fails to
identify different kinds of aeroplane he says:

> You *look* more or less like a human being. . . You *must*
> have had a brain at some time in your past. What have
> you done with it? Where d'you keep it? A sheep would
> know more than you do, Postey. You're lamentable. You
> are less use than an empty tin can, you dowey old
> cassowary.

and, a little later

> Postey, I believe you think with your nose. . . You
> haven't the mental capacity of a white mouse.

This is not the proper way, in the society that Kipling is depicting
(nor in any other), to talk to an older woman in a subordinate position.
But Mary Postgate seems not to resent it. Nor, though Miss Fowler
quizzes her, does she seem to admit to sexual feelings. Miss Fowler
reminisces shockingly with tales 'not always for the young', but her
companion listens unflinchingly and drops the subject, 'for she prided
herself on a trained mind which "did not dwell on these things"'; when
Miss Fowler comments that she is now over forty and asks whether
she ever thinks about 'the things that women think about' Mary Postgate avoids a direct answer, and says: 'I've no imagination, I'm afraid.'
    Her reaction to Wynn's death is the stoic acceptance of loss, the stiff
upper lip shown by the bereaved in 'The Gardener', too, but it is
mingled with a regret of a strikingly specific and non-rhetorical kind;
'"Yes," she said. "It's a great pity he didn't die in action after he had
killed somebody."' The choice of this phrase rather than, as might be
expected, something more grand and general about throwing back
invaders or doing one's duty, tends to make us conscious of a number
of hints of resemblance between Wynn and the German, who *has* killed
somebody. His uniform is described as 'something like Wynn's' and
he has fallen through trees and 'Wynn had told her that it was quite
possible for people to fall out of aeroplanes. Wynn told her too, that
trees were useful things to break an aviator's fall.' She has, after all,
remembered something from those conversations in which Wynn
jeered at her. It would be too simple to say merely that in watching
the German die she is taking revenge for slights and jeers as well as
for the wrongdoing of the enemy, nor that her final ecstasy can be

simply defined as the pleasure of sadism after a lifetime of subordination, but the conclusion of the story, with its sexual overtones, does not allow us to deny that both these are present in a complex effect more powerful than anything else in Kipling. She goes on burning Wynn's things, while listening for the airman's groans:

> There was a dull red glow at the bottom of the destructor not enough to char the wooden lid if she slipped it half over against the driving wet. This arranged, she leaned on the poker and waited, while an increasing rapture laid hold on her. She ceased to think. She gave herself up to feel. Her long pleasure was broken by a sound that she had waited for in agony several times in her life. She leaned forward and listened, smiling. There could be no mistake. She closed her eyes and drank it in. Once it ceased abruptly.
>   'Go on,' she murmured, half aloud. 'That isn't the end.'
>   Then the rain came very distinctly in a lull between two rain-gusts. Mary Postgate drew her breath short between her teeth and shivered from head to foot. '*That's* all right,' she said contentedly, and went up to the house, where she scandalised the whole routine by taking a luxurious hot bath before tea and came down looking, as Miss Fowler said when she saw her lying all relaxed on the other sofa, 'quite handsome!'

Notes

1. *Kim*, epigraph to Chapter 8:
     Something I owe to the soil that grew –
       More to the life that fed –
     But most to Allah Who gave me two
       Separate sides to my head.

   I would go without shirts or shoes,
     Friends, tobacco or bread
   Sooner than for an instant lose
     Either side of my head.

2. First published in Russian in 1926, in translation in America in 1929 and in Great Britain in 1957. The quotation is from the first story in the collection, 'Crossing into Poland'.

3. I give the date of publication of stories in the first collections.

4. See L. Trilling, *The Liberal Imagination* (1943). The essay is reprinted in *Kipling's Mind and Art*, edited by Andrew Rutherford (1964), a very recommendable collection.

5. The stories are to be found in the following volumes: 'The Three Musketeers', 'The Taking of Lungtungpen', 'The Daughter of the Regiment', and 'The Madness of Private Ortheris' in *Plain Tales from the Hills* (1888); 'The God from the Machine', 'Private Learoyd's Story', 'The Big Drunk Draf', 'The Solid Muldoon', 'With the Main Guard', 'In the Matter of a Private', and 'Black Jack' in *Soldiers Three* (1890); 'The Incarnation of Krishna Mulvaney', 'The Courting of Dinah Shadd', and 'On Greenhow Hill' in *Life's Handicap* (1891); 'My Lord the Elephant', 'His Private Honour', and 'Love o' Women' in *Many Inventions* (1893); 'Garm – a Hostage' (which can barely be included in the series) in *Actions and Reactions* (1909).

6. I am assuming either that the stories are read in the order of publication or that the reader bears in mind an order which he may not originally have kept.

Chapter 5
E. M. Forster: The Proclamations of the Liberal Agnostic

A Passage to India (1924) is a full-blown political novel, dealing with that theme of imperialism which recurs so often in English fiction as the natural setting for issues of power and responsibility; Forster's early novels are social comedies which turn on private and personal feelings. Yet this shift of interest is, if we consider the books more closely, a good deal less striking than it seems, largely because the concerns of Forster which manifest themselves in the early books reflect what are essentially relationships of power. Classification is a fundamental principle in the presentation of his characters. Lionel Trilling, in the first significant criticism of Forster, discusses them as sheep and goats, though he also comments that goats sometimes turn sheepish and sheeps goatish[1]; but it is notable that usually the distinction is not simply between individual personalities but between groups defined by nation or social class. We do not have to read far before we meet such classificatory judgements as: 'Ansell isn't a gentleman' in *The Longest Journey* (1907) or 'She knew that the intruder [Mr Emerson in *A Room with a View* (1908)] was ill-bred' or, in *Where Angels Fear to Tread* (1905),

> And Philip had seen that face before in Italy a hundred
> times – seen it and loved it, for it was not merely
> beautiful, but had the charm which is the rightful heritage
> of all who are born on that soil. But he did not want to
> see it opposite him at dinner. It was not the face of a
> gentleman. (2)

The dialectic of the books develops on lines which confirm the terms though with Forster on the side of the supposedly lower groups; his enemy is the English upper-middle class which defines itself in terms of its superiority to other groups.

Social distinctions, snobberies, comic misadventures with foreigners are, of course, the stuff of much fiction, especially of this period, but in Forster's work the basic categories of life and death, feeling and insensitivity, salvation and condemnation involve the lining up of opposed sides, with snobbery and social exclusion. The resemblance to the imperial theme of *A Passage to India* is obvious enough; the certainty which justifies Mrs Herriton in playing God to her family and inspires Charlotte Bartlett's kidnapping of the baby is not dissimilar from that which causes Mrs Moore to remark that in India 'Englishmen like posing as gods' (5). Forster links the suburban and the imperial specifically by the public school; it is appropriate that in *The Longest Journey* at Sawston school 'portraits of empire builders hung on the wall' so that 'it seemed that only a short ladder lay between the preparation-room and the Anglo-Saxon hegemony of the globe' (17) and that Ronny, in his mood of self-righteous certainty, 'reminded her [Mrs Moore] of his public-schooldays'.

This relationship between class consciousness and imperial power and the role of schools in creating it is not an idiosyncratic view of Forster. The immense development of public schools in the nineteenth century frequently had as a conscious purpose the training of men who would go out to rule the Empire, and one of the consequences of thus training a caste is the implied insistence that those not so trained are excluded from it. There are, of course, other reasons for the outgrowth of snobbery which is so marked a feature of the later nineteenth and early twentieth centuries. The greater fluidity of society and the consequent need to assert one's superior position in a society in which birth alone did not give it was clearly an important factor, but the sense of membership of a superior group, formed by a particular kind of somewhat Spartan education, marked its recipients from their tender years. Forster's intense dislike of the public school ethos and his alliance with those who reject it or who are outside it are very closely akin to his view of the imperial functionaries and the Indians in *A Passage to India*.

The first published of Forster's novels, *Where Angels Fear to Tread*, opens with as entertaining and finely balanced a presentation of discriminations and snobberies as anything he ever wrote. There are passages which will reveal more meaning as the book progresses: for example, Philip's list of little towns that Lilia must see, ending with Monteriano and his emphasis that 'the people are more marvellous than the land' combined with the fact that when he speaks of the 'supreme moments of her coming journey' he recites a list of views from which the population is absent. But the contrast between Lilia, 'sprawling out of her first-class carriage' and Miss Abbott, 'a rather nice-looking young lady', Mrs Theobald who cries and 'Mrs Herriton herself', defined in the first sentence by that personal pronoun, who gossips felinely with her son for just so long as she wishes and then, tired of the praises of Italy, changes the subject, is succinct and, even after the social changes of three-quarters of a century, definitive. What is also clear about this opening is that it is written, so to say, from inside the subject-matter. Mr Forster would not yield even to Mrs Herriton in his awareness of the distinction between 'Granny' and 'Grandmother' or the implications of being able or not being able to keep one's servants. He knows more than Mrs Herriton, of course; he knows the delights of Baedeker, but he is not an alien to her world. She is by any judgement the most wicked of all the characters, yet he gives his devil her due, and there are moments when her insight appears to be praised quite genuinely. At the end of the analysis of the misery of Lilia's marriage with Gino, for example, he says:

> generations of ancestors, good, bad, or indifferent, forbade
> the Latin man to be chivalrous to the northern woman,
> the northern woman to forgive the Latin man. All this
> might have been foreseen: Mrs Herriton foresaw it from
> the first.   (4)

But by this time we are concerned with a prejudice which is national (and actually envisaged by those who share it as in some sense racial); Mr Kingcroft might never have 'done', but Gino Carella belongs to a lower race.

Forster himself (and the narrative voice of the book is distinctive enough for us to call it Forster), though he will elevate Gino most eloquently as a father and a friend, is not averse to such a generalization about national types as 'his morality was that of the average Latin'. As always, Forster's prose appeals to one of his own kind, to a member of his own social group – that is, the same group as Mrs Herriton, but with more education and a warmer heart.

It is in the exploration of these national differences that he first, in this book, breaks through the mode of social comedy which is so firmly yet lightly established from the beginning. That vulgar Lilia should go to Italy to imbibe a little culture and be separated from what the Herritons regard as an inappropriate suitor and then marry the flashy son of a dentist is inherent in the tone of the novel from the very first page. The culmination of Chapter 2 sets the seal on this with Lilia's denunciation of her treatment at Sawston, Philip's certainty that his self-control will triumph and the reversal which comes when Gino, apparently regretfully, refuses the money offered him to desist from his courtship and, pushing Philip over jocularly on the bed, reveals that he and Lilia are already married. But the next two chapters are somewhat different; the comic note is not absent, as in the implications of Lilia's joining 'the Roman Catholic Church, or as she called it, "Santa Deodata's"', but a different tone is set by: 'It was in this house that

the brief and inevitable tragedy of Lilia's married life took place.' The
alien place is as frightening to Lilia as Gino's incomprehension and
violence, and this disorientation culminates in her attempt to run away
and her collapse as the diligence sweeps past her:

> She did not call any more, for she felt very ill, and
> fainted; and when she revived she was lying in the road,
> with dust in her eyes, and dust in her mouth, and dust
> down her ears.   (4)

Her death in childbirth is soon put behind us as the book turns to the
hypocrisies of Mrs Herriton's desire first to deny the existence of the
baby and then, when this proves impossible, to endeavour to fail in
what must seem a conscientious attempt to rescue it from its father;
nevertheless some lurking horror remains at the back of our minds.

Critics have often commented on the sudden deaths in Forster's
novels, most often citing as an example Gerald's being 'broken up in
the football match' in *The Longest Journey*. In fact death often comes
without advance notice in real life, but in fiction we are usually
prepared for a character's disappearance. Forster's defiance of the
fictional convention is one manifestation of his habit of raising certain
expectations and then frustrating them by changing the mode. It is
certainly arguable that not all these sudden changes are successful but
they are clearly part of a deliberate purpose. One such reversal which
recurs is the presentation of a landscape which appears to stand for a
comprehensible social life but which is suddenly felt to be a disorientating, threatening cause for panic. This is most developed, of course,
in *A Passage to India*, but it is there in Lilia's realization that the countryside around Monteriano is hardly country at all but is 'terrible and
mysterious all the same' with its 'vast slopes of olives and vineyards,
with chalk-white farms, and in the distance other slopes, with more
olives and more farms' and her collapse into the dust (very near where
the baby will die, as we realize on rereading). There is one phrase in
the description of Philip and Harriet's expedition to rescue the baby
which sums up this effect; it comes at the end of a jocular description
and a conversation about how pleasant the temperature is and how
nonsensical are people who talk about how hot it is in Italy; 'And on
the second day the heat struck them, like a hand laid over the mouth,
just as they were walking to see the tomb of Juliet' (6).

The comic is never abandoned. The expedition to Monteriano
which involves us in death, torture, grief, and despair also includes the
set piece of the performance of *Lucia di Lammermoor* in the opera house
with nymphs above the proscenium supporting a clock, of whom it
is said 'these ladies with their clock would have nodded to the young

men on the ceiling of the Sistine'. But there is one big change; as the book goes on Forster is obliged more and more often to assert significances in his commentary rather than allowing them to emerge from dialogue or ironic social observations. In the early sections Caroline attacks Philip's big phrases; when he says:

> There is no power on earth that can prevent your
> criticizing and despising mediocrity – nothing that can stop
> you retreating into splendour and beauty – into the
> thoughts and beliefs that make the real life – the real
> you.   (5)

she answers – and the implications of the answer and Philip's belief that it marks her lack of logic are devastating – 'I have never had that experience yet. Surely I and my life must be where I live.' But when she sees Gino with the baby Forster feels the need for big phrases himself; he ends the scene with Caroline, Gino, and the baby so arranged after the bath that Philip sees them as 'to all intents and purposes, the Virgin and Child with Donor' (7). There is little in this which is ironic; Caroline is elevated above the common world by her very admission of common feelings and there is much in the immediately preceding pages which strikes me as strained because Forster seems to see himself as a teacher. His philosophizing about the nature of fatherhood might well find a place in an essay but it asserts more than is demonstrated; we do not quarrel with Caroline's revelation that 'wicked people are capable of love', for it is in the nature of the experience she is having that she should realize that the man whom she has regarded as wicked does indeed love his son, but the generalizations about parental feelings are delivered by the author *in propria persona* and they are oddly unrealized:

> a wonderful physical tie binds the parents to the children;
> and – by some sad, strange irony – it does not bind us
> children to our parents. For if it did, if we could answer
> their love not with gratitude but with equal love, life
> would lose much of its pathos and much of its squalor,
> and we might be wonderfully happy.

Forster is so concerned for his message – that love matters more than propriety, that coldness of heart is the worst sin, that Sawston and all it stands for is evil and that Monteriano, with all its selfishness and brutalities is good – that he is prepared to break right out of the comic mode and address us directly in the most solemn language known to him, which is, at bottom, that of the religion in which it is clear that he does not believe. Caroline saves Philip from Gino's murderous anger and speaks as a goddess – 'I will have no more intentional evil' – and tells Gino to give to Philip the milk which had been prepared for the baby. 'Philip looked away. . . . He was saved' (9).

This opposition between the powers of life and those of death continues as the animating spirit of the next two novels. *The Longest Journey* (1907) sets the values of Sawston, though here primarily those of the public school rather than of what he calls the 'sububurb', against both the intellectual freedom of Cambridge and the love of life somewhat unconvincingly embodied in Stephen Wonham, who makes Ansell feel 'that he had been back somewhere – back to some table of the gods, spread in a field where there is no noise, and that he belonged for ever to the guests with whom he had eaten' (26). This was Forster's own favourite novel; with the evidence of *Maurice*, the posthumously published novel of homosexual love, before us it is difficult not to see it as an attempt to deal with many of the implications of his sexual feelings without making them overt. Rickie Elliott's sense of being different from the majority, his attempt to fit in through marriage with Agnes and work with her brother, the embodiment of Sawston, the appeals to him by Ansell not to pretend to be what he is not and his sacrifice of his life to save the life-giving but apparently cruder man whom he has denied – all these make much more coherent sense if we think of them as related to a love which dared not then speak its name. Schematically, too, it has an interesting resemblance to *Maurice*: Ansell's dismay at Rickie's marriage parallels Maurice's sense of betrayal by Clive; Stephen Wonham's appeal to Rickie parallels Alec's to Maurice.

A Room With a View followed in 1908, though it had been begun earlier and redrafted; it takes us back to the Anglo/Italian polarity, with English allies of the Italian virtues in the Emersons and the possibility, therefore, of a marriage between Lucy Honeychurch and George Emerson. This is celebrated, like Philip Herriton's salvation, in terms of the utmost eloquence. Lucy, having entered the 'armies of the benighted' when she denies loving George Emerson is won back by his father and saved from muddle by such appeals as 'Marry him; it is one of the moments for which the world was made' and 'we fight for more than Love or Pleasure: there is Truth. Truth counts, Truth does count.' Forster reinforces the proclamation: 'He gave her a sense of deities reconciled, a feeling that, in gaining the man she loved, she would gain something for the whole world' (19).

All three of the early novels are about admitting something, about being brave enough to defy convention and proclaim the truth, and when the characters do so we are given a sense not merely that they are likely to be happier and more decent but that the powers of truth and love have triumphed. The triumph, however, often seems excessive. Lucy's admission that she loves George Emerson, Caroline's that she loves Gino, and Rickie's that he has an illegitimate brother are certainly, by the standards of the snobberies and proprieties of the day, significant, but our attention is taken away from the feelings of the people and directed towards a general principle of taking sides, proclaiming love and truth, being ennobled, winning the good fight. It is tempting to suggest that all such admissions are 'really' surrogates for an admission of that homosexual nature which could not be admitted and a proclamation of the value of such love. The restrictions placed upon his nature must surely make Forster especially aware of the oppressions of society and the meannesses of convention; they place him with the rebels and the minorities. But it also forces him to write of love as a triumph of principles rather than of bodies and feelings and leads him into rhetorical excesses in an attempt to arouse a response to what is, for him, not real.

Maurice, completed in its first form in 1914 but not published, with some revisions, until 1971, shows that this sense of love as proclamation goes very deep, as indeed we might expect, given the uncivilized attitude to homosexuality prevalent in Forster's youth. He complained that he had to write 'marriage novels' and so gave up writing because he would not do this. But his homosexual marriage is no more convincing. The unreality of Maurice and Alec living freely in the 'greenwood' has often been pointed out. But it is inevitable as an ending because Forster cannot conceive of love between them as finding any place in society; the expression of their love is against the law, they are not willing to love furtively and, despite the advice given to Maurice by the hypnotist, they will not take refuge abroad. The proclamatory and even defiant nature of heterosexual commitment in the early novels is there not merely because Forster needs to disguise to his readers that his real interest is homosexual, but because, even when he proclaims it in *Maurice*, he must needs see love as defying the world.

But though his lovers may defy the conventional world, Forster himself has a keen awareness and great interest in social minutiae and he also has a highly developed social consciousness; he is, I think, at one with Maurice in being intensely English and he feels that England is worth saving. *Howards End*, which appeared in 1910, was greeted by several critics of the time as a foray into the territory associated with Bennett and Wells and Galsworthy and it is certainly a 'condition of England' novel.

It is often overtly didactic; the epigraph – 'only connect' – which at its occurrence in Chapter 22 is a demand that love should include both the flesh and the spirit, is usually taken as proclaiming the need to combine the world of practicality, Wilcoxes, telegrams, anger, work with that of feeling, Schlegels, personal relationships, intuition, the arts. The scheme of the novel – and it is very schematic – asserts this. The house which gives the title comes to represent England; starting as the possession of the yeomen Howards, it is inhabited temporarily as a result of his marriage by the business man Wilcox, who then acquires its ownership by fraud; but he cannot hold it and it comes, as Mrs Wilcox the yeoman-aristocrat had desired, to the liberal artistic Schlegels (with a place in it for Henry Wilcox); but it will descend to the offspring of Helen Schlegel and Leonard Bast, who is, as Forster says, the nearest that his imagination will take him to the poor. To establish his scheme Forster is prepared to make use of fantastic coincidences: the Wilcox exploitation of the poor and their inability to love without hypocrisy is signified by the fact that Jacky happens to be Henry Wilcox's mistress; Leonard Bast happens to arrive just in time to die under a tumble of books and the flat of the Schlegel's father's sword, wielded by Charles Wilcox; there are repeated motifs and symbolic circumstances which underline the pattern. Mrs Wilcox is first seen with her hands full of hay and at the end of the book Helen rejoices that they have cut a splendid load of hay; Henry Wilcox is secluded indoors with hay fever, which he shares with all Wilcoxes and also with the Schlegel brother, Tibby, who is a dry aesthete and goes to Oxford (a bad sign in a novel by Forster). At the concert early in the book (6) Beethoven's Fifth Symphony is described (profoundly for some readers and whimsically for others) in terms of goblins, 'phantoms of cowardice and unbelief', walking over the universe and though scattered by the climax of the last movement, remaining as a potentiality for 'panic and emptiness'; at this concert Leonard Bast's umbrella is accidentally taken by Helen Schlegel. This brings him together with the sisters and his reaction also demonstrates the way in which small things, possessions, losses, fears, inevitably loom large in the minds of the poor and may spoil the great spontaneous feelings, and be, as the women see it, a 'goblin footfall'. Helen has already spoken of 'panic and emptiness' in Paul Wilcox and she defines the hollowness that she sees in supermen in the same words and also uses the phrase when told that Margaret is going to marry Henry. Helen describes Jacky as having lost her husband like an umbrella and thinks of her appearance as like 'a goblin footfall'.

But the elaborate symbolic scheme is set to work within a novel which demands a convincing social and psychological reality and this it does not possess. Readers have often commented that Helen's one-night love-affair with Leonard is totally unconvincing; it is indeed a very clear example of the proclamatory sexual love which I have noted in the three earlier novels; Helen's desire for Leonard or Leonard's for

Helen is so much less important than the assertion of the right to equal treatment for all and the justification of love for social inferiors. But at least it happens off-stage and we can strive to imagine pity and heroine-worship and outraged principles combining to create passion. Margaret's marriage to Henry Wilcox happens in the full light of day and at every point we feel that she is acting out of character; when she finally denounces Henry because he expects to be forgiven for having had a mistress while condemning Helen for her affair with Leonard we can only feel that if she has had to wait as long as this before recognizing how matters stand then we cannot respect her good sense and good feelings as much as the book demands.

Equally damagingly, *Howards End* constantly reveals how little Forster knows about the society of which he is writing and how persistent in him is the power of social stereotypes. His earlier books are strong on social observation, but they do not stray outside the world which was familiar to him; the Herritons and Abbotts are what he knows and he is not concerned to deal with such matters as the sources of Mrs Herriton's income or the family relationships of the servants who first give and then withdraw their notice. But he is committed in *Howards End* to a wide view and to a presentation of the processes of social change. The scheme, as I have indicated, is concerned with this and a multitude of comments assert his intention of dealing with it. Of the farm labourers whom Leonard passes on his way to his death at Howards End we are told:

> They are England's hope. Clumsily they carry forward the
> torch of the sun, until such time as the nation sees fit to
> take it up. Half-clodhopper, half board-school prig, they
> can still throw back to a nobler stock, and breed
> yeomen.   (41)

A little later he is passed by an 'Imperial' type in a motor car and Forster says: 'He is a destroyer. He prepares the way for cosmopolitanism, and though his ambitions may be fulfilled, the earth that he inherits will be grey.' When Margaret realizes the full weakness and cruelty of her husband, it is blamed on 'the inner darkness in high places that comes with a commercial age'. But the society which we see is largely mythological. Leonard Bast is probably the most obvious weakness: he is presented to us more as a representative example than as an individual:

> Hints of robustness survived in him, more than a hint of
> primitive good looks, and Margaret, noting the spine that
> might have been straight, and the chest that might have

broadened, wondered whether it paid to give up the glory
of the animal for a tail coat and a couple of ideas.   (14)

At times he talks like a parody of a Cockney and at others like one
of Tibby's friends. Forster warns us not to feel complacent in our
greater wealth and education and he may wish us to dislike Helen's
snobbish jokes about 'Mrs Lanoline' but he does not avoid patronizing
his stereotype when he tells us that, arriving home, Leonard 'cried
"Hullo" with the pseudo-geniality of the Cockney' or that he 'hoped
to come to Culture suddenly, much as the Revivalist hopes to come
to Jesus'.

Taken in isolation, a number of the social comments are perceptive
and striking: for example, the Schlegels' lack of need to worry about
such items as lost umbrellas is contrasted with the manner in which,
for the poor, little things get in the way of spontaneity, symbolized
by the fuss about Leonard's umbrella. Similarly, Margaret's reflection
on the importance of money:

> I'm tired of these rich people who pretend to be poor, and
> think it shows a nice mind to ignore the piles of money
> that keep their feet above the waves. I stand each year
> upon six hundred pounds, and Helen upon the same, and
> Tibby will stand upon eight, and as fast as our pounds
> crumble away into the sea they are renewed – from the
> sea, yes, from the sea.   (7)

It may be Margaret's (and Forster's) intention to show that she and
other *rentiers* actually do imagine that money renews itself effortlessly,
but it cannot be said that when Margaret links her fortunes with Henry
Wilcox's or when Forster aims to deal with the world of business and
finance which is central to the book that his business men seem much
better informed. We hear a good deal about the business type but
virtually nothing about what they actually do; we do not get much
more than Margaret's assertion: 'I like Mr Wilcox. He is taking up his
work – rubber – it is a big business.' It is no great surprise to us that
except when she is playing the little woman Margaret is better at
dealing with crises than her husband. But this means that most of
England is missing in this study of 'the whole island at once, lying as
a jewel in a silver sea, sailing as a ship of souls, with all the brave
world's fleet accompanying her towards eternity' (19), and that all the
values of the Schlegels have to connect with is a mass of clichés. It is
no wonder, then, that the rhetoric with which Forster endeavours to
carry us away is overstrained to a degree greater than anything he has
written before. Surely only such a struggle to write about what he

knows so little can explain the famous evocation of England seen as
a ship from the summit of the Purbeck Hills (and is it not significant
that such a view excludes rather a lot of this country? The Pennines,
for example, are unimaginable here not to speak of Birmingham and
Liverpool) or the description of Leonard's body – 'Let squalor be
turned into Tragedy, whose eyes are the stars, and whose hands hold
the sunset and the dawn' (43).

There was a long wait before the publication of Forster's next novel
– though *Maurice* was, as we now know, written in this period – and
A Passage to India, published in 1924, was to prove his last. The theme
of the book is akin to that of the early works; all the issues of power,
orthodoxy, snobbery, and emotional blindness are there. Fielding,
indeed, even reflects that Indians are like Italians. But for the others
the contrast between outlooks is an overtly racial one with all that the
difference of skin colour could mean in an imperial age.

The choice of India and an imperial theme for his novel was of the
greatest importance for Forster; his interest in India was not confined
to the novel and he wrote a great deal else about the country and about
the political problems faced there. The most significant effect on his
fiction seems to me to be that the need to come to terms with something so totally new and to create it in the novel liberated him from
those stereotypes of both character and situation which were damaging
in *Howards End*. Moreover the particular kind of fable of confrontation
which he uses frees him from the necessity to write of feelings to
which he could not respond. The most impressive moments of the
novel are not, as in his earlier novels, climaxes of feeling and admission, but anticlimaxes of baffled acceptance of limitation. These,
though set within the framework of the public nature of the conflict
extend beyond it, but it is the public nature and the distance which this
opens up even between friends which permit Forster to tread between
his weaknesses. He sets up many expectations – about the kind of story
he is telling, about what sort of feelings we will be expected to have
– and frustrates our expectations. *Howards End* is very predictable; *A
Passage to India* is the reverse. The opening chapter sets a tone which
we recognize as akin to his early novels, dramatizing the dominant
theme of separation in comic terms. The total lack of knowledge of
the Anglo-Indians about the reality of Chandrapore, which has been
described as if from a great height in the first paragraph – 'The streets
are mean, the temples ineffective' – is registered in a crescendo of
misdescriptions in increasingly flamboyant prose:

> On this second rise is laid out the little Civil Station, and
> viewed hence Chandrapore appears to be a totally different
> place. It is a city of gardens. It is no city, but a forest

sparsely scattered with huts. It is a tropical pleasaunce,
washed by a noble river.

Thereafter Forster makes his best points about racial prejudice and
incomprehension in a comic mode. Mrs Moore tells her son that she
has been talking to a doctor and is met by bafflement until she tells
him that the doctor could not come to the club and he realizes that she
is talking of 'a Mohammedan'; Aziz's demonstrative friendliness
towards Fielding is expressed by the loan of a back collar-stud and
Ronnie draws confident conclusions about the inefficiency of Indians
because Aziz's collar rides up; discovering that some of the Indian
ladies have visited Paris causes Mrs Turton to comment on this 'as if
she was describing the movements of migratory birds'.

But we are also shown that the differences between the cultures of
England and of India exist even for those who are willing to try to
bridge them. When Professor Godbole sings at Adela's request the
song is meaningless, 'the ear, baffled repeatedly, soon lost any clue,
and wandered in a maze of noises, none harsh or unpleasant, none
intelligible. It was the song of an unknown bird. Only the servants
understood it' (7). When he explains it no greater clarity is produced.
Young Mr Sorley, the devoted missionary, who is 'advanced' and
never goes to the club, cannot feel happy at an admission into heaven
which extends below mammals. Above all, the landscape of India
baffles and disturbs even the most well-meaning of the English and
does not seem to depend upon the divisions caused by the imperial
relationship.

This is made most clear in the excursion to the Marabar Caves
which starts as farce, with immense preparations, missed trains, inappropriate food for the time of day. The sunrise in sight of the Marabar
Hills promises to be superb but fizzles out, leaving Mrs Moore and
Adela to yearn for 'dearest Grasmere' whose 'little lakes and mountains
were beloved by them all. Romantic, yet manageable, it sprang from
a kindlier planet' (14).

But it is this scenery – specifically the Marabar Caves – rather than
the people who inhabit the country which makes that intrusion into
a basically comic mode which was a part of Forster's vision from the
earliest novels. The comic disorientation of finding that the sun has not
risen where it was expected is soon replaced by the horrifying disorientation of both Mrs Moore and Adela in the caves. Mrs Moore, who
has for some time been feeling tired, is overwhelmed by a sense of
futility, a nightmare in which whatever is said will turn into the same
meaningless echo. This is rather like Godbole's view turned on its head
and Mrs Moore finds it only destructive. Thereafter in the book she
becomes grumpy, feels that 'poor little talkative Christianity' has failed

her, makes no effort to save Aziz, though she believes him innocent, and is shipped off home to die on the voyage.

Adela goes into the cave thinking about marriage and regretting that 'neither she nor Ronny had physical charm' and realizing that she does not love him and that they will have to make do with esteem and common sense (15). In discussing the book Forster spoke of there being a mystery about what happened in the cave, but it does not seem to me that the book leaves room for more than one interpretation – that it is a fantasy by Adela. This is surely made clear in a scene which occurs while they are waiting for the trial of her supposed assailant. Adela is talking with Ronny and his mother, and Mrs Moore mutters in her disgruntled way: 'And all this rubbish about love, love in a church, love in a cave, as if there is the least difference.' Adela suddenly exclaims: 'Aziz is good. You heard your mother say so.' Endeavouring to go back over the conversation she says:

> 'When her voice dropped she said it – towards the end,
> when she talked about love – love – I couldn't follow, but
> just then she said: "Dr Aziz never did it."'
>   'Those words?'
>   'The idea more than the words.'   (22)

Later, when she and Fielding are talking after the trial, she interprets Fielding's suggestion that she suffered from a hallucination as 'the sort of thing – though in an awful form – that makes some women think they've had an offer of marriage when none was made' (26).

Forster states quite specifically that she is not attracted by Aziz, but the prominence given in her perceptions at the trial to the physical perfection of the punkah wallah suggests that we are to feel that some obscure sense of deprivation has emerged in Adela as a fantasy of attempted rape.

For both Mrs Moore and Adela it seems that the Marabar Caves are the culmination of that disorientating function of India, especially manifested for them in the Indian countryside and climate, which destroys the certainties which they brought to India and undermines their sense of their own personalities and the standards by which they have lived. Mrs Moore dies, though not before she has seen on her journey out that there is more yet to India than she had thought, and Adela has to undergo the torment of the trial and the hatred of one side and ostracism of the other before she can return chastened to England. In the course of that ordeal she learns a great deal and in her conversations with Fielding we come, I think, very close to the quality in this book which makes it so superior to anything else that Forster wrote.

In the earlier novels Forster leads his characters to a climax of admission which frees them from the constraints of society and this is hailed by him in terms appropriate to the religion in which he did not believe. Ansell and Rickie classify people into those who are 'saved' and those who are not and I have shown the use of this word in *Where Angels Fear to Tread* and of phrases like 'inner darkness' in *Howards End* and the 'armies of the benighted' in *A Room With a View*. Fielding and Adela have, so to say, passed all the tests which are imposed upon the characters of the early novels, and yet they feel dissatisfied. Forster is very definite about this, speaking *in propria persona* as he so often does:

> Both man and woman were at the height of their powers
> – sensible, honest, even subtle. They spoke the same
> language and held the same opinions, and the variety of
> age and sex did not divide them. Yet they were
> dissatisfied. When they agreed, 'I want to go on living a
> bit', or 'I don't believe in God', the words were followed
> by a curious backwash as though the universe had
> displaced itself to fill up a tiny void, or as though they
> had seen their own gestures from an immense height –
> dwarfs talking, shaking hands and assuring each other that
> they stood on the same footing of insight.   (29)

This harks back to Fielding's mood after he has taken a stand on the side of Aziz, relying upon that belief in personal relationships as against the code of the group – in this case the club – which is at the heart of so much of Forster's view of what matters in life:

> After forty years' experience he had learnt to manage his
> life and make the best of it on advanced European lines,
> had developed his personality, explored his limitations,
> controlled his passions – and he had done it all without
> becoming either pedantic or worldly. A creditable
> achievement, but as the moment passed, he felt he ought
> to have been working at something else the whole time –
> he didn't know at what, never would know, never could
> know, and that was why he felt sad.   (20)

Such moods are in keeping with the emphasis throughout the book on anticlimax. Again and again what is expected does not occur, events tail off, confrontations do not quite happen. This is true not only in small incidents – Godbole seems about to say something significant but does not, for example; Fielding is not quite assaulted when he leaves the club nor is he quite able to leave with dignity – but also in the larger matters. The trial ends in a muddled withdrawal of charges; the riot which seems likely to break out is checked by Dr Panna Lal's humiliating himself and playing the fool and by the Nawab Bahadur's sense that in riots property often suffers and he is a man of property; the conclusion of the religious ceremony in 'Temple' is a ludicrous capsizing of the boat and uncertainty whether the worshippers are shouting in wrath or joy, while fireworks fail to go off and rain spoils the decorations.

The effect of muddle is indubitable, but the question is raised early as to whether there is such a thing as a mystery which is not, in Fielding's phrase 'only a high-sounding term for a muddle' (7). On this matter readers have differed a great deal; there are certainly some who believe that Forster has written a book to glorify the mystical sense. There is a good deal in the book which seems to support this interpretation. There are odd coincidences: Mrs Moore looks at a wasp and murmurs 'Pretty dear', and long after her death Godbole remembers a wasp with love and then an old Englishwoman; Mrs Moore murmurs 'a ghost' to explain the accident on the Marabar road, though the others have said that the obstacle was probably a hyena, but the Nawab Bahadur believes that the ghost of a man whom he had run over nine years before haunts the spot; Ralph seems to be able to sense the feelings of others and instinctively directs Aziz to the one place on the lake at Mau where the statue of the dead Rajah can be seen. Moreover, there are a considerable number of slighting references to reason. When Fielding feels that he will never be intimate with anyone Forster comments that 'experience can do much, and all that he had learned in England and Europe was an assistance to him, and helped him towards clarity, but clarity prevented him from experiencing something else' (11). Within this line of thought the last section shows the triumph of the oceanic feeling, clad in mingled splendour and tawdriness which is only found comic because of a Western demand for seemliness and decorum and a narrowing value for rationality. Even though Mrs Moore does nothing to help Aziz, the Indians are therefore right to transform her into 'Esmiss Esmoor' because her spirit broods over the latter part of the book, and Dr Godbole has a wisdom hidden from those, like Fielding, who are at home in the Mediterranean, 'the civilization that has escaped muddle'.

But this line of thought, the opposition of Western rationalism to Eastern wisdom, is only possible, I believe, if much of the book is ignored. The lines of racial and cultural battle are much less clearly drawn than at first it seems. Fielding may feel that he will never be intimate with anyone and Forster may suggest that it is European clarity which cuts him off, but it is very clear that when he springs to Aziz's side it is not reason which moves him and, indeed, it is of

Hamidullah that Forster says 'faith did not rule his heart'. Moreover this faith of Fielding makes him ask for facts, by contrast with the other Anglo-Indians who are carried away by hotly irrational feelings: 'he was still after facts, though the herd had decided on emotion. Nothing enrages Anglo-India more than the lantern of reason if it is exhibited for one moment after its extinction is decreed' (17).

Above all, so much in the authorial presentation is in the sceptically ironic tone which is announced on the first page in the apparently throwaway comment that 'the Ganges happens not to be holy here'. It seems to me inconceivable that a book which begins thus should, however respectful it may be of the religion of others, actually be presenting mystical experience as true and available.

Yet the coincidences, the odd correspondences, are present and there is no doubt of the sense of deflation of Fielding and Adela and their desire for some belief that they do not possess. This mood is dominant in their talks after the trial, in such authorial comments as 'She was at the end of her spiritual tether, and so was he. Were there worlds beyond which they could never touch, or did all that is possible enter their consciousness? They could not tell' (29). The matter is put at its clearest, I think, when they are talking of Mrs Moore, whom they still believe to be alive. Fielding says:

> 'it is difficult, as we get on in life, to resist the
> supernatural. I've felt it coming on me myself. I still jog
> on without it, but what a temptation, at forty-five, to
> pretend that the dead live again; one's own dead; no one
> else's matter.'
> 'Because the dead don't live again.'
> 'I fear not.'
> 'So do I.'
> There was a moment's silence, such as often follows the
> triumph of rationalism.   (26)

It would be a mistake to take that last comment as dismissive of what Fielding and Adela have said; it is rather an awareness that human beings may want experiences which they do not believe are possible. Some people, Forster seems to be saying in this novel, can see life, India, the universe as mystery and for them Godbole is wise, if sometimes infuriating. Those who cannot and for whom memories of wasps and guesses about ghosts are coincidences may still feel, as Fielding does (and Forster, too, by implication) that they would like there to be a meaning. But, as Fielding says, the desire for it does not make it true.

Notes

1. Lionel Trilling, *Forster, a Study* (Norfolk, Connecticut, 1943; revised edition 1967).

Chapter 6
Fictional Politics and some Minor Forms

The choice of a public, political, even of an urgently controversial theme was the way in which Forster liberated himself from many of his limitations. He could create the India of his fiction from personal observation and from the comments and writings of those who knew it well, rather than from inherited stereotyped views of England. Moreover, the theme of anticlimax is congenial to his outlook. The proclamations of allegiances which are central to all his books are in this novel both convincing and politically significant. For Lucy to admit that she loves George Emerson requires a patch of rhetorical assertion about her rightness; Fielding's alliance with Aziz against the Anglo-Indians can be trusted to carry its own weight.

But, as I have suggested, one of Forster's deepest preoccupations in *A Passage to India* is a personal dilemma, the plight of the agnostic who nevertheless experiences moments of yearning for a supra-personal reality which may be provoked by the impact of India but which is not political. Similarly, the conclusion of the book is the rueful realization that while Britain rules India it will hardly be possible for Englishmen and Indians to be friends; the political reality of dominance and subordination will spoil personal feelings. The hope, however, is that one day this may not be so. This is, in effect, to hope that one day individuals will be able to ignore politics; that, in a sense, politics will cease to exist.

Nothing could be further from the outlook of Conrad, who takes it for granted that the dynamics of power are logical and inescapable and who traces their ramifications throughout a society. Orwell who, in *Burmese Days* (1934), wrote a novel about imperialism which is unconvincing as a novel but very effective as didactic analysis, said that Kipling never really understood where power lay, that his administrators despised the 'box-wallahs', the merchants, and never realized that they themselves were there to guard commercial interests.[1] Forster, it has often been noted, has little concern even for the work done by the Anglo-Indian administrators – indeed, a number of Indian civil servants made the point when the book first appeared – and it is certainly true that we usually only see his characters when they are at their leisure. There is one occasion, however, when he does tell us something of their work and his comment on this reveals most clearly the limitations of his understanding.

Ronny returns to his bungalow after trying to dispense justice in the knowledge that his work will probably be frustrated by venality and tells his mother that he is not in India to be pleasant but to run the country. Mrs Moore sees the point of what he is saying, but her admission is quickly overtaken by irritation at his self-satisfaction; she sums up her reaction in phrases which give the impression of being Forster's own judgement, for the tone is far more appropriate to him than to her: 'One touch of regret – not the canny substitute but the true regret from the heart – would have made him a different man, and the British Empire a different institution'(5).

It does not seem to occur to Forster here – or elsewhere in his judgements of his characters – that normally people, unless they are a great deal more monstrous than his Anglo–Indians, can only rule over others if they believe that they are right to do so. A conviction that they do not need to feel regret is a necessary part of the state of mind which enables them to wield power. For Forster political power is not inevitable and this is surely because he belongs to a group which can either exercise power or choose not to; he does not belong to a group which has such power exercised over it.[2] He took a very different political line from Kipling, but both of them are alike and profoundly different from Conrad in thinking in terms of how 'we' ought to behave towards 'them'; it is inconceivable for both, however hard they may sometimes try, to feel as naturally as Conrad can in terms of what 'they' may do to 'us'.

Conrad never conceives of a political situation as one in which well-meaning people in positions of authority are called upon to make the right choices. His strategy is to set certain political assumptions before us and then to undermine them. But he leaves no room for any belief that some other assumption, some other organization, would resist undermining. In *Nostromo* he assumes that his readers are likely to start with some sympathy for Gould as the English hero of this tale of South America and with some dislike for those referred to as a 'mob' (it might be said that his own conscious and publicly proclaimed views would lead him in this direction), and he then undermines the position of both Gould and the Blancos. But if we started with different premises and fitted the novel into a somewhat different framework, re-arranging it in our minds and asserting that it is clear from the start that invested capital in an underdeveloped country necessarily involves the support of tyrannical – albeit sometimes discreetly tyrannical – regimes, we would find it hard to idealize the revolutionary masses.

Conrad still believes, in these novels, though much less than in earlier ones, in the short-term virtues of reliability and doing one's job, but he sees no government and no possible government as naturally worthy of allegiance. In the short term one situation may be preferable to another, but none will last and each bears within itself the seeds of its degeneration. In *The Secret Agent* we start with easy contempt for the anarchists but the more striking, because the less expected, attack is on Chief Inspector Heat and Sir Ethelred and his adoring Toodles. *Under Western Eyes*, beginning with its revelations about the Tsarist secret police, might lead us to expect a sympathetic portrayal of the conspirators against it, but this expectation does not survive our introduction to Peter Ivanovitch and the group in the Château Borel.

The range of experience with which Conrad is at home in his political novels is far, far wider than that of any English novelist of the time. They may deal with similar situations but only Conrad convinces us by his tone that he is completely familiar with that of which he writes. We know that much of his knowledge was, despite the protestations which he made at the time, derived from other people and other books; the debt to Dostoevsky, especially in *Under Western Eyes*, is very great, and Eloise Hay and Norman Sherry, among others, have documented his debts in *Nostromo* to a number of writers.[3] But the tone of recognition, sometimes weary, sometimes ironic, usually sardonic, is what carries conviction. If one had to choose examples, two which stand out are the entrapment of Razumov by the Tsarist police and the account in *Nostromo* of Monygham's torture and inter-rogation by Father Beron, ending 'His confessions, when they came at last, were very complete, too' (III. 4). The quality which is most effective, and most horrifying, is the lack of surprise.

It is difficult not to believe that Conrad's outlook on politics, and especially this preparedness for the abominable comes from his national situation. Possibly one could be more precise and relate it to his individual personality as a child of a Polish revolutionary in a part of Poland ruled by Russia, who, after his father's death, became the ward of an uncle who made his peace with his rulers. But, like most biographical criticism, much would be speculative and such speculations are not necessary. It is enough to say that any Pole of the ruling classes at the time of Conrad's childhood and youth would have grown accustomed to the knowledge that his country, partitioned between three great powers, was exploited and that its exploitation was assented to by the rest of the world. For a thinking man there was only the choice between hopeless, and hence useless, revolution and collab-oration with an alien rule, and this plight must touch the private as well as the public man. It is not surprising, then, that a child of Poland should, in his three great political novels, show a world in which no government can claim the kind of legitimacy which, for English novelists, could be taken for granted, regardless of whether they agreed or disagreed with particular policies.

There were, of course, citizens of the United Kingdom who felt that they had no say in what was done, but very few of these wrote novels. Robert Tressell's novel of working-class life, *The Ragged Trousered Philanthropists* (1914), is an exception and Hardy, most strikingly in *Jude the Obscure*, explores the plight of the powerless. The trenches in the Great War taught some writers the common experience of powerlessness to make decisions and, in the case of Frederic Manning, enabled a minor *littérateur* to write what is certainly a minor master-piece, *The Middle Parts of Fortune*.[4] But the vast majority of our writers belonged, by birth or achievement, to those classes which, at some level, decided matters.

Conrad, cultured, educated, naturally sympathetic to order and decorum and a sense of historical continuity, yet belongs among those to whom, politically, things are done. His attitude of disdainful and disillusioned scepticism is akin to that which, in England, puts its possessor on the side of the status quo, on the grounds that change will probably be for the worse and reformers and revolutionaries are prob-ably posturing cranks with a grievance. But this English kind of conservatism can only arise if the status quo at least has some historical legitimacy and, normally, suits the possessor personally. Tsarist Russia did not provide these requirements and Conrad is therefore as sceptical of the powers that be as of revolutionaries. It is this which explains his sudden ferocious attacks on received wisdom and his contempt for those – whether the peaceful citizens of the European capital of 'Heart of Darkness' or the teacher of languages in *Under Western Eyes* or the chairman of the railway company in *Nostromo* – who believe that they will always be exempt from the lessons which he learned as a child.

If one holds, as I and many other readers do, that *Nostromo* is the finest political novel of this (and, some would say, any) period of English literature, our judgement is on the face of it an oddity. The social and political changes of the nineteenth century stimulated a number of our greatest novelists to explore the effects of them upon fictional characters. The half-century from 1890 saw changes in tech-nology, patterns of work, power, class relationships which would seem to provide a rich field for the novelist. Yet there is in this period no large-scale treatment of English society which in any way approaches the sense of an understanding of the modern world which is given by this presentation of quasi-imperial relationships in South America by a man for whom English was his third language.

This is not because major writers were necessarily uninterested in politics and social developments but because they seemed unable, and in some cases unwilling, to embody this interest in large political fictions. Those novelists who did make the attempt were not very successful. In the early part of the period with which I am dealing the best-known novelists of society were probably John Galsworthy and H. G. Wells. Galsworthy, though a heavy documenter of his chosen field, the upper-middle commercial classes, presents only a very tawdry conception of the values for which he claims to be fighting and ends up more or less in love with what starts as the object of his attack. Wells, a more significant writer, has great gifts for science – or speculative – fiction, of which I shall speak later in this chapter, but his realistic novels have little interest beyond the documentary. His depiction of small shopkeepers and clerks, for example, is a great deal more convincing and interesting than Forster's Leonard Bast, but the books as a whole lack a consistent viewpoint from which to examine human interactions, and his stylistic resources do not permit him to penetrate far below the surface. The writer by the side of whom these limitations are most clearly revealed is not, it should be emphasized, Henry James, despite the famous wrangle between Wells and James about the provinces of journalism and art, but Arnold Bennett. In the 1930s another novelist who, like Wells, was an interesting polemicist who achieved success in the form of the novel of ideas or Utopia, George Orwell, displays similar weakness in his attempts to embody his convictions about society in terms of people and their relationships.

When the great social changes are touched on by the major writers they tend to appear within an exploration of personality which focuses chiefly on non-social and often intensely personal issues, as does the whole agonized question of Parnell and Irish independence in the Christmas dinner scene in Joyce's *A Portrait of the Artist as a Young Man* or of the changing position of women in Ursula Brangwen's experience as a schoolteacher in Lawrence's *The Rainbow*.[5]

It is perhaps pointless to seek reasons for the scarcity of good political or, more generally, social novels in this period. It may be answered that, given the rarity of great writers, generalizations about their subject-matter always rest on inadequate data. Yet there are a few guesses which I would like to hazard.

The social background and education of many writers were such as to make it hard for them to come to terms with the changes which were taking place around them. Ivy Compton-Burnett said that she did not feel able to write about anything after 1910 and, in fact, the society about which she writes is rarely even as modern as that. She is an extreme case, but I have already instanced Forster's lack of knowledge of more than a very limited segment of English society, which is equally true of Virginia Woolf and, in a later generation, of Evelyn Waugh.

The modern world, moreover, gives an intimidating impression of complexity. English society was, of course, far from simple in the mid-nineteenth century, but for a number of reasons, mostly to do with the increasing range of communications, the complexity has in this century become more obvious. For novelists, I suspect, the chief reason is that, as a consequence of universal education, more and more groups of people have risen into unchallengeable visibility. It is harder to ignore the reality of men and women if, say, the newspapers which they read are continually before one's eyes. Too many groups of people whom he should know but does not are clamouring for the novelist's attention.

Some writers, of whom Virginia Woolf is one, have turned away from any conception of man as a social being and seen him as an individual in a society which is essentially alien; this concept of society as an external force of which those individuals who deserve our attention are not really a part is sometimes combined with a sense that things have not always been thus and that there was once a harmonious society in which the sensitive and the intelligent could find a place.

The proper response to the plight of the modern novelist confronted by a society which he does not feel that he can capture in a novel is, I think, one of respectful sympathy. The great nineteenth-century novelists of society proceeded with such confidence as often as not because they could not conceive of their ignorance; they marched forward with stereotypes or they turned blind eyes to whole areas of society. Their successors are perhaps more obviously insecure because they have a greater awareness of what they do not know.

If the novel seems often, in enlarging its range in the exploration of inner states of mind and feeling, to have restricted it in the world of affairs, there is one specialized form of fiction in which public issues find a place. The novel of ideas takes on the form of science fiction in this period and produces a form of Utopia particularly well suited for speculation.

H. G. Wells, though he did not invent science fiction, was the first writer to make serious use of the form – the first, that is, to take plausible scientific discoveries or tendencies and to extrapolate from them so as to reveal their social or moral potentials. Here he can make full use of that interest in ideas which in his straight novels lie uneasily side by side with inadequately realized characters. His interest in science is genuine; it stirs his imagination, but his concern is with the consequences for humanity rather than technology or gadgetry. He ensures that the technicalities will not strike us as too monstrously implausible and he sets his happenings within an extremely mundane framework. It is typical that when, in *The War of the Worlds* (1898), Martians appear, equipped with heat-rays, they first land in a sandpit near

Woking. But, as is inherent in novels of ideas, Wells focuses our attention on general speculations, social implications, and political consequences and not on individuals, following in this the tradition of More, Swift, and the Butler of *Erewhon*.

The most effective of the stories are the ones in which our sympathies shift, so that we admit the conflicts within our social and political beliefs, and in which Wells successfully taps a vein of traditional, almost mythical, feeling. We are not likely to sympathize with the Martians in *The War of the Worlds* but the strength of *The Island of Dr Moreau* (1896) comes from mingled pity and horror roused by the half-human victims of vivisection and the strange blurring of obsessional experimentation and imposed ritual. In *The Time Machine* (1895) the extrapolation of contemporary tendencies is at its clearest. The Time Traveller's first interpretation of the world to which he journeys is one where the tender, elegant, and weak are served by helots who live underground but this is turned on its head when he discovers that the refined have become the prey of their apparent servants. The force of the story comes both from speculations about the future organization of society and the relationship between workers and employers, speculations very much in the air at the time Wells was writing, and also from the old opposition between higher and lower selves, the children of light and their darker partners.

The other explorer of Utopia who has provided us with a fable which still seems to have some validity is Aldous Huxley. His early novels are all ones where characters exist largely as the bearers of ideas and the satisfaction which we receive is predominantly intellectual, the experience of feeling what it would be like to entertain such ideas. In 1932 he published a pure Utopian fiction, *Brave New World*. This world is created by an exaggeration of various tendencies which Huxley sees as likely pointers to the future: ideas about planning economies, eugenics, 'free love' and efficient contraception, emotional conditioning, psychoanalysis, and a general belief that reason and science can solve all problems. The mentally conditioned, test-tube-born inhabitants of this world are named eclectically after the great men of the past who strove to bring about a more enlightened, more prosperous, less superstitious, happier society – Bradlaugh, Hoover, Marx, Mond, Darwin, Helmholtz, with appropriate feminine endings for such names as Lenina. The book is very funny with its choice of 'Our Ford', sometimes modulated to 'Our Freud', as the object of ritual worship, its entertainments, the scent organ and the cinematic development of 'the feelies', and the ultimate opium of the people, the happy drug 'soma'.

Those within the society who have doubts have nevertheless been too conditioned to be real rebels and if they prove too much of an irritant they are banished to islands where, surrounded by their own kind, they can enjoy themselves in what amount to open-minded seminars in permanent session. The only truly intransigent opponent is a man who has by accident been brought up in a reservation for savages in New Mexico where he has adopted a religion which is a mixture of fertility ritual and flagellant Christianity and has formed his idea of a world elsewhere from his only book, the complete works of Shakespeare. Found and brought to London, he is appalled by this brave new world which has such innocently fornicating, guilt-free, conforming hedonists in it. He claims, eventually, the right to suffer, despairs of others and, after he has succumbed to the wiles of a girl who does not understand what the problem is (what any problem could be), kills himself.

Only a fanatic, it seems, can oppose this horrifying world which – and this is, I think, what makes *Brave New World* so much more convincing than Orwell's Utopia, *Nineteen Eighty-Four* – has not been created by monsters of cruelty or corruption. Mustapha Mond, the Controller, a cousin, we may say, of Dostoevsky's Grand Inquisitor, explains the reasoning behind the brave new world and we see that every one of us has gone some way down the slope towards the easy nightmare. If we would not deny tranquillizing drugs for the deranged, would we deny them to the intensely worried? To the slightly upset? To anyone who feels less than totally relaxed? If we do not drive fallen women out into the snow, do we tolerate extramarital sexual activity? Do we condone promiscuity? Do we find celibacy suspect? Do we encourage sexual experimentation from an early age? If we believe in giving our children the right background, do we see that they do not make the wrong kind of friends? Do we make them aware of what will be expected of them? Do we prepare them for a role in life? Do we reward or punish them? Do we effectively condition them? We may wish to reject Mustapha Mond's lucid explanation that:

> Actual happiness always looks pretty squalid in
> comparison with the over-compensations for misery. And,
> of course, stability isn't nearly so spectacular as instability.
> And being contented has none of the glamour of a good
> fight against misfortune, none of the picturesqueness of a
> struggle with temptation, or a fatal overthrow by passion
> or doubt. Happiness is never grand.   (16)

But most of us have at one time or another tried in some specific way to bring about a world that seems if not brave and new at least less miserable and old.

There are other specialized forms of fiction which have developed in this period to which we might go if we wish to consider the relationship between the writer and society. Indeed, the very existence and popularity of specialized forms demands that we should do so, partly because of the social implications of these forms themselves and partly because of the light that their rise may cast on other forms of writing.

The most striking literary novelty in this period was undoubtedly the enormous development of the detective story. An interest in crime and the sensational is nothing new; the title page of *Moll Flanders*[6] offers all the attractions of the now traditional Sunday newspaper and at different times there have been Newgate Calendars, broadsheet confessions, and Gothic romances in plenty. The distinguishing characteristic of the detective story, the element of puzzle, developed during the nineteenth century and can be seen in Wilkie Collins's *The Moonstone* (1868) and even as early as 1843 in Poe's *The Murders in the Rue Morgue*. It is with Conan Doyle's Sherlock Holmes, who first appeared in *A Study in Scarlet* in 1888, that the modern detective is born and he largely determines many of the characteristics of his successors. Those successors have been legion and their popularity extraordinary; the name of Agatha Christie is probably known to more people than that of any writer to whom I devote a chapter in this study and she has certainly had immeasurably more readers.

One is tempted to wonder, since detective stories have such popularity, what people did before they were invented, which is another way of asking what particular circumstances brought about their rise. Many suggestions have been made, of which two seem to me worth considering. The extension of education brought about by the Act of 1870, it has been said, produced a crop of partially educated people whose tastes were catered for by the rise of the popular press and of such magazines as *Tit-Bits* and *Answers*. Puzzles of various kinds fitted their tastes; the first crossword puzzle, for instance, was produced in the United States in 1913 and in Great Britain in 1924. Puzzle stories – detective fiction – catered for the same interest and, once established, snowballed. The same case could be made at the present time for the astonishing increase in the reading of science fiction. It is difficult to know how seriously to take this argument; it starts with somewhat simplified sociology and fails to explain the popularity of such writing with educated and sophisticated readers. The other suggestion, of a more solemnly psycho-sociological kind, is that, in an age of increasing uncertainty about values and worry about threats to order, the function of the detective story is to locate wrongdoing in the criminal, to assure us that he will be found out and that threatened order will be restored. The detective is the guardian of stability who is cleverer than the criminal. Leaving on one side the question of whether the stability of society actually was more threatened than previously, we can certainly say that many people, faced by social changes which they did not like, thought so. Most detective story writers actually do seem to be conformist in their views and to encourage conformity in their readers. The form requires a closed environment for the exclusion of accidental factors, but the typical story tends to locate the necessary locked room within such closed societies as the smugly traditional version of the English village or country house or club or college.

But if, at the conclusion of the detective story, we can safely return to the garden party or our port, there is one kind of popular fiction, often considered as an offshoot of the detective story, where this is by no means always true – the thriller. Historians of the detective story have traced a line of descent for the thriller and here the key names are Dashiell Hammett (1894–1961) and Raymond Chandler (1888–1959). Both are Americans, though Chandler had what he, at least, regarded as the advantage of an English education; both write of corrupt and violent societies and both are still dealing with the solution of problems, though the solution is brought about less by the painstaking working out of clues than by violent actions. At the conclusion society remains corrupt and violent and the next guarded telephone call will not be an appeal to help authority but, as likely as not, to protect someone from it.

But the thriller can claim another ancestry, too. The English novel has a considerable tradition of action and adventure, often violent. We find it in Fielding and Scott and Thackeray and Dickens and in this century most strikingly in Conrad. There has also been a tradition of adventure stories, usually set in foreign parts, by such writers as Stevenson and Rider Haggard, for whom it is not always possible to make high literary claims but which have surprising powers of survival from generation to generation of readers. Many of these, together with the works of Kipling and Conan Doyle, are often first encountered in childhood though not all of them were originally intended for children. One successor is clearly John Buchan whose highly patriotic and essentially authoritarian views find expression in tales of the thwarting of spies and other enemies of the State. In this he is one of the first practitioners of that form of thriller, the spy story, which continues to fill the bookshops.[7]

But there are also a number of writers of a more sceptical disposition who have placed substantial gifts, including intelligence and particularly political intelligence, at the service of the minor form of the thriller. One may speculate that their choice has been made in part because the general tendency of the novel since the end of the nineteenth century has been to move inwards, to concentrate on individual psychology and to turn away from public themes and has thus made them feel that what they have to say does not find a place in the main-stream of fiction.

Here the influence of Conrad, whose outlook is, as I have shown, so different from his English contemporaries, has been very great. So true is this of Graham Greene, the most obvious example of the tendency, that in his early book, *It's a Battlefield* (1934), he pays his debt with ostentation: the Christian name of one of his characters is Conrad because his parents once had a lodger, an officer in the merchant navy, of that name. *It's a Battlefield*, like a number of Greene's other early books, was labelled 'an entertainment'. They are all based on intrigue, murder, problems which can – or cannot – be solved by strong action and police work, yet in them all political and social issues are dealt with from a lively and critical point of view. The effect is a strange and rather unsettling one; it is almost as if the novelist were saying that such matters can no longer find a place in the 'serious' novel.

Greene, who continued for some time to distinguish between his novels and his entertainments, is the most celebrated example of this tendency to explore what is serious in a form which is deliberately minor, but there are others. Patrick Hamilton, an unduly neglected writer, is one, and if asked where to find political speculation and a sense of individuals as both private and social beings, presented with a degree of intelligence in any way comparable with that shown in *Nostromo*, my own choice would be for books which lay no claim to major status, the thrillers of Eric Ambler.

Notes

1. See 'Rudyard Kipling', in *The Collected Essays, Journalism and Letters of George Orwell*, edited by S. Orwell and I. Augers (1968), II.

2. As a homosexual he might feel persecuted, but by nation and by class he belonged to the rulers; he might wish to throw in his lot with the less fortunate, but he is a Schlegel and not a Bast, a Fielding and not an Aziz.

3. See Bibliography.

4. *The Middle Parts of Fortune* was published under the pseudonym 'Private 19022' in a limited edition in 1920, followed by an expurgated edition under the title *Her Privates We* in 1930. An unexpurgated general edition appeared in 1977.

5. I am aware that Lawrence may be thought to be a striking refutation of the case which I am making. I discuss his work at length in Chapter 12. It is enough to say here that what he writes about society in general seems to me to be the least convincing part of his work, to such an extent that I would deny it the term 'politics'.

6. 'The Fortunes and Misfortunes of the Famous Moll Flanders. Who was born in Newgate, and during a Life of continu'd Variety for Threescore Years, besides her Childhood, was Twelve Year a Whore, five times a Wife (whereof once to her own Brother), Twelve Year a Thief, Eight Year a Transported Felon in Virginia, at last grew Rich, liv'd Honest and died a Penitent, Written from her own Memorandums'.

7. It is at least sociologically interesting that many spy novels and some detective stories have in recent years become much less certain of the value of that order which their heroes are supposed to uphold.

Chapter 7
Arnold Bennett on the Pentonville Omnibus

'The man is most honest, and anxious to do justice,' wrote Arnold Bennett in his *Journal* on 28 May 1896, in reference to the publishers reader's report on his first novel by John Buchan, 'but he clearly has not been able quite to sympathize with the latest disciple of the de Goncourts.' There is perhaps something a little dandyish in thus labelling oneself but Bennett makes it abundantly clear in his letters and elsewhere in his *Journal* that, though he does not regard the de Goncourts as the best writers who have influenced him (that place probably goes to Turgenev), he would never dissociate himself from the basically realistic aims of the brothers. This was for him a matter both of technique and attitude. In his *Journal* for 15 October 1896 he describes the first requirement of a novelist as an all-embracing Christlike compassion and, whether he can emulate the Deity or not, his range of sympathies is remarkably wide and extends very far into the mundane. His original field of study and the one at which he most excelled was the Midland middle class, sometimes in very comfortable circumstances but essentially ordinary. When Frank Harris complained that Sophia Baines in *The Old Wives' Tale* (1908) did not rise to a great passion so as to make a contrast between her and her sister – 'the contrast between the mangy tabby-cat and the superb wild animal' – Bennett replied: 'At bottom I regard your attitude as flavoured with a youthful sentimentality. At bottom I am proudly content with the Pentonville omnibus.'[1]

There is a similar conscious down-to-earthness in his attitude to his craft; he was very much the professional man of letters. He knew perfectly well that his reputation, and even his long-term income, would depend upon those novels which he took seriously; in this he was right and, though some of the novels which he liked have not stood the test of a few generations' reading, in general his judgement of his own work was remarkably sound. But he also wrote avowedly commercial novels and plays, going so far as to use the word 'pot-boiler' and explaining that he found that he could write them easily and regarded such writing as an honest trade. In so far as Bennett has

been greatly misunderstood and grossly underrated, it is his pot-
boiling novels and journalism which have been partly to blame. His
attitude to them – the extent to which he did not let them use up much
of his energy – is indicated by the fact that he wrote *Buried Alive* in
eight weeks during the composition of *The Old Wives' Tale*.

Throughout his career Bennett also wrote literary and other journalism and here, likewise, the degree of seriousness and value varies
greatly, though what impresses one most is his range of interests. If
we glance through *Books and Persons* (1917), a selection of the weekly
articles which he contributed as 'Jacob Tonson' to *The New Age*
between 1908 and 1911, we find not only discussions of general topics
and now forgotten writers but also essays on Mallarmé, Chekhov,
Turgenev, and Dostoevsky as well as more expected ones on Wells,
Kipling, Conrad, Meredith, Anatole France, Galsworthy, and Mase-
field. His tastes were astonishingly wide. In the period in which he was
writing *Clayhanger* (January to June 1910), for example, his *Journal*
records not only what might be expected of any educated man of his
time – regular visits to the theatre and the opera, a lot of sketching in
Florence, the reading of Flaubert's correspondence and of Stendhal –
but also discussions with friends of Matisse, Bonnard, Etruscan tombs,
Picasso, particular enjoyment of Monteverdi and Richard Strauss, and
the entertaining to tea of Ravel (with whom he played duets) and his
mother. He was a writer about limited and provincial people who was
one of the least limited and least 'provincial' of English writers.

He staked out his chosen territory with his first novel, *A Man from
the North* (1898), and consolidated his hold in his first novel of real
value, *Anna of the Five Towns*, published in 1902. By 'territory' here
I do not only mean that, like most of his significant novels, *Anna* is
set in his re-creation of the Potteries but also that it touches on most
of the major themes which were to preoccupy him. The Potteries,
indeed, are only of interest for him as an outward form for a whole
set of assumptions and a way of life. As he wrote to Lady St Helier
on 22 June 1912: 'One can only tolerate them by living in them.' The
novel has a melodramatic snap ending for the last two or three pages
which is altogether unworthy of the book, but apart from that it is
characterized by the even-paced sobriety appropriate to that stifling of
spontaneity which he sees as lying at the heart of the society which
he depicts. This evenness of tone is broken from time to time, as it
is throughout his major work, by sudden, almost epigrammatic flashes
of harsh insight which give the effect of great energy underlying the
inhibited surface. These flashes normally concern the victims of
complacency and philistine acquisitiveness. The most striking example
in this book comes in the description of the old servant, Sarah Vodrey:
'After fifty years of ceaseless labour, she had gained the affection of

one person, and enough money to pay for her own funeral' (12).
Bennett has, indeed, great understanding of the narrowed and the
shrunken, and in this novel he treats at length what is to be one of his
major themes – jocularly in *Helen with the High Hand*,[2] seriously in the
late novel about London, *Riceyman Steps* (1923), and most successfully
in *Clayhanger* (1910) and *The Old Wives' Tale* – the effects of avarice.
Miserliness, as the enemy of spontaneity and joy, is shown not as a
wanton aberration but as the extreme end of that respectable, chapel-
attending, dutiful, and self-respecting thrift which that hypothetical
man on the Pentonville omnibus would not wish to deny.

Bennett also has a much more real sense than most contemporary
novelists of the reality of poverty, of the want which makes money
the first step towards a decent life. Nowhere is this more effective and
moving than in his treatment of Darius Clayhanger. The reader is
shown the destitution of Darius's childhood, the shame of being sent
to the 'Bastille', the workhouse, which lies beneath his obsession with
security of possessions; his son Edwin knows nothing of this and can
despise his father's tight-fistedness. Bennett comments, when Darius
dies: 'The vast and forlorn adventure of the little boy from the Bastille
was over. Edwin did not know that the little boy from the Bastille was
dead' (III. 17) and, a little later 'They were all in clover, thanks to the
terrible lifelong obstinacy of the little boy from the Bastille' (IV. 1).
But if we reflect for a little on that 'in clover' we shall also see that
it is not totally contemptuous. Bennett *is*, as Virginia Woolf said, a
materialist; he knows perfectly well that people are defined in part by
their jobs, their habits, their possessions, and also that they define
themselves thus. Edwin Clayhanger, for example, is fascinated by the
new house which has the magic of new potentialities of activity and
quietly proud of that success in his work which enables him to set
Hilda's affairs straight. It would have been inconceivable for Bennett
to have sought our approval for a character denouncing possessions,
as Birkin does in Lawrence's *Women in Love*, while relying on the
secure competence of 'about four hundred a year.'

I shall have more to say later about the famous attack of Virginia
Woolf on Bennett on the grounds that he was a 'materialist' but it is
necessary to point out here that materialism, in some senses, is central
to Bennett's whole aim. Forster's Margaret Schlegel, in *Howards End*,
speaks of standing on £600 a year, and Forster agrees with her that it
is dishonest not to recognize that civilized life depends upon a secure
income. But this is a very abstract realization; Forster cannot, and
admits that he cannot, really imagine what life would be like for those
with, say, £120 or £250 and how a man who moved from £120 to
£600 would change his ideas and aspirations in the process. Bennett
said in an essay on 'The Middle Classes' that what distinguished them

was that 'they never look twice at twopence'. He himself was never poor, though his father had been and, unlike Darius, had not concealed the fact, but he had seen poverty and, good follower of the de Goncourts that he was, had done his homework. He thought it his duty as a novelist, as well as a man, to understand what life was like for those who had to count twopence or had had to do so.

This is one aspect of the fact that Bennett, unlike most novelists of his time, writes novels about those who are very different from himself and, by most judgements, less intelligent, less experienced in the world, and less sophisticated. It is unusual in a twentieth-century novelist to deal so consistently, in serious works, with characters at a 'lower' level than both the writer and the hypothetical readers. It was not, of course, uncommon in earlier fiction. I do not have in mind those studies – *Emma* and *Middlemarch* may stand as examples – in which the writer and the implied reader are conceived as older and wiser than central characters who are potentially of their own emotional and intellectual stature, but those in which the central character is, inherently and permanently, less intelligent or sophisticated. Tom Jones, however old he grows, will not be as shrewd as Fielding; none of Trollope's characters will see all round things as he does; Tess and Jude exemplify the tragedies of those whose plight we can understand but could not share. Henry James is more typical of modern fiction in his avowed interest in those who can comprehend their plights, and most English novelists of our own century have concerned themselves with emotional and intellectual experiences akin to their own. The revelations which they offer us are the revelations of their own characters – of Paul Morel and Birkin, of Margaret Schlegel and Fielding, of Mrs Dalloway and Lily Briscoe. Even those who sometimes offer us an understanding which is denied any of their characters, as Conrad does in his political novels or Joyce in *Ulysses* and *Finnegans Wake*, also offer us the insights of Marlow and Stephen Dedalus. Bennett never does this in his major works; the understanding which we have of the Baines sisters or Anna Tellwright or Edwin Clayhanger is something which we share with Bennett and not with the characters themselves. Doubtless this has something to do with his declared realistic method and the great influence on him of French fiction. He shares it with Balzac and Flaubert and Stendhal. It also has to do with his temperament, which we may reasonably call democratic, in the sense that he accepts the Pentonville omnibus and has little sense of an emotional or spiritual élite.

Nowhere is this more clear than in what most readers would regard as, with *Clayhanger*, his best work, *The Old Wives' Tale*. The obvious danger for a writer who chooses as his subject the lives of two provincial, slightly educated, and rather unimaginative women is that

he will allow us to patronize them, either because he is patronizing
them himself or because his narrative tone is not sufficiently secure to
keep us in order; the dangers, in short, are either that we will connive
with him in patronage or that we patronize both the characters and
their creator. Bennett runs both risks at the start of the novel. The
opening sentence is striking, implying that we already have some
community of experience with the narrator – 'Those two girls, Constance and Sophia Baines, paid no heed to the manifold interests of their
situation, of which, indeed, they had never been conscious.' We realize
its purpose fairly soon, though; Bennett is telling us, rather jocularly,
a good deal about Staffordshire and about the time in which the
opening of the novel is set ('The crinoline had not quite reached its full
circumference, and the dress-improver had not even been thought of')
but mostly he takes up the position of a commentator from within the
adult world of the Five Towns who is contemplating the inexperience
of the young. He is shrewd and humorous though his approach is
inoffensive and, it might seem, in danger of cosiness. Of Mrs Baines,
for example, we are told: 'She was stout; but the fashions, prescribing
vague outlines, broad downward slopes, and vast amplitudes, were
favourable to her shape. It must not be supposed that stout women
of a certain age never seek to seduce the eye and trouble the medi-
tations of man by other than moral charms' (I. 3).

But he takes us closer to his personages and engages our sympathies
by an acute psychological penetration into the feelings of girls discovering what their feelings are. Sophia, preached to by her paralysed
and bedridden father, discovers that the 'grotesqueness of her father's
complacency humiliated her past bearing'. Constance discovers,
muddledly, that she does not want Samuel Povey mocked. It is only
when we are no longer in any danger of sneering at his characters and
rather may feel that Bennett is accepting the outlook of Bursley that
he begins to widen the possible frame of reference. He does it, at times,
harshly. The best example is, I think, what he says near the beginning
of the second part of the novel about the servant Maggie, who is
giving notice in preparation for her marriage:

> Constance looked at her. Despite the special muslin of
> that day she had traces of the slatternliness of which Mrs
> Baines had never been able to cure her. She was over
> forty, big, gawky. She had no figure, no charms of any
> kind. She was what was left of a woman after twenty-two
> years in the cave of a philanthropic family.   (II. 1)

His treatment of Samuel Povey is throughout a fine example of how
he holds the balance: Povey *is* limited, he *is* often ineffectual; he only

comes to be recognized by his community as a solid and successful man when he refuses to sell his best cloth to make a coat for a miner's dog and orders the man out of his shop – a scene where our judgement is likely to be very different from that of his fellow-citizens; he has, as we are specifically told, 'a certain officious self-importance' when he wakes Constance to break the news to her of Daniel Povey's killing of his wife; and yet, in this very matter of Daniel's crime and sentence, he brings about his own death by his efforts and earns, from us as well as Bennett, the epitaph: 'He was a very honest man' (II. 5).

It is in the treatment of the two old wives of the title that we may study more effectively that implied conflict between two kinds of judgement. I have already quoted Bennett's repudiation of Frank Harris's characterization of the two as a tabby cat and an at least potential wild animal, but it is true that the great separation of their lives means that, however far he may wish us to see that they are both deeply rooted in St Luke's Square and its values, he is nevertheless contrasting, overtly or by implication, the woman who seems not to have to make choices with the woman who has. It is in the character of Sophia, therefore, that we meet most often the moment of choice at which more than one judgement of value, more, sometimes, than one whole way of life, is in question.

We might ask Frank Harris's question, I think, without its being simply a rhetorical one. She is at the start lively, beautiful, and with a quality of sexual energy which Bennett brings out in a superb erotic image when he describes Gerald kissing her:

> However, the powerful clinging of her lips somewhat startled his senses, and also delighted him by its silent promise. He could smell the stuff of her veil, the sarsenet of her bodice, and, as it were wrapped in these odours as her body was wrapped in its clothes, the faint fleshly perfume of her body itself. (III. 1)

She ends, back in St Luke's Square, feeling that 'not for millions of pounds would she live her life over again' (IV. 2), squabbling with her sister, childless and wishing that she had a son and cosseting an aged dog. Why? Bennett shows her enduring a number of experiences which might frustrate any impulse towards sexual love: Gerald proves totally feckless, takes her to the public execution, and goes off with another woman while leaving Sophia in a squalid room, overhearing the 'whisperings; long sighs suddenly stifled; mysterious groans as of torture, broken by a giggle' (III. 3) of her neighbours while they wait for the guillotining; later he proves not only unfaithful but treacherous. When she is ill she is looked after in the house of Mme Foucault, the

bedizened and ageing courtesan; when she is running the boarding
house it is Niepce, who seems virtually senile, who tries to make love
to her; Chirac touches her feelings, but she is by this time worn out
by strain and slightly contemptuous of his self-dramatization. He dies
in the balloon flight out of besieged Paris. By this time she is efficient,
proud, isolated. I think that nowadays most of us would feel not only
that the sexuality of a woman like Sophia would be more urgent,
would overcome these obstacles, but also that her sexuality would be
only a component part of an urge towards companionship, friendship,
some shared human activity. But Bennett's temperament did not make
him see matters this way; the tradition of French fiction, which was
so important to Bennett, has always tended to take sexual love as an
isolated, definable, and possibly unrelated feeling, more a matter of a
specific visitation than a leaning, and the standards of the fiction of
1908 made it easy for him to follow this course. Naturally enough the
standards by which she judges the inadequacy of her husband or the
kind incompetence of Mme Foucault are, basically, those she has
acquired in Bursley. It is inevitable, surely, that when Chirac helps her
in the hotel after the guillotining, while Gerald lies drunk asleep, she
reverts to the shop to express her feeling – 'he had successfully passed
through the ordeal of seeing the wrong side of the stuff of her life'.
What is significant is that the values which are strongest and which
enable her to survive are those which we feel to be ambiguous, just
as Samuel Povey's self-assertion to the collier is for his peers a proof
of independence and strength (and we respect this) and simultaneously
a judgement on the limitations of that society.

Hard practicality and self-respect save Sophia; looking at the wreck
of Mme Foucault she thinks: 'If I had been in her place, I shouldn't
have been like that. I should have been rich. I should have saved like
a miser. I wouldn't have been dependent on anybody at that age'
(III. 5). We applaud; to speak of saving like a miser is hyperbole. But
it is not long before, during the siege of Paris, she is described in the
classic posture of the miser:

> And she went up to her room every night with limbs
> exhausted, but with head clear enough to balance her
> accounts and go through her money. She did this in bed
> with thick gloves on. If often she did not sleep well, it
> was not because of the distant guns, but because of her
> preoccupation with the subject of finance. (III. 6)

There is a significant echo of a much earlier time during her stay with
Mme Foucault; she goes, shaky and convalescent, to explore the flat
and

> pressed her face against the glass, and remembered the
> St. Luke's Square of her childhood; and just as there from
> the showroom window she could not even by pressing her
> face against the glass see the pavement, so here she could
> not see the roof; the courtyard was like the bottom of a
> well.   (III. 5)

What the reader remembers is that when we first encountered Sophia
with her sister looking out at St Luke's Square it is so that they can
watch the drudge Maggie and make fun of her grotesque romance. It
is not surprising that, though Sophia is scrupulously honest to her
clients and generous when she can afford to be, she establishes Fren-
shams by 'employing two servants, working them very hard at low
wages' (III. 7).

The virtues of Bursley are what save Sophia from disaster and we
cannot but sympathize with her practical dealing with Mme Foucault
and the boarding house; but the virtues are limited and have their own
price. There is, I think, nothing sadder in the book than her reflection,
after she has been told of Chirac's presumed death and has realized that
though she feels loss it is not acute, for Chirac would never have
attracted her powerfully: 'She continued to dream, at rare intervals, of
the kind of passion that would have satisfied her, glowing but banked
down like a fire in some fine chamber of a rich but careful household'
(III. 7).

She meets her match, however. Her toughness, growing as it does
from the roots of Bursley, is no proof against the similar tenacity of
her sister; the struggle between them provides another conflict in
which we see that what makes for restriction and inhibition comes
from attitudes which we have been made to respect and that we have
so far absorbed the values of St Luke's Square that we ourselves are
dubious about what offers enjoyment. Sophia and the doctor discuss
what would be best for Constance; she is a rich woman; she need not
continue living in the old dark house; she and her sister could live
anywhere. Their conversation is reasonable but we know that they are
enjoying themselves knowing best. We recognize that they are right,
and yet everything in their conversation grates. When the doctor says:
'What she needs is the bustle of life in a good hotel, a good hydro,
for instance. Among jolly people. Parties! Games! Excursions! She
wouldn't be the same woman' (IV. 3), we feel that he is vulgar and
obtuse. When the conflict between the sisters comes into the open it
is notable that Constance has little to say, and that she needs to say
little. The quarrel is both upsetting and, in its lack of logical encounter,
comic. Sophia says:

'There are several places I should like to visit –
Torquay, Tunbridge Wells. I've always understood that
Tunbridge Wells is a very nice town indeed, with very
superior people and a beautiful climate.'
'I think I shall have to be getting back to St. Luke's
Square,' said Constance, ignoring all that Sophia had said.
'There's so much to be done.'   (iv. 3)

What most strikes us here is a sense which is central to the whole
book of minds made up and decisions taken without conscious reflection, and of the privacy of individual experience.

The only reasons which Constance can give as to why she should
not seize the opportunity of having an altogether easier life are obviously inadequate ones about the need to keep the house clean. Not only
does Bennett remind us of what we know already, that people habitu-
ally give inadequate or irrelevant reasons for what they do, but he
is also able to make us feel the strength of her feelings because we have
acquired, in the course of the book, a striking sense of an individuality
which has grown unwatched and unknown to others and we know
that this individuality is inextricably joined to the house.

It has often been said that the main theme of *The Old Wives' Tale*
is the passage of time and this is obviously true; Sophia's awareness,
as she looks at her husband's dead body, of what life has done to him
is the clearest example, and the point does not need labouring. But this
sense of privacy, of a world in which people keep their own counsel,
of essential loneliness, is equally strong. We find out about decisions
like Sophia's elopement and Mrs Baines's decision to go and live with
her sister after they are made in secrecy. The world of the novel is one
where people shut up their thoughts from others, partly because of a
desire not to be talked into or out of things and partly because sometimes to reveal them would be damaging. The most dramatic revelation of the book occurs in the chapter, 'Another Crime', which follows
on from 'Crime' which recounts the discovery that Constance and
Samuel's son has been pilfering from the till of the shop. It seems to
me typical that Bennett plays fair with the reader by labelling what we
are to expect but doing so in such a way that we are misled precisely
because, like his characters, we do not expect disaster. The second
crime, however, is truly disastrous; Samuel Povey learns that his
cousin's wife is an alcoholic and that Daniel Povey has killed her in
a fit of·rage at her neglect of their sick son. But before Samuel
discovers this he sees the bakehouse in his cousin's yard with 'naked
figures strangely moving in it'. For Daniel this is normal night baking
and he does not see that for Samuel it is a sudden revelation of a whole

area of life just as unknown to him as the squalid secret which has not yet been revealed, so that he never again, we are told, ate a mouthful of bread without remembering that 'midnight apparition'.

It is fitting that the conclusion of the novel, Constance's death-bed ruminations, should maintain this pattern. She reviews her life and her feelings about those close to her. All her reflections would surprise the objects of them: her pity for Sophia's wasted life, her knowledge that she has spoiled her son and that it would probably have made no difference if she had not, and, finally, her judgement on her favourites, Dick and Lily. 'The secret attitude of both of them towards her was one of good-natured condescension, expressed in the tone in which they would say to each other, "the old lady". Perhaps they would have been startled to know that Constance lovingly looked down on both of them' (IV. 5).

This theme is reinforced, as I have suggested of the scene in the bakery, by the imagery of the book and especially by the symbolic significance which accretes around places. Bennett is not given to producing obvious symbolic properties unless, like the shop signboard and the changes made to it, they are public symbols chosen as such by the characters. His method is normally to describe things in terms of their use or their significance to the characters and to leave the resonances to emerge. The shop and the house, in particular, are central and we grow accustomed to seeing them as carrying meanings for the characters and for us. When Constance lets the shop go and keeps the house and, irritated by dilatory workmen and dust, watches the bricking up of the doorway between them, it is clear to us because it is clear to her that a portion of her past is being shut off.

Houses do become symbolic to us in just this way and in this book, as in life, the house plays its part in the *rites de passage* of its inhabitants: Book I ends with the departure of Mrs Baines as the new generation takes charge in the persons of Constance and Samuel Povey; Book II ends with the departure of Cyril for London and his mother's return to the house (this was the section which Bennett said was his favourite); Book III, being devoted to Sophia, cannot end with the house – the return of Sophia to St Luke's Square must wait for the Book which she is to share with Constance and there the house is of immense significance to both of them.

The mental wanderings of Constance in the delirium of her death-bed bring to the fore one of the images of the house which most underlines the sense of the hidden and secret nature of individual experience:

> In all her delirium she was invariably wandering to and
> fro, lost, in the long underground passage leading from
> the scullery past the coal-cellar and the cinder-cellar to the

back yard. And she was afraid of the vast obscure of those
regions as she had been in her infancy.   (IV. 5)

Though we have visited those cellars in a practical frame of mind
to discover, for example, Cyril hiding there and covered in coal dust,
this image re-creates that sense of mystery which is described – with
the echoed phrase 'the vast obscure of those regions' – as the childhood
feeling of the sisters.

There is an even more explicit symbolic suggestion of what lies
hidden in human experience in the presence of the empty room which
is never entered and which is described at the very beginning of the
book:

> Another window, on the second story, was peculiar, in
> that it had neither blind nor pad, and was very dirty; this
> was the window of an unused room that had a separate
> staircase to itself, the staircase being barred by a door
> always locked. Constance and Sophia had lived in
> continual expectation of the abnormal issuing from that
> mysterious room, which was next to their own. But they
> were disappointed. The room had no shameful secret
> except the incompetence of the architect who had made
> one house out of three; it was just an empty,
> unemployable room.

It is typical of Bennett that, having offered a symbolic empty room
in the middle of their house – next, indeed, to their bedroom – , he then
explains it in terms of architectural incompetence. It is equally typical
that, much later in the novel, after describing Constance watching the
door being bricked up we are told that

> Constance had been out into the Square and seen the
> altered sign, and seen Mrs. Critchlow's taste in window-
> curtains, and seen – most impressive sight of all – that the
> grimy window of the abandoned room at the top of the
> abandoned staircase next to the bedroom of her girlhood,
> had been cleaned and a table put in front of it. She knew
> that the chamber, which she herself had never entered,
> was to be employed as a storeroom, but the visible proof
> of its conversion so strangely affected her that she had not
> felt able to go boldly into the shop, as she had meant to
> do, and make a few purchases in the way of
> friendliness.   (II. 7)

The room is, after all, something more than an architectural incompetence.

Such echoes and repetition are also important, regardless of how much symbolic resonance we see in them, as a way of giving a sense of shape or rhythm to a story which, in the nature of things, must be in danger of seeming simply chronological. Bennett's concept of form and structure was a rather loose one in the novels which he took seriously. He produces neat and essentially traditional plots in pot-boilers like *Helen with the High Hand* or *The Card* (1911). But in his serious novels he is seeking a much less fixed sort of pattern; when the novel, for one reason or another, fails the result is scrappiness. *The Pretty Lady* (1918), for example, is an astonishing hotchpotch. There is a scene in which the prostitute, Christine, who is taking a mad officer to the station to catch his train back to the front, loses him. Her chase through the streets and the growing sense of suppressed panic gives a striking, almost surrealist image of the discontinuities of experience; the description of the Zeppelin raid, some of the war-committee scenes, the relationship between Christine and her maid are all first-rate. But they are set, cheek by jowl with other sections of the book which are often downright dull or unconvincing (the central male character who should link things together fails totally to do so, except in the most mechanical way) and which do ñot appear to belong together. What we have is a jumble with good bits. In places it reminds me of such early novels by intelligent writers as Virginia Woolf's *The Voyage Out* where scenes are inserted because the writer has something he, or she, wants to say and is determined to put it in regardless of any sense of formal propriety.

The Old Wives' Tale, similarly, has very little fixed pattern. Bennett is committed to showing the lives of 'those two girls' and this implies a chronological succession. He is obliged to leave Sophia in abeyance while he deals with Constance, rather than intercutting sections of their lives, because it is part of his view that each is separate and he will not risk letting us feel that Sophia is more than a memory for Constance. Moreover such intercutting (the possibility of which he was well aware of, to judge from his critical comments on various writers) would direct attention towards his shaping and take it away from our sense of the slow development of the people, would, in short, detract from the temporal for the benefit of the spatial. Furthermore, though he must, to do justice to what is significant for them, deal with the major events of their lives – Sophia's elopement, Samuel's death, Cyril's birth – he often chooses to deal with them rather briefly and we are more often aware of how he seems to have come to the same conclusion as did Virginia Woolf, that the novelist should not take it for granted 'that life exists more fully in what is commonly thought big than in

what is commonly thought small'. The set pieces which we remember
– the children's party, for example – are often such apparently small
matters. Often, too, they highlight an emotional process which is then
left to happen off-stage and whose culmination is treated very briefly.
Gerald's foolish squabble in the restaurant and his blustering return to
Sophia and the squalid deceits of the guillotine party are vivid; after
that, Bennett seems to imply by his omissions, the steady erosion of
love and trust goes on in a more subterranean manner.

Many of the more important sections are quite deliberately non-
climactic. In Book IV, Chapter 3, for example, what seems most
important is Sophia's reproach to Cyril for not having come home to
see his mother and the way that this becomes a cosy chat between
them, but this is muddled in with the plan for the sisters to go to a
hotel and with the bad behaviour of the servant Amy, provoked by
Sophia's rebuke, itself provoked by Amy's having kicked Sophia's
poodle. The deepest feelings of the characters are roused but they are
mixed with the daily clutter and are transformed into apparent trivi-
alities. The basic structure of most novels comes from a sense of a
problem to be solved or a quest or a trial with the author judging the
characters, who often also judge themselves, on their success or failure.
Bennett shows his characters making sense of their lives as they live
them, but there is little sense of assessment. Sophia suddenly thinks,
as she runs the Pension Frensham, 'How strange it is that I should be
here, doing what I am doing!', Constance comes to feel that she will
always be an intermediary between her husband and her son, but such
perceptions do not encourage us to plot these moments as points on
a chart leading somewhere. It is this sense of moments of insight
coming in the midst of ordinariness which presumably caused Bennett
to choose for Book IV what seems at first an almost excessive title
'What Life Is'.[3]

But there are patterns, though tentative and never obtrusive; often,
though not always, we share the perceptions of the characters. Cyril
is to Constance as Sophia is to Mrs Baines; we see this because Constance sees it. As the demonstration against Daniel Povey winds through
the town, Bennett reflects that 'Since the execution of the elephant,
nothing had so profoundly agitated Bursley' (II. 5). Not only do we
think of the innocence of the elephant but also remember that but for
it Sophia would never have met Gerald. Looking from a window in
Paris in convalescence is for Sophia like looking from a window in
Bursley as a child; the back regions of the house, as we have seen, link
childhood and old age. When Sophia returns to Bursley Constance
takes a circuitous route to the station, 'so that, if stopped by acquaintances, she should not be too obviously going to the station' (IV. 2);
this links with various other evasive manœuvres, like Mrs Baines going

out to see the altered signboard and not, as Constance thinks, her husband's grave, but it also reminds us more specifically of Sophia's excursion to see Gerald, without which there would have been no occasion to meet her on a return from a long absence.

The Old Wives' Tale is characteristic of Bennett in its sad but not despairing vision. No doubt any complete life story is likely to produce an effect of some gloom, for it is bound to end with ageing and death and in this book there are two main characters to die. But his view throughout his career is consistent. His pot-boilers may be jolly, but the serious works all share an awareness, not only of inevitable age and death but also of opportunities lost and joys forgone. Edwin Clayhanger is successful in his career and he marries the woman whom he loves, but for most of the book he is suppressed and his marriage, when at last it comes, produces an effect of only measured happiness. Clearly Bennett thought with Thoreau that most people lead lives of quiet desperation. What makes him remarkable is, as I said at the beginning of this chapter, that he writes of very ordinary people and does not allow us to condescend to them. He is the least autobiographical of novelists and his vision is an unusually democratic one. He believed in realism and he believed that realism was moral. He is very specific about this in a little book, not in general of a great deal of interest though, like all his books, containing good things, called *The Author's Craft* which was published in 1914.

> One is curious about one's fellow creatures: therefore one watches them. And generally the more intelligent one is, the more curious one is, and the more one observes. The mere satisfaction of this curiosity is in itself a worthy end, and would alone justify the business of systematised observation. But the aim of observation may, and should, be expressed in terms more grandiose. Human curiosity counts among the highest social virtues (as indifference counts among the basest defects), because it leads to the disclosure of the causes of character and temperament and thereby to a better understanding of the springs of human conduct. Observation is not practised directly with this high end in view (save by prigs and other futile souls): nevertheless it is a moral act and must inevitably promote kindliness – whether we like it or not.

Notes

1. Bennett's letter is of 30 November 1908 in answer to Harris's letter of 27 November in which he refers to Ruskin's animadversions on 'the sweepings of a Pentonville omnibus'. Both letters are to be found in *Letters of Arnold Bennett*, edited by J. G. Hepburn (1968), II.

2. He dashed this off in five weeks in 1907; though a pot-boiler which he referred to in his *Journal* as 'my humorous novel', it is worth reading for some of its social observation of life in the Five Towns and for such strokes of wit as the comment on the skinflint Ollerenshaw: 'He disliked show, with a calm and deep aversion. He was a plain man with a simple, unostentatious taste for money.'

3. The phrase, italicized, occurs as part of Constance's ruminations on her death-bed and here it is a standard banality: 'With whom would she be willing to exchange lots? She had many dissatisfactions. But she rose superior to them. When she surveyed her life, and life in general, she would think, with a sort of tart but not sour cheerfulness: "*Well, that is what life is!*"'

Chapter 8
Virginia Woolf and the Search for Essences

It was in relation to Arnold Bennett that Virginia Woolf most clearly declared her aim as a novelist, and even a cursory glance at later studies of fiction shows that it is common to accept their confrontation as typical of that between (in her own terms) 'Edwardian' and 'Georgian' novelists or, very often, 'modern' as opposed to 'traditional'. In the next chapter I shall consider some effects of this general adoption of her argument, but here I shall discuss what she says only so far as it throws light on her own work.

Her argument is set out in two notable texts – the various versions of 'Mr Bennett and Mrs Brown' and the essay, 'Modern Fiction'. The first of these was provoked by Bennett's review of *Jacob's Room* in which he declared that the creation of character was the foundation of good fiction and that the characters of Virginia Woolf's novel 'do not vitally survive in the mind'. 'Mr Bennett and Mrs Brown' first appeared in the *Nation and Athenaeum* in 1923 and was later enlarged into a lecture and an article, in which form it is more commonly known. It is here that the famous statement 'in or about December, 1910, human character changed' appears. She finds the evidence for this in Samuel Butler's *The Way of All Flesh*, the plays of Bernard Shaw, and (with a frivolity which she may well have regretted later) the behaviour of one's cook:

> All human relations have shifted – those between
> masters and servants, husbands and wives, parents and
> children. And when human relations change there is at the
> same time a change in religion, conduct, politics, and
> literature.

The rest of the essay asserts that Bennett and Wells and Galsworthy have so much emphasized the social situation, the belongings, the economics of the situations with which they deal that the Georgian writers cannot follow them. Here she repeats what she said more briefly and more stylishly in 1919 in 'Modern Fiction'.

This essay has become perhaps the most famous text by a practising novelist on the subject of fictional technique. In it she rejects Bennett, Wells, and Galsworthy on the grounds that they are 'materialists' who cannot catch life because they are constrained to construct plots which must have an air of plausibility, and that they aim at this by emphasis upon externals.

By contrast, she says:

> Look within and life, it seems, is very far from being 'like this'. Examine for a moment an ordinary mind on an ordinary day. The mind receives a myriad impressions – trivial, fantastic, evanescent, or engraved with the sharpness of steel. From all sides they come, an incessant shower of innumerable atoms; and as they fall, as they shape themselves into the life of Monday or Tuesday, the accent falls differently from of old. . . . Life is not a series of gig lamps symmetrically arranged; life is a luminous halo, a semi-transparent envelope surrounding us from the beginning of consciousness to the end. Is it not the task of the novelist to convey this varying, this unknown and uncircumscribed spirit, whatever aberration or complexity it may display, with as little mixture of the alien and external as possible? . . . Let us record the atoms as they fall upon the mind in the order in which they fall, let us trace the pattern, however disconnected and incoherent in appearance, which each sight or incident scores upon the consciousness. Let us not take it for granted that life exists more fully in what is commonly thought big than in what is commonly thought small.

In relating her technical innovations to changes in the way of seeing human beings and perceptions, and conceiving of these as a kind of shared *Zeitgeist*, Virginia Woolf is not only declaring the seriousness and necessity of the innovations but also responding to the observable fact that a number of writers, largely in isolation from one another, came to use a form of presentation which has commonly been called the 'stream of consciousness' or 'interior monologue'. She herself first developed it in *Jacob's Room*, published in 1922, though she had obviously been brooding about it for some time before. *Ulysses* was published in the same year, though sections had been appearing previously; *A Portrait of the Artist as a Young Man* had been published in 1916 and the first of Dorothy Richardson's sequence of novels, *Pointed Roofs*, a year earlier. Joyce claimed that Edouard Dujardin's *Les Lauriers Sont Coupés* (1887) was an influence on him and Virginia Woolf mentions Proust as a fellow explorer and Chekhov's 'Gusev'. There are differences between the methods of these writers and they would certainly not have agreed in all points on their aims, but they all share the intention in at least some parts of their works of giving the reader a sense of receiving the direct flow of a character's perceptions, unmediated by a narrator and giving thus some sense of the richness, untidiness, and associativeness of the mind.

It is not difficult to find such earlier examples of the uses of this technique as the first paragraph of Dickens's *The Mystery of Edwin Drood* (1870), and frequent occurrences in Dostoevsky, but what distinguished these earlier examples is that they are incidental effects, normally rather short, and in all of them the perceiving mind is in an abnormal state – drugged, delirious, or drunk. J. J. Mendilow, in *Time and the Novel*, gives a number of examples of an awareness by nineteenth-century writers of the theoretical possibilities, most strikingly one by Stendhal, but they remain theoretical; Stendhal's clear and analytical style could hardly be further from an internal monologue, and Maupassant specifically rejects it on the grounds of the need for selection. But Virginia Woolf uses basically the same method for the sane Peter Walsh and the mad Septimus Warren Smith. Leopold Bloom, musing as he goes out to buy breakfast, is not treated totally differently from his wife when she is three-quarters asleep. Gone is any feeling that the sane and waking mind is best represented by coherent sentences given to us by a narrator who shares with the reader a belief that the mind is potentially knowable and best explained as clearly as possible. To produce this technical change required two concomitant influences. The first is, obviously, those changes in the conception of human personality which found expression in depth psychology and which are most often associated with the name of Freud; the second is a view of fiction which sees its aim as approximating as closely as possible to an imitation of reality. Just as novelists had increasingly made their characters talk differently from one another so they now set to work to make them think and perceive differently. The stream of consciousness novel is, in this sense at least, a natural continuation of realism.[1]

Indeed, despite her repudiation of Bennett's kind of realism, Virginia Woolf's way of talking about her novels and her practice within them clearly starts from certain realistic premises. Her objection to Bennett is that he tells us so much about the social or physical circumstances of Mrs Brown (or, when she uses an example from Bennett's own work, Hilda Lessways) that he cannot convey the reality of the character herself. It has often been suggested that *Jacob's Room* is rather unsatisfactory because in it Virginia Woolf discovers her technique for rendering experience but does not do very much with it. This criticism might well have meant less to her than to her critics; the rendering of perception with a feeling of immediacy and freshness might seem self-sufficient and self-justifying. Lily Briscoe, in *To the Lighthouse* (1927), when she is trying to remember Mrs Ramsay, feels that 'what she wished to get hold of was that very jar on the nerves, the thing itself before it has been made anything' (III. 12). We do not have to rely for our conviction that this expresses Virginia Woolf's own feelings upon our sense that Lily Briscoe resembles her creator, for in her diary in 1926 Virginia Woolf writes:

> This is what the book would be that was made entirely
> solely and with integrity of one's thoughts. Suppose one
> could catch them before they became 'works of art'? Catch
> them hot and sudden as they rise in the mind.

It must, of course, go without saying that what I have called 'technique' is equally subject-matter and that to discuss what the novels are 'about' may seem to give an unjustified primacy to a concept or an argument or a philosophy which predates and is more important than the work itself. Virginia Woolf's claim for the necessity of a method is equally a claim for a subject.

Yet, though she omits it from her argument in 'Modern Fiction', Virginia Woolf knows perfectly well that the atoms falling upon the mind do not, of themselves, produce a pattern. We select and Lily Briscoe, taking up her unfinished painting, might be speaking for the novelist when she formulates it thus:

> Beautiful and bright it should be on the surface,
> feathery and evanescent, one colour melting into another
> like the colours on a butterfly's wing; but beneath the
> fabric must be clamped together with bolts of iron. It was
> to be a thing you could ruffle with your breath; and a
> thing you could not dislodge with a team of
> horses. (III. 6)

Given Virginia Woolf's feeling for Impressionist and Post-Impressionist painting, the resemblance is not surprising, but here, again, we do not have to rely upon an assumption that this is her way of conceiving a novel, for it echoes what she had written in her diary for 8 April 1925 about Proust: 'he is as tough as catgut and as evanescent as a butterfly's bloom. And he will, I suppose, both influence me and make me out of temper with every sentence of my own.'

Having decided that a traditional form of plot misrepresented life, however, she was committed to finding some other – to discovering what form emerged from the revelation of the characters upon whom she focused her attention, following where this inspiration led. In practice this meant that even a frolic like *Orlando* (1928) has an unconventional structure and if we consider her mature novels we see very clearly that, more perhaps than any other novelist, she feels that each experience requires a different form for its expression. These forms are all not only highly individual, but also highly elaborated. *Mrs Dalloway* (1925) follows two characters who never meet and yet whom we are meant to link; *To the Lighthouse* creates a scene and a mood in the first part which, after a short section which disposes of ten years and a number of major happenings, is recovered and, as one character says, 'unfolded' by survivors; *The Waves* (1931) gives a rather dematerialized account of six lives, counterpointed with the rising and setting of the sun over the sea; *The Years* (1937) is a variant on a highly selective family chronicle and it is tempting to speculate that this novel cost her more than any other in terms of work and agony because the form resisted her urge to dematerialize, to move ever further inwards into her personages; *Between the Acts* (1941) sets an amateur pageant play, interpreting the history of England, against the feelings of characters facing the threat of war.

To the Lighthouse has generally been thought the best not only by those devoted to her individual vision but also by those who have some reservations about much of her work, and I therefore propose to discuss it in some detail, exemplifying through it the main characteristics of her writing.

The two elements of the technical method used in this novel – the presentation of moment-by-moment sensation and the underlying structure – are inseparable; the one necessitates the other and they both imply the subjectivity of time. As if to emphasize this, Virginia Woolf sees to it that the opening pages are less readily locatable in time than anything else in the book. It seems to me unlikely that any reader at first acquaintance will realize immediately, when she writes: 'it was odious of him [Tansley] to rub this in, and make James still more disappointed; but at the same time, she would not let them laugh at him' that the words 'at the same time' have more or less the opposite of their literal meaning. We have moved here from the specific moment (Mrs Ramsay talking about the chances of going to the lighthouse tomorrow, Mr Ramsay saying that the weather will not allow it) to a general reflection which means something like 'nevertheless, despite the typicality of this behaviour on Tansley's part, she reflected that she was not in the habit of allowing her family to mock him'. From this we go to an apparent immediacy, – '"Nonsense," said Mrs Ramsay, with great severity' – which is actually a specific moment in a previous discussion with her children about Tansley. Then we modulate to description of a repeated action 'When she looked in the glass and saw her hair grey, her cheek sunk, at fifty, she thought, possibly she might have managed things better', then back to the moment when she said 'Nonsense' and find that this was at a meal, for we are told that her family are looking up from their plates. We are at last, after about two pages, brought back to the original time by Tansley's speaking about the lighthouse, only, a few lines later, to find that her memory has again brought the past into the present – 'He was a sarcastic brute, Andrew said.' Thereafter, until the end of the first section everything is memory, including a lengthy description of a visit to the town with Tansley, though some is not her memory but that of Tansley himself. Section 2 is only six lines and is all in the present, acting as a kind of summing up, perhaps giving the reader a chance to feel for a moment unquestioningly fixed, before going on to Section 3, which again begins in the present but once more wanders back into the remembered experience of Mrs Ramsay.

Virginia Woolf, throughout her writing, is preoccupied with time. Sometimes this is an apparently technical matter; she writes in her diary about the problem of ending the novel so that the boat's reaching the lighthouse and Lily Briscoe's completing her picture seem to come together. 'Could I do it in a parenthesis? So that one has the sense of reading the two things at the same time.' The expedition of Paul and Minta to the shore with Nancy and Andrew is given in a six-page parenthesis (I. 14) between the asking of a question – 'Did Nancy go with them?' – and its answer. But in general it is far more than technical. Virginia Woolf is both obsessed with a sense of the flux of experience and with the mind's desire, and ability, seemingly to abolish time, to recover the sharp immediacy of past experience. The paradox at which she aims is the simultaneous recognition that everything flows and that only by accepting this flowing can some permanence be achieved.

I have used the common expression 'stream of consciousness' to express the manner in which Virginia Woolf presents the experiences of her characters, but, as previous critics have often emphasized, the term, though virtually indispensable, covers a multitude of devices. If we compare Virginia Woolf's method with that of Joyce, we find vast differences. Joyce is careful that no word, no idea, no idiom should occur in Molly Bloom's soliloquy which she would not have recognized. The aim is to give us as far as possible (bearing in mind that Joyce can only say one thing at a time while Molly can think several and feel them, too) the sense that we are watching the atoms as they fall upon the mind. Virginia Woolf certainly wants to give us this sense of partaking in a character's intimate thoughts and sensations, but she quite frequently chooses to register them not as a sequence of discrete reactions but as a·metaphor or simile. Mrs Ramsay, having given her husband the 'reassurance that he wants', feels that 'there throbbed through her, like the pulse in a spring which has expanded to its full width and now gently ceases to beat, the rapture of successful creation' (I. 7), and this image is followed through for some forty lines. These images, it could be argued, are those of the character herself. But what are we to say of one which immediately precedes it: 'Immediately, Mrs Ramsay seemed to fold herself together, one petal closed in another, and the whole fabric fell in exhaustion upon itself'? Does she see herself thus? And in the splendidly funny sequence in which we see Mr Ramsay trying to think out his problem in philosophy and then finding that he is thinking about himself trying to think and so will not think any more, we are often in doubt. That he sees himself as a doomed explorer may be appropriate to Mr Ramsay in his self-dramatizing mood (and to that great mountaineer Sir Leslie Stephen, as his daughter no doubt intended), but what can we make of the likening of logical thought to repeating the alphabet from A to, say, R (I. 6)? This is surely an author's image; it is inconceivable that Ramsay himself would translate whatever his problem is into this terminology.

It might seem that to chop logic thus is pointless; does it matter whether it is Mr Ramsay's own image or his creator's? I think that it does (for if Ramsay did function in this way he would be a much stranger kind of philosopher than he is intended to be) but that few readers think the image is his own and thus the problem is normally solved in the reading. But elsewhere there are more puzzling and potentially more damaging matters. When Mrs Ramsay goes down to dinner, preoccupied with the question of whether Paul had proposed to Minta, her descent is presented thus:

> So she must go down and begin dinner and wait. And, like some queen who, finding her people gathered in the hall, looks down upon them, and descends among them, and acknowledges their tributes silently, and accepts their devotion and their prostration before her (Paul did not move a muscle but looked straight before him as she passed), she went down, and crossed the hall and bowed her head very slightly, as if she accepted what they could not say: their tribute to her beauty.   (I. 16)

Mrs Ramsay manœuvres people and she wants to be the centre and to make people happy, but she cannot, surely, be such a self-regarding monster as this. Given what we have been told about her before, it seems more likely that what Virginia Woolf is saying, a little playfully, is that this is how she has often appeared to other people and that she cannot be totally unaware of the effect which she makes upon others. But this cannot be demonstrated and, even taking the view which I do, it is uncertain what tinge of irony may be implied in the description. What is certain is that Virginia Woolf is often present, appealing to us directly, in what at first sight look like accounts of the experiences of her characters. Consider, for example, the function of the word 'one' in the following account of Mr Ramsay:

> He stopped to light his pipe, looked once at his wife
> and son in the window, and as one raises one's eyes from
> a page in an express train and sees a farm, a tree, a cluster
> of cottages as an illustration, a confirmation of something
> on the printed page to which one returns, fortified and
> satisfied, so without his distinguishing either his son or his
> wife, the sight of them fortified him and satisfied him and
> consecrated his effort to arrive at a perfectly clear
> understanding of the problem which now engaged the
> energies of his splendid mind.   (I. 6)

Her frequent use of 'one' in such passages usually has this effect as does her frequent use of the present participle – a form of speech which asserts a continuity of a happening but does not attach it to any person.

Again and again we find ourselves in the position of saying that a perception could be in the mind of a character, that no signal has been given to us that we have passed out of this character's mind into that of another, and yet to accept the perception as part of this character's stream of thought and perception would call for a marked shift of our attitude. It seems clear that what is often happening is that Virginia Woolf is herself commenting without making any very clear separation between the character and the creator. Her way of dealing with her characters is, if one accepts this view, seen to be similar to the way in which she deals in her essays with real people.

The attitude which we take up to the second part, 'Time Passes', is of importance in determining our judgement of how present she is throughout. It is possible to see it as a necessary interlude, a way of making ten years pass, and therefore stylistically different from the rest, but the more we see it in relation to the other two parts the more will we feel the persona of the author permeating the whole novel, for in it this element of the writer brooding or ruminating or dreaming her characters is most pronounced.

All the elements of Part II are to be found in the other two parts, though sometimes in more developed and sometimes more attenuated forms. It starts and ends with personal experience, rendered in dialogue or reflection by named characters. In between there are fanciful anthro-

pomorphisms about the winds, the furniture, the seasons, the mythol-
ogization of Mrs McNab into the archetypal charwoman, parenthetical
accounts of happenings elsewhere. Throughout, surfacing in various
forms, there is a Protean consciousness which weaves the whole
together. This perceiving persona is sometimes the asker of rhetorical
questions ('What power could now prevent the fertility, the insensi-
bility of nature?') sometimes 'one', sometimes 'any sleeper', sometimes
'the dreamers', sometimes 'those who had gone down to pace the
beach and ask the sea and sky what message they reported or what
visions they affirmed' (II. 6).

Virginia Woolf seems to be implying that there is a shared experience, a collective awareness, which breaks down the barriers between
individualities, so that in solitude powers for which we hardly have
names can move us. This is to express matters metaphorically, as she
herself does. She implies in *The Waves* (1931) that there is some kind
of common consciousness which can make people feel that they are
all parts of some larger, undifferentiated being; Mrs Dalloway
conceives of her continuance after death in memories and the continued
existence of places at which she has looked; in *To the Lighthouse*, Mrs
Ramsay returns in the consciousness of Lily and of her family. Less
metaphorically we can say that she is prepared to stand in the middle
of her novel, flowing in and out of her characters, but also, at times,
speaking in her own person in descriptions which cannot be those of
any character, or in perceptions unattached to anyone or in images
which direct our feelings. Often such passages are very ornate,
sustained set pieces, such as the description to which I shall revert later
in my discussion of the structure of the book, of the effect of the
lighting of the candles at dinner.

It is clear that such a narrative method carries inevitable risks of
ambiguity; we will not receive an answer, for example, if we ask
whether or not the rumours of Mrs Ramsay's earlier unhappy love
affair are true. We can only say, as we might of some person in real
life, that we do not know but that she is the sort of person about
whom people speculate thus. I do not think that in this novel, unlike
some of her others, these uncertainties are damaging, for the shared
ground which is indisputable is great.

This element of lifelike ambiguity is embodied also in the structure
of the novel. Essentially it is the rediscovery, the re-creation in Part
III of a moment which is created in Part I but which might seem to
have been made irrecoverable by the passage of ten years in Part II.
In various places Virginia Woolf draws attention to the pattern in terms
which make sure that we shall not overlook it. Lily Briscoe, remembering Mrs Ramsay and speculating about how she had come to marry
Mr Ramsay, feels that 'She was not inventing; she was only trying to

smooth out something she had been given years ago folded up' (III. 12). That could stand very well for a description of the effect of the book. So could Mrs Ramsay's own feeling when, in the middle of dinner, William Bankes reminds her of some old friends, the Mannings, and she remembers them and 'it fascinated her, as if, while she had changed, that particular day, now become very still and beautiful, had remained there, all these years'. A little later, in the middle of a babble of conversations, she feels that her remembering the Mannings 'was like reading a good book again, for she knew the end of that story, since it had happened twenty years ago, and life, which shot down even from this dining-room table in cascades, heaven knows where, was sealed up there, and lay, like a lake, placidly between its banks' (I. 17).

The choice of metaphor by Mrs Ramsay points to one important structural characteristic of *To the Lighthouse* – that it is largely incomprehensible at a first reading and only achieves its significance at a second and thus demands a spatial understanding. Just as Mrs Ramsay can only know in retrospect that the Mannings's room will acquire significance for her as it is contrasted with the 'cascades' of present life, so we will only recognize what is significant in Part I when we look back to it from Part III.

A movement towards the spatial, towards what Henry James called 'the figure in the carpet', has been observable in much fiction of this century. It goes along with a diminishing interest in narrative and, paradoxically, with a desire for an effect of immediacy. Its triumphs are obvious and *To the Lighthouse* is one of them. But the paradox entails a price. Here, for example, we find that to understand the book we must read it more than once but that on a second reading we cannot forget what we are supposed not to know. We cannot enter into Mrs Ramsay's wonderings as to whether the evening at dinner will be remembered without an undesirable knowledge that she will shortly die but that the evening will be remembered ten years later, just as we cannot forget that the Rayleys will not be a happy couple and Prue will not have for long the happiness that her mother foresees for her.

But though we cannot totally re-create the freshness of first acquaintance and though the sense of the remembered moment is, finally, what matters, we should not undervalue the book's effect of complexity and even of that muddle against which Mrs Ramsay fights. We need to remember, for example, that for some time at the dinner table William Bankes is bored and Charles Tansley has a good case in feeling that there is something infuriating in the prevailing social manner. Mrs Ramsay herself is well aware of this and it is her task to create unity. 'Nothing seemed to have merged,' she feels at table, 'They all sat separate. And the whole of the effort of merging and

flowing and creating rested upon her' (I. 17). The moment when things
do merge is produced when she orders candles to be lit; she sees them
illuminating the arrangement of fruit and a shell on the dish in the
middle of the table, in a sudden passage of baroque description of it
as 'a trophy fetched from the bottom of the sea, of Neptune's banquet'.
She sees Augustus Carmichael looking at the plate of fruit and reflects;
'That was his way of looking, different from hers. But looking
together united them.' But, in the manner which I have already
discussed, the centre of perception moves away from her, we float in
and out of several minds and though we come back to Mrs Ramsay's
as the presiding mind, we first have an assertion of a general perception, shared by them all:

> Some change at once went though them all, as if this
> had really happened, and they were all conscious of
> making a party together in a hollow, on an island; had
> their common cause against that fluidity out there.   (I. 17)

Thereafter Mrs Ramsay feels secure. When she leaves the room she
casts a glance back and feels that it has already become the past, but

> They would, she thought, going on again, however
> long they lived, come back to this night; this moon; this
> wind; this house: and to her too. It flattered her, where
> she was most susceptible of flattery, to think how, wound
> about in their hearts, however long they lived she would
> be woven. . . .   (I. 18)

The third part of the novel is to demonstrate the truth of this intuition; at its opening we are told that the expedition to the lighthouse
is planned again and that Lily Briscoe is returning to the painting
which she had started ten years before. In both actions Mrs Ramsay
is rediscovered but in neither is the remembrance simple; Lily, in
particular, admits to very mixed feelings about her and about that day
in the past. The link which for her joins it to the present is the
recollection, suddenly, that

> When she had sat there last ten years ago there had
> been a little sprig or leaf pattern on the tablecloth, which
> she had looked at in a moment of revelation. There had
> been a problem about a foreground of a picture Move the
> tree to the middle, she had said.   (III. 2)

This motif had indeed preoccupied her but the revelations associated with it were far from simple. First it was linked with her feeling that Mrs Ramsay sometimes misunderstood people – in particular that she had pitied William Bankes in a manner which 'seemed to be instinctive and to arise from some need of her own rather than other people's. He is not in the least pitiable. He has his work' (I. 17) – and then she had thought reassuringly that she, too, had her work, her picture. Later at dinner, it was linked with her being nice, at Mrs Ramsay's unspoken request, to Charles Tansley and feeling that so many human relations are insincere. Later still, it came to her in the middle of violent images about Minta and Paul Rayley and love and the sense that 'she need not marry, thank Heaven: she need not undergo that degradation'. And amid the complexity of her memories of Mrs Ramsay comes, very strikingly, the recollection of 'this mania of hers for marriage' and how she, Lily, would triumph over her now by telling her that the Rayleys had not had a happy marriage. Above all,

> She had only escaped by the skin of her teeth, she
> thought. She had been looking at the tablecloth, and it had
> flashed upon her that she would move the tree to the
> middle, and need never marry anybody, and she had felt
> an enormous exultation. She had felt, now she could stand
> up to Mrs Ramsay – a tribute to the astonishing power
> that Mrs Ramsay had over one.   (III. 6)

But as she goes on painting, trying to stay immersed in the painting but coming to the surface of what surrounds her and to memories, she feels grief for Mrs Ramsay and anger at having to feel grief again, and details about the daily life of the Ramsays impose themselves upon her, including a very vivid recollection of Mr Ramsay stretching out his hand and raising his wife from her chair, and she feels that this is how they must have been when she agreed to marry him. What we observe here is that Lily, who has fled marriage, seems only to be able to complete her picture – to remember clearly enough the shadow on the steps which is Mrs Ramsay's shadow and which will give a centre to her painting – by reconstructing something of the relationship of husband and wife.[2] She walks to the edge of the lawn with her paintbrush in her hand and looks for the boat, feeling that she must share her vision – 'Where was that boat now? Mr Ramsay? She wanted him.' Remembering from that same morning that he had sought sympathy and that she had been unable to give it directly and that when she wanted to give it he no longer demanded it and the time for it had passed, she feels at the very end of the book that 'Whatever she had wanted to give him, when he had left her that morning, she had given him at last' (III. 14).

A similar complexity and a similar resolution is experienced by Cam
and James in the boat. United in embarrassment at their father's pecu-
liarities and in resistance to his domination they too remember what
we have been shown in Part I. James, not fully understanding what
it is, remembers the image of a beak striking which in Part I
represented his father's hated interruption of his mother's reading to
him; but, intruding upon this is another image which reminds us of
Mr Ramsay's own vision of himself as he walked on the terrace and
tried to think and dramatized himself as a lonely thinker:

> Yes, thought James, while the boat slapped and
> dawdled there in the hot sun; there was a waste of snow
> and rock very lonely and austere; and there he had come
> to feel, quite often lately, when his father said something
> which surprised the others, were two pairs of footprints
> only; his own and his father's. They alone knew each
> other.   (III. 9)

Cam, falling asleep, dreams of the island they have left as 'a hanging
garden; it was a valley, full of birds, and flowers, and antelopes' (III.
13). This echoes directly what her mother had said as she talked her
to sleep as a child frightened by the pig's skull, which has been covered
with a shawl:

> It was like a beautiful mountain such as she had seen
> abroad, with valleys and flowers and bells ringing and
> birds singing and little goats and antelopes.   (I. 18)

She has already virtually abandoned her rebellion, though she would
wish to maintain it for the sake of loyalty to James. But at the end they
are both in a situation akin to that of Lily when she cannot give
sympathy and then is enchanted by Mr Ramsay's tirade about boots
and then wants to give when Mr Ramsay no longer asks. Here, too,
we end with Mr Ramsay as a lonely and impressive figure and the
description of him shows that his children are in effect seeing him as
his wife must have seen him:

> He rose and stood in the bow of the boat, very straight
> and tall, for all the world, James thought, as if he were
> saying: 'There is no God,' and Cam thought, as if he were
> leaping into space, and they both rose to follow him as he
> sprang, lightly like a young man, holding his parcel, on to
> the rock.   (III. 13)

Mrs Ramsay's triumph, here, her last, is that her feeling about her husband survives all other views of him.

The novel is so organized that it concludes with two simultaneous revelations and it is appropriate that its last word is 'vision', for it is beyond question a novel which seeks a meaning beyond the simply representational. It is notable that, while most nineteenth-century novelists were content to leave fundamental beliefs to take care of themselves while they dealt with questions of ethics which do not demand religious scrutiny, many twentieth-century novelists, writing in a period when religious orthodoxy has been in decline, have probed this question of fundamental meaning. Here it is Lily who, as a character, formulates what Virginia Woolf, throughout her work, takes as central:

> What is the meaning of life? That was all – a simple
> question; one that tended to close in on one with years.
> The great revelation had never come. The great revelation
> perhaps never did come. Instead there were little daily
> miracles, illuminations, matches struck unexpectedly in the
> dark. . . . Mrs Ramsay making of the moment something
> permanent (as in another sphere Lily herself tried to make
> of the moment something permanent) – this was of the
> nature of a revelation.   (III. 4)

It is a tenuous revelation, that memory and love can survive and give emotional significance after the passage of time and, as if to make clear beyond question her own awareness of just how limited it is (though no less precious for its limitation), Virginia Woolf introduces into the book a repeated image of quite extraordinary horror – the mackerel which they use as bait. We know from her diary, 14 May 1925, that this was part of her plan from the beginning:

> But the centre is father's character, sitting in a boat
> reciting 'We perished, each alone', while he crushes a
> dying mackerel –

In the novel the mackerel, which is given a complete parenthetical section to itself, is treated less mercifully:

> [Macalister's boy took one of the fish and cut a square
> out of its side to bait his hook with. The mutilated body
> (it was alive still) was thrown back into the sea.]   (III. 7)

There are, Virginia Woolf seems to be saying, some agonies which even the memory of Mrs Ramsay cannot redeem. We should not be surprised at this harshness, though she may wish us to be shocked at the gruesomeness, for throughout the book there has been a sense that her characters must seek a meaning in life just because of a horror which attends us all the time. When Marie, the Swiss girl, speaks of the beauty of the mountains she does it with tears in her eyes and Mrs Ramsay knows it is because her father is dying of cancer. The sound of the sea, which for Mrs Ramsay 'for the most part beat a measured and soothing tattoo' will suddenly 'like a ghostly roll of drums remorselessly beat the measure of life' and make her 'look up with an impulse of terror' (I. 3).

This image of the sea reminds us that a sense of impermanence and threat and a sometimes rather desperate seeking for some belief or experience which can keep it at bay, is central, also, to *Mrs Dalloway*, the novel which she wrote before *To the Lighthouse*. Mrs Dalloway, too, seeks some stability in the midst of flux and the sea which she imagines as comforting her (paradoxically, through the dirge from *Cymbeline* with the message that none of us are exempt from death) is also there in the mind of Septimus Warren Smith, for here, more openly than anywhere in *To the Lighthouse*, Virginia Woolf suggests that minds may in some way flow into one another and communicate without ever the people meeting. Mrs Dalloway's belief, reported by Peter Walsh, is akin to Lily Briscoe's feelings about Ramsay, but with an outright descriptiveness replacing the slowly emerging suggestion:

> It ended in a transcendental theory which, with her horror of death, allowed her to believe, or say that she believed (for all her scepticism), that since our apparitions, the part of us which appears, are so momentary compared with the other, the unseen part of us, which spreads wide, the unseen might survive, be recovered somehow attached to this person or to that, or even haunting certain places, after death.

What vitiates *Mrs Dalloway* as an exploration of a similar range of feelings to those of *To the Lighthouse* is in part the obtrusively obvious element of contrivance in the parallelism of Clarissa Dalloway and Septimus Warren Smith and partly a radical ambiguity. It is said that Virginia Woolf had originally intended to have Mrs Dalloway die at the end of the book and that, changing her mind, she introduced Septimus as a surrogate. Whether or not this is true, it is certainly how he functions; but the interrelationships between the two groups are often asserted with a slickness which obtrudes. That Peter Walsh, returning to his hotel, should hear the bell of the ambulance which will deposit Smith at the mortuary and reflect that it is one of the triumphs of civilization, comes too pat; it is the kind of irony which belongs more to the world of Graham Greene's 'entertainments'. That Sir William Bradshaw should bring to Clarissa's party the news of Septimus's death and should provoke in Clarissa the same feelings which Septimus has had about him is too obvious. The whole linkage with 'Fear no more the heat o' the sun' and the dog barking draws attention to itself. In the work of a writer like Hardy who is overtly constructing plots as the framework of a story there may be no harm in such contrivance, but if the writer comes before us as tracing the marks of the atoms as they fall we cannot accept such neatnesses. We certainly have a sense of Virginia Woolf's presence in her novels, but in speaking of her 'brooding or ruminating or dreaming her book' I have tried to draw attention to the way in which we feel that her consciousness is part of the book without being an overtly controlling, far less a contriving, device.

But there is an ambiguity in *Mrs Dalloway* which seems to me even more damaging. I have suggested that Virginia Woolf's narrative method leads inevitably to ambiguities. It is possible (though insensitive) to produce a reading of *To the Lighthouse* in which Mrs Ramsay is a contriving and ageing beauty, totally mistaken about other people's feelings, Mr Ramsay an equally ageing and also outdated pedant who bullies women and children and is admired intermittently by those who have some taste for being bullied, and Lily Briscoe a sexually frustrated but also timid spinster who compensates for these disadvantages by high-flown rapture about water-colour painting. It is *possible* to take this view because there is often no logically incontrovertible way of assigning feelings and beliefs to the right people; it is insensitive and, for a receptive reader, difficult to do this because to take up such a perverse view leads eventually to an awareness that one is pushing one logic against the pressure of other suggestions; the book pulls itself back into shape. It leaves us, reasonably enough, with that range of ambiguities to which we are accustomed in real life. But in *Mrs Dalloway* there is a radical ambiguity in the judgements which we are invited to make. Put with crude brevity we might say that we can see Mrs Dalloway as a woman who, haunted by the knowledge of death and reminded on this day of an irrecoverable past in which her feelings flowed more deeply, bravely throws her party in the face of fear and, reminded of death in the middle of her party, acknowledges its power and feels a link with all who die; others, from Scrope Purvis at the opening to Peter at the very end, are given some joy and love by her gallantry and her power to feel. Or we can see her as a remarkably self-dramatizing woman (note how she thinks that her maid Lucy sees her as a brave knight going out with her parasol to conquer), despising Hugh Whitbread but basically no different (how she is hurt by Lady Bruton's non-invitation to a luncheon party which any sensible person would avoid at all costs), who tries to inject significance into her worldly party (how glad she is to have the Prime Minister and how mean she is to Ellie Henderson) by claiming kinship with the unknown dead young man (he has thrown away his life and she likens it to throwing a shilling in the Serpentine). I do not think that one can get the book into focus because the two utterly opposed views constantly jar on one another. The ambiguity is not such as we deal with in life but rather the ambiguity which evades the issues, which refuses to decide between incompatible views and which seeks therefore to dazzle us with momentary set pieces.

Virginia Woolf's resolute avoidance of 'issues' tends to make such ambiguity not only possible but inevitable. Clarissa's inability to distinguish whether her husband's committee is concerned with the Armenians or Albanians is typical. We might take this as a good satirical jab at a political wife, and hence move towards my second account of the book and of Clarissa's character, were it not that Virginia Woolf similarly disposes of such facts throughout her writing. There is a very striking example in *The Years*. Eleanor, in the 1891 section of the book, attends a committee meeting; we are never told what the committee meeting is about, Eleanor is never shown thinking about the issues involved, although the obvious assumption is that its purpose is to do good to the poor. Eleanor is, however, aware of her position of some prestige as compared with the other committee members and the section ends with ludicrous abruptness: 'She pulled herself together and gave him her opinion. She had an opinion – a very definite opinion. She cleared her throat and began.' The effect of this is not merely to assert that Virginia Woolf has no interest in the purpose of the committee and feels that we do not need to know what it is; it is also to make us feel, whether Virginia Woolf desires this or not (and I do not think that she wants us to despise Eleanor), that Eleanor herself has no interest, that she is concerned only with a conception of herself as a member of the committee. It is an unwanted triumph of 'life-style' over life.

No writer can include everything, but if we compare the nature of her omissions with those of Bennett, with whom she contrasted herself, we can see very clearly the consequences of her choices. There is much not revealed in *The Old Wives' Tale* but it is private, intimate. We feel that perhaps we should not explore it or even, almost, that the writer does not know. There is an irreducible privacy to the human personality. What is not explored in *To the Lighthouse* is usually not intimate at all but we may feel that we need it if we are to understand the characters. Often, of course, it is external and unnecessary, but the omission of the external may very easily suggest mysteries to us. We are given no reason why, ten years after his wife's death, Mr Ramsay chooses to return to the island. But we have enough sense of his personality to envisage a need to memorialize and even to exacerbate his feelings. But why does he ask Lily Briscoe and Augustus Carmichael? Both would seem, from what we know of him, rather odd choices, unless he is trying to reconstruct so far as possible the circumstances of his last visit. But if so why is Mrs Beckwith there? I do not think that there can be any answer; the guests are there because they are there and the re-creation of the past is what the book is about. But if we once begin to wonder – and in a book which proceeds by flashes of insight we cannot be blamed if we do wonder – we are in danger of spinning theories and imputing motives and making mysteries.

The novel in which she most eschews that concern for social issues which she mocks in Bennett is *The Waves*. To such an extent are the characters and their circumstances dematerialized that it has often been suggested that the best way to look at the book is to think of the named personages less as individual characters than as aspects of one character. Virginia Woolf's habit of dissolving the boundaries between the perceptions of different characters and between those of the characters and of the creating mind tempts one to this suggestion, but it is difficult to see that this means more than that all the characters have in them some of her own sympathies and preoccupations. It is surely more plausible to think of her as having gone as far as is possible in removing the tiresome accidentals and rendering the essence of characters, as in *To the Lighthouse* Mrs Ramsay feels herself at times to be a 'wedge-shaped core of darkness, something invisible to others' (I. 11). But in omitting so much of what makes up our daily life – work, routines, opinions, beliefs, convictions, everything that is socially conditioned as well as much which comes from day-to-day human relationships – in omitting both the opportunities and the restrictions which spring from relationships (not just love relationships, but working ones and neighbourly ones and even political ones) she creates not true essences but shades who appear psychotically self-regarding. In not having to take into account most of the rest of the world the characters. appear as people who choose not to consider them. The weirdly snobbish effect of some parts of *The Waves*, the apparent lack of any sense that those outside a magic circle could be human, is less an individual characteristic of Louis or Bernard than an inevitable consequence of Virginia Woolf's aim.

It seems that in agreeing with Bennett that the creation of character is the basis of value in fiction Virginia Woolf was right but that she was wrong in thinking that there could be an essence detached from accidentals. Her own masterpiece, *To the Lighthouse*, is such because there she is concerned not only with essence but with experience; the search, by the characters as well as by their creator, for essence comes up against the hard, unyielding, formative experience of relationship, the sense that other people exist.

Notes

1. No generally agreed tidy definition can be given of literary terms which, like 'realism', have been used as both banners and weapons as well as tools. My use of it here refers to a fictional technique which aims to show us the actions, the thoughts and the feelings of plausible characters conceived at the level of daily life. I discuss various implications of the term and also those cases in which it becomes unusable in Chapters 3 and 4 of *The Approach to Fiction: Good and Bad Readings of Novels* (1972).

2. Some critics have suggested that the line which Lily draws on her painting 'in the centre' represents the lighthouse. This may tie her picture more closely to the title of the book but the description of her last brush stroke in the culminating paragraph of the novel must surely indicate that it is placed on the steps and that it represents a visible sign of Mrs Ramsay's presence. Moreover the line, if it is to be as significant as it is said to be, must be the focal point of the picture; it is harder to imagine a vertical line above the horizon fulfilling this function rather than something nearer the central area where we know there are a number of masses representing 'the wall; the hedge; the tree' (III. 2).

Chapter 9
Modernism and its Implications

Virginia Woolf's attack on Bennett and her proclamation of the need to break with what she saw as his adherence to a 'materialist' tradition has been of surprising importance in later discussions of fiction and especially in discussions of the nature of 'Modernism'. 'Mr Bennett and Mrs Brown' and, even more, 'Modern Fiction', which I quoted at length in my last chapter, have figured largely in critical studies and critical anthologies. There are several very obvious reasons for this. They are very quotable and very attractively written; how often must readers have heaved a sigh of relief when they have fought through more rebarbative matter to reach them! They provide a brief account by a novelist of how a 'stream of consciousness' is envisaged. They have, moreover, a certain rarity value. It is easy to find general statements about modern poets by Pound, Eliot, Yeats, and others, but few novelists have proclaimed a Modernist aesthetic. Joyce was not given to general statements, Conrad is rarely very specific, Lawrence is usually either talking about the novels he is reviewing or about his own novels, or he is making general statements about the novel with no particular reference to modernity. Virginia Woolf, by contrast, writes about her own fictional technique and about its inevitability for modern writers in terms of changes in society and our perception of human nature. She is, in short, producing exactly what is needed in the way of exemplification by anyone seeking a theory of Modernism which will implicitly suggest that it is comprehensive.

I have already suggested that so far as the adoption of the 'stream of consciousness' is concerned she is right in recognizing a *Zeitgeist* which influences a number of writers; but the implications of her case go further than this and here the logical objections to it are relevant, as they are not when we think only of her argument in relation to her own practice. The essays imply a great deal which is not examined. The two central points are the rejection of the traditional realistic form of the novel in favour of tracing the atoms as they fall upon the mind and the rejection of the assumption that life exists more fully in what is commonly thought big than in what is commonly thought small.

But more atoms fall than we can register, so that their pattern is created by the writer in terms of what he or she thinks significant, and what is commonly thought big is so considered because human experience has had it so. The beliefs which lie behind the choice of which pattern to trace are just as real as those paraded by authorial commentators, though they may not be as immediately recognizable, and the choice of what is commonly thought small amounts very often to a rejection not of fictional conventions but of common experience.

But many later critics who are documenting what they see as 'Modernism' have been happy to accept her statements without reservations about their logic. It is not my purpose to take issue with individual writers who have written on this subject, more particularly because the generalizations with which I am concerned have now filtered down so widely and have become so much received wisdom that the general impression is more significant than any specific analysis. Suffice it to say that I have in mind such a view as that which is enshrined in the *Fontana Dictionary of Modern Thought*[1] or in the writings, listed in my Bibliography, of Gabriel Josipovici, Malcolm Bradbury, and Richard Ellmann and Charles Feidelson.

Despite minor differences such accounts seem to be in agreement that from some time late in the nineteenth century onwards (for Virginia Woolf's date of 1910 is clearly too late, at least for the Continent) artists in all media broke decisively with their predecessors, abandoning tonality in music, and turning away in painting and literature from the representational and the mimetic to the abstract and the autonomous. Certain major figures are always associated with this movement – Kafka, Picasso, Pound, Webern, Eliot, Joyce; the names alone assure us that one of the striking characteristics of the movement is that it is international. It is normally seen as including within it various lesser trends: surrealism, dadaism, imagism, vorticism, cubism, acmeism. It is seen as a response to a general breakdown in agreement about continuity and order in society and is consequently marked by fragmentation, discontinuity, and introversion.

It is in this last matter – the relationship of artistic novelty to social changes – that Virginia Woolf's line of thought has proved so useful. Her emphasis on the need to move away from the public to the private, the social to the introspective, the political to the individual, fits well with that rejection of the public sphere which characterizes so many of the artists who are central in all accounts of Modernism.

This may at first sight appear paradoxical. Has it not been characteristic of many of the artists of this period that they have been embroiled in political issues, some because they took up political positions and some because their works were regarded as inherently subversive or decadent? Here, I think, it is essential to remind ourselves that it is totally unhistorical to postulate a relationship to society which applies to Wilhelminian Germany, Habsburg Austria, Czarist Russia, post-Risorgimento Italy, Edwardian England, and America in the 1890s. There may be some common factors, but the differences between Kafka's alienation from Prague, say, and the situation of Pound or Eliot in America and Great Britain, or Yeats's in Ireland, are far greater than the similarities. What is striking about the English writers who are commonly thought of as Modernists is that they are, indeed, often concerned with social and political issues but they are at odds with their societies in a very distinctively unpublic and unsocial way. They are mostly inherently anti–democratic, in the sense that they do not feel themselves to be part of a society or of a section of society (unless that section is 'artists') which they accept and which rightly demands of them some political responsibility. Moreover their political principles normally rely upon a strikingly unhistorical yearning for a supposed past golden age. It is easy to laugh at the conception of the English working man held by Auden and his fellow Communists in the 1930s. Eliot's conception of traditional English society is equally ludicrous, and so is Yeats's vision of the 'indomitable Irishry'. The tendency to grasp at extreme and apocalyptic interpretations and creeds – whether Pound's Mussoliniesque fantasies or the self-regarding despair so fashionable on the campus – is a characteristic of those who do not wish to test their highly individual visions against the perceptions of their fellow citizens. We may not unreasonably see this as a survival of that strain in Romanticism which exalts the unique individual vision after its libertarian drive has perished.

But if Virginia Woolf's rejection of the public has fitted well with this view of Modernism and, in particular, has made it easier to suggest that English writers were responding to the same pressures as those in other, often widely different, cultures, the question remains as to whether it fitted equally well with what she was writing about – modern fiction in Great Britain. It is a characteristic of large generalizations that we cannot expect a perfect fit. But here, I think, the fit is very bad. Do the novelists whom she calls 'Georgians' share her rejection of that documentation which insists that the personality of a man or woman is to a considerable extent determined by what she calls 'house property', the external economic, social, and public aspects of their life? Do they share her sense that human nature changed in 1910 (or whatever period we choose to replace this metaphorical date)? Do they share her belief that 'issues' are death to the novel and the pursuit of the flow of momentary sensation alone a worthy aim?

The answer to the first question can be most briefly given in the form of a quotation:

> What homothetic objects, other than the candlestick,
> stood on the mantelpiece?
>
> A timepiece of striated Connemara marble, stopped at
> the hour of 4.46 a.m. on the 21 March 1896, matrimonial
> gift of Matthew Dillon: a dwarf tree of glacial
> arborescence under a transparent bell-shade, matrimonial
> gift of Luke and Caroline Doyle: an embalmed owl,
> matrimonial gift of Alderman John Hooper. (James Joyce,
> *Ulysses*, p. 668)

Nor is it merely in the 'Ithaca' section that Joyce's almost maniacal love of detail appears. Hilda Lessways was never documented like Leopold Bloom or Stephen Dedalus.

Nor does Joyce's use of a stream of consciousness method in various parts of his work seem to derive from a belief that human nature changed in a dramatic manner during or shortly before his lifetime. It is a device to record the mind, and though it is perfectly true, as I have said, that it would not have been available to him much earlier, we are surely meant to feel that Molly's great-great-grandmother, lying drowsily in bed, would have ruminated and fantasized much as her twentieth-century descendant does. Similarly, H. C. Earwicker's experience proclaims that human nature does not change, that H. C. E. is manifested as Haveth Childers Everywhere because Here Comes Everyone.

D. H. Lawrence did believe that he lived in an age of crisis and to this extent may have agreed with Virginia Woolf that human nature had in some senses changed; but it cannot be said that he regarded 'issues' as contaminants. Conrad (whom she mentions in 'Modern Fiction' but does not talk about on the rather frivolous grounds that he is a Pole) may be thought the greatest political novelist in the language; the last words of Forster's *A Passage to India* assert as clearly as possible that human relationships can be spoilt by political issues.

It is unlikely that Virginia Woolf herself would have been surprised at these divergencies; she was trying to work out her own literary method and taking part in a local argument and it is hard to have one's periodical essays or evening lectures scrutinized as Holy Writ half a century and more afterwards. What I am concerned with is the way in which her statements were taken up and used in the construction of an ideology which ignores some of the evidence. Let us suppose for a moment that we abandoned the commonly asserted pattern: alienation from society, fragmentation, stream of consciousness, Woolf, *The Waste Land*, *Finnegans Wake*, Gertrude Stein, and replaced it by: awareness of the lives of those less gifted than the writer, *Jude the Obscure*, Bennett, Leopold Bloom, Henry Green's *Living*, Lewis

Grassic Gibbon, would this tradition not be just as convincing? And just as tendentious? Could we not, by different selections, produce many patterns?

Various suggestions have been made of late by such critics as Donald Davie and Philip Hobsbaum for a possible reinterpretation of the tradition of poetry in this century which would give more prominence to those writers who do not fit into a 'Modernist' tradition – Hardy, Edward Thomas, a number of the poets of the Great War, Larkin. My suggestion is of the same kind though I do not think that we need necessarily lean towards the mildly chauvinist opposition of international Modernism and sturdy Englishness. Parts of Thomas Mann's novels can be accommodated within the orthodox Modernist pattern, but much cannot; the same is true of Faulkner and Svevo and Proust. It may be that fiction is too much of a social art to reject society for very long. What is quite certain is that the orthodox generalization seems always to acquire its force when dealing with literature and especially with fiction by assimilating minor and sometimes rather bad writers to a tradition constructed from selective elements of some major ones. Martin Green in *Children of the Sun* exemplifies this very neatly when he says: 'they [Brian Howard and Harold Acton] were impresarios of others' talents and of the international modernist movements. They were friends of the Sitwells and Gertrude Stein and Jean Cocteau and others.'

I would not wish to be understood as saying that there was no such thing as a Modernist movement; it is not possible to discuss much which has happened in the arts during the last century without making use of the term, not least because so many of the artists of the period proclaimed the need to 'make it new'. But it is not a comprehensive tradition and it applies much less to fiction than to the other arts, so that it is vital to distinguish propaganda from analysis and to avoid the undue neatness and tidiness achieved by blurring distinctions between minor symptoms and major aims and by omitting some writers from the record. Moreover the need to challenge simple ideas of 'movements' is particularly pressing, as I indicate in Chapter 11, because the concept of 'Modernism' has grown up in the age of the professionalization of literary study and it has acquired the kind of academic acceptance handed on from teacher to pupil, with which the Romantics, for example, were not so speedily threatened.

I would place a good deal of emphasis in any discussion of the evolution of the concept of Modernism in England on the social circumstances which caused a number of writers and critics to take kindly to the idea of a conflict between the perceptive few and the insensitive masses. It is inevitable that anyone fighting for the acceptance of new works will expect to meet incomprehension and often downright hostility. But it is notable that many of the leading English 'impresarios' (to use Martin Green's term) – editors, publishers, literary journalists, critics – were marked by their origin from a small section of the community, by an education at public schools and, often, the older universities, which not merely limited their experience but tended to make them feel that the mass of the population was both unknown and inferior. It is surely obvious that Virginia Woolf's case against Bennett is not only against his realism or his supposedly inert documentation but against taking seriously the kind of people about whom he writes. Why else in 'Mr Bennett and Mrs Brown' should she feel that Mrs Brown, with whom we are to sympathize, though impoverished, 'came of gentlefolks who kept servants' while Mr Smith, with whom we do not sympathize, 'was of a bigger, burlier, less refined type . . . very likely a respectable corn-chandler from the North'.

There are other ways besides social snobbery of feeling that one is part of an élite and consequently of distorting one's reactions to works of literature, and I deal with some of these in Chapter 11. But in the England of the period with which I am dealing one of the unconscious motives behind the view that artists must break with convention was surely a sense of belonging to a socially defined minority of superior souls. The paradox which escaped the observation of such critics was that the greatest novelists of the period were those least likely to be in sympathy with this outlook.

Notes

1. The entry is too long to quote in full but the following extracts should give some ideas of the content:

> '"Modernism" (or "the modern movement") has by now acquired stability as the comprehensive term for an international tendency, arising in the poetry, fiction, drama, music, painting, architecture and other arts of the West in the last years of the 19th century and subsequently affecting the character of most 20th century art. The tendency is usually held to have reached its peak just before or soon after World War I, and there is some uncertaintyabout whether it still persists or a subsequent age of style has begun. . . . As a stylistic term, modernism contains and conceals a wide variety of different smaller movements. . . . A number of these movements contain large theoretical differences among themselves, but certain stylistic similarities. . . . Modernism had a high aesthetic and formed

constituent, and can often be seen as a movement attempting to preserve the aesthetic realm against intellectual, social and historical forces threatening it. . . . Its forms, with their elements of fragmentation, introversion, and crisis, have sometimes been held to register the collapse of the entire tradition of the arts in human history . . . the modernist arts require, for their comprehension, criteria different from those appropriate to earlier art.'

Chapter 10
James Joyce, the Professors and the Common Reader

Before beginning a discussion of James Joyce it is essential – as it is not essential for any other novelist of this period – to consider the terms of the discussion, to decide how one is going to read him. He is reported to have commented that he had given plenty of work for the professors and it is clear that he expected to be studied by Joycean specialists as well as by that common reader to whose attention previous novelists had aspired. This is placed beyond question by a number of jokes built into the story, some of which have been elucidated by Robert M. Adams in *Surface and Symbol: The Consistency of James Joyce's Ulysses*. The knowledgeable account of various horses by Nosey Flynn in Davy' Byrnes pub is perhaps the clearest example: only a professor is likely to check the accuracy of this by contemporary records and discover that Joyce has changed the sex of the Derby winner. Joyce's laughter must have echoed over the decades to the first discoverer of this discrepancy, planted so that it would only be noticed when Joyce studies had been added to Joyce readings.

If appreciation of that joke or other effects like it is an inherent and necessary part of a proper response to the novel then it is certain that only after a great deal of co-operative study will *Ulysses* be anything like fully understood, and we can say that Joyce did indeed write for the professors. If so he is a very different kind of novelist with very different aims from any other writer of significance (including many who are not obviously simple: Conrad, James, and Lawrence, for instance) and *Ulysses* is a different kind of novel from their works.

If we say that the joke and a multitude of other effects which only become clear after a great deal of research are not necessary elements then we must mean either that there is much in the book which is in the nature of optional extras or that the elaboration is, despite the incidental rewards, at bottom likely to be regrettable because it distracts us from what matters more.

The theory of optional extras, it should be clear, is not merely a manifestation of what we all know about most literary works – that serious reading is more rewarding than superficial and that we can sometimes be surprised even in works which we know well by a sudden perception of a shade of meaning or a resonance previously overlooked. A glance at either of the schemata for *Ulysses* which Joyce showed to Stuart Gilbert and to Carlo Linati indicates that there is a vast amount which can only be detected as the result of much detailed study and even a cursory glance at most criticism of Joyce leaves no doubt that most discussion is exegetical and assumes that what is revealed by co-operative scholarly effort is what deserves print. If Joyce gave the professors plenty to do, they have taken up their burden with a will and demonstrated their ability to bear it. If they are on the right lines then Joyce was indeed lucky that his works began to be established when the expansion of English Studies as an academic discipline ensured an adequate supply of professors to do the job. Nor is there any question, as there may be with some other writers, of over-ingenious critics reading things into the text; Joyce spent most of his lifetime elaborating his works and no critic is likely to be more ingenious than he was himself. But if everything which can be extracted from the text is important then the optional extras bulk as large as what an intelligent but non-scholarly reader can ever perceive and this is bound to make us feel that the common reading is an incomplete one.

My own opinion is that much of the elaboration is inert, intellectually rewarding in the same way that puzzles are, and that we have the right to regret this, and so far as we can, to ignore it.[1] We are accustomed to the critical claim that we are justified in seeing things in a book of which the author was unaware; it seems equally justifiable to seek to reject some matters which the author introduced if we believe that they take attention away from the qualities which make him a great novelist.

My conviction rests upon two assumptions. One is that there is a limit to the attention which can be paid by any reader – specifically that we cannot combine different *kinds* of attention to more than a very limited degree; it is not possible to attend concurrently, for example, to the feelings and perceptions of a realized fictional character and to the proliferation within the prose of covert references to various organs of the body or precious stones. Consecutive readings may allow us to move from one to the other but I do not believe that these consecutive readings can ever be combined in one. My second reason helps to explain why they cannot be combined. Characters, if we are to take any interest it them, must affect us as autonomous beings; even if the writer sees them as constrained by social forces which lessen their autonomy, as Conrad does in *Nostromo*, these forces are conceived as having an existence outside the arbitrary will of the novelist, perceived by him in society and in principle conceivable to the characters themselves. Joyce very naturally sees his characters as determined by their Catholic upbringing and the political state of Ireland in the early years of this century. But the *fuga per canonem* which was claimed by Joyce as the form of the 'Sirens' episode of *Ulysses* and the sequence of pastiche/parodies in 'Oxen of the Sun' emerge from neither the perceptions of the characters nor the circumstances of society, and attention to them goes far to abolish all sense of the characters as people about whom Joyce certainly wishes us to have various feelings. This is particularly so because many of the elaborations bear all the marks of having been superadded to a work whose energies lie elsewhere, most evidently in such traditional pleasures as the deployment of characters and the establishment of the social scene. But much criticism of Joyce produces the odd paradox of critics avoiding all mention (presumably as too elementary) of these triumphs while expatiating at length on ingenuities which, in truth, should be well within the compass of any intelligent literary person. The chapter of parodies, for example, could surely have been produced, once the idea is there, by many a contributor to literary competitions, and the idea itself is strikingly mechanical.

There is one critical line of thought which accepts the mechanical nature of many of the effects and claims it as an inherent part of the totality of the book. Hugh Kenner, seizing on Wyndham Lewis's attack in *Time and Western Man* (1927) and turning it on its head, asserts that Joyce is a backward-looking pessimist who believes that the world has been drained of meaning, so that the basic strategy of *Ulysses* is precisely an accumulation of inert detail which smothers everything. Kenner's argument is marked by great erudition and great play of logic; in my opinion it falls to the ground because the tone of *Ulysses* is not in the least despairing but, on the contrary, humane, liberal, and celebratory.

The line traced by Joyce's work is a strange and paradoxical one: he begins his significant work with short stories about a variety of people and, despite some complications under the surface, the stories can be read with ease; he then writes a novel about a highly intelligent and academically minded young man, and this, too, is now relatively easy to read; this is followed by the further adventures of that same young man, to whom are added as central characters, a strikingly ordinary man and his wife, and this is still, after sixty years, a difficult book; he ends by writing about the most ordinary man imaginable and produces a book which is unreadable, although it is studiable. I do not mean by this that *Finnegans Wake* is in all ways unrewarding, but my observation has been that professionals study it and a few others make it a cult book – that is, one in which a sense of being members of an initiated group provides its own somewhat dubious satisfaction – but it shows no signs of acquiring that readership which other notoriously 'difficult' works of the first half of this century have had for some decades.

Yet even in that first volume of stories there can be seen, warring against its triumphs, elements of inert ingenuity with which we must come to terms. *Dubliners*, first published in 1914, lingered with the publishers for a number of years of complicated negotiations, the subject of much anxiety and frustration. It is often suggested that we are fortunate, even if Joyce felt that he was not, because the delay enabled two good stories to be added – 'A Little Cloud' and 'Two Gallants' – and Joyce's best story, 'The Dead' to conclude the volume. What is perhaps not always realized is the extent to which the additions changed the balance of the whole volume, highlighting certain qualities and diminishing the significance of others. I would go further and suggest that 'The Dead', though indeed the best story, does not really belong as clearly as the others within the volume and that a good deal of discussion of it has gone astray because of the attempt to fit it in.

The original twelve stories form a loose unity, as Joyce said, stories of childhood, followed by adolescence and mature life and culminating in 'stories of public life in Dublin', ending with 'Grace'.[2] As might be expected of a collection called 'Dubliners' written by one educated by the Jesuits, the first and the last stories are concerned with aspects of Dublin Catholicism; they are both concerned with the religion and they are both extremely funny. 'The Sisters' is certainly about much else besides – the small boy's first encounter with death and his mixture of shrewdness and incomprehension about the reciprocally uncomprehending world of adults and his fascination with those big matters which he does not understand. But its title, which has often puzzled readers, should direct attention towards the two old women who gossip ignorantly about their dead brother – ignorantly because, whatever they might superstitiously believe, no priest who is able to put the boy through his paces about such 'intricate questions' as are dealt with by the fathers of the Church (who wrote 'books as thick as the *Post Office Directory* and as closely printed as the law notices in the newspapers') could possibly believe, as his sisters say, that the accidental breaking of a chalice, whether empty or not, has the dread significance which they give to it. The effect which the story leaves upon us has far less to do with the oddity of Father Flynn than with the comic banality of the sisters. There are few things in the whole of Joyce's output more penetrating and funnier than the way in which the stilted conversation proceeds via every necessary cliché (from 'Ah, well, he's gone to a better world', through 'there's no friends like the old friends' to 'It's when it's all over that you'll miss him') to the moment for which all this has been a preparation:

> She stopped, as if she were communing with the past,
> and then said shrewdly:
> – Mind you, I noticed there was something queer
> coming over him latterly.

'Grace', the story of 'public life', would have fittingly concluded the volume. Mr Kernan, having disgraced himself by falling down the lavatory steps in a bar, is persuaded by his friends to 'wash the pot' – make a retreat. To the accompaniment of glasses of stout and the 'light music of whisky falling into glasses' his friends proclaim the victory of religion and right thinking, all expressed in a farrago of inaccurate history, misquotation, ludicrous discussion of Papal mottoes ('Lux upon Lux' succeeded by 'Crux upon Crux'), snobbery, and some toadying. As in 'The Sisters', their conversation is conducted in a succession of owlish clichés, and the story culminates in the sermon of Father Purdon (whose name is that of the Dublin street famous for its brothels) who addresses them as if he were 'their spiritual accountant' on the text.

> For the children of this world are wiser in their generation
> than the children of light. Wherefore make unto yourselves
> friends out of the mammon of iniquity so that when you
> die they may receive you into everlasting dwellings.

The first collection of *Dubliners* is thus opened and closed by stories of the almost farcically superstitious debasement of a Catholicism which is as inescapably social as it is religious. There is much in the intervening stories, like the canvassers in 'Ivy Day in the Committee Room' listening to the fustian poem on Parnell to the accompaniment of the popping of corks in stout bottles, which is comic, too. But there is much else: even in the example which I have chosen there is the perception that men may be genuinely moved by fustian, and many of the stories – 'Araby', for example, or 'Clay' or 'A Painful Case' – are predominantly sad. What they share with 'The Sisters' and 'Grace' is a sense of debasement and staleness, of a society from which many of the characters desire to escape but in which they are trapped by poverty or habit or family. But whenever religion rises to the surface the tone is likely to become comic, even if pathetically so, as in the end of 'Counterparts' where the small boy cries: 'I'll say a *Hail Mary* for you, pa, if you don't beat me . . . I'll say a *Hail Mary*.' It seems that in this volume the religion of Dublin, whether seen as the debasement of the highest claims or as the manipulation of the greatest trap, can only be confronted by irony and farce. And, because it is the biggest claim, the volume opens and closes with it.

'The Dead', written after the first collection had been put together, is different in many ways from all the other stories, including the other two later ones. Not only is it much longer and more complex in structure but it is – to put it in the simplest terms – about someone who has escaped from the constrictions which entangle the characters of the other stories; Gabriel Conroy is a successful teacher at the college, prosperous, happily married, a reviewer for an English newspaper and accustomed to take his holidays on the Continent. He has, indeed, moved so far away from the general outlook of Dublin that he feels at times awkwardly out of place among the guests at his aunt's party, though at other times he is warmly affectionate towards the family. This unease is, indeed, what the story explores; it might be said that he is constantly putting his foot (extracted from its continental goloshes) in it. His attempted jocularity with the maid, Lily, falls flat, he is put out by Miss Ivor's teasing about being a 'West Briton', and finally he discovers when he returns with his wife to their hotel that she has been reminded by a song heard at the dance of a man who had loved her in her youth and had, as she puts it, died for her. His frustration and anger die away first in an excessive self-contempt and then in a feeling of unity with the dead young man and with all the dead, culminating in an ornate and highly rhythmical prose which has not previously been found in *Dubliners*:

> [The snow] was falling on every part of the dark central plain, on the treeless hills, falling softly upon the Bog of Allen and, farther westward, softly falling into the dark mutinous Shannon waves. It was falling, too, upon every part of the lonely churchyard on the hill where Michael Furey lay buried. It lay thickly drifted on the crooked crosses and headstones, on the spears of the little gate, on the barren thorns. His soul swooned slowly as he heard the snow falling faintly through the universe and faintly falling, like the descent of their last end, upon all the living and the dead.

This snow with which the story ends is the most important of a number of central images which run through the story; appearing first as stuff to be scraped off Gabriel's goloshes (which makes him seem finicky, perhaps, and certainly un-Irish, to judge by the jokes about them), the snow transforms everything: 'A light fringe of snow lay like a cape on the shoulders of his overcoat and like toecaps on the tops of his goloshes.' Later, as Gabriel speculates a little apprehensively on the speech which he is to make, he looks out of the window and thinks how pleasant it would be to walk outside – 'The snow would be lying on the branches of the trees and forming a bright cap on the top of the Wellington Monument' and on their way to the hotel they see the statue of O'Connell, 'the Liberator', turned into 'a white man' from the snow lying on it. It is right, then, that snow should fill Gabriel's mind at the moment when his feelings are transformed. It joins, too, with another theme which has surfaced intermittently throughout the story – the contrast between the East, England, the Continent (most clearly presented by the paradox of Gabriel's being called a 'West Briton' by Miss Ivors) and the West of Ireland, the region of Gretta's childhood, of the language advocated by Miss Ivors, of the primitive which Gabriel thought he had left behind and which he does not wish to visit, and finally of the snow-covered churchyard in the far West which Gabriel imagines and towards which his feelings go out.

Gabriel's moment of revelation – or 'epiphany', to use Joyce's own word – is the culmination both of finely observed and presented psychological detail and also of a train of imagery created with the story and perceived by the characters. It is in its nature the very opposite of sterility and lack of contact and shabbiness which are the climaxes of the other stories. The only possible parallel is the realization of the narrator at the end of 'An Encounter' that he is glad to see the companion whom he has always despised a little.

Nevertheless the story has not always been read thus and if we consider how else it can be read, we move to the central point of my argument about professors and common readers. William York Tindall, in *A Reader's Guide to James Joyce*, for example, describes it as 'at once the summary and the climax of *Dubliners*', and in this judgement he is far from alone. If we take this view we are obliged to assert that Gabriel is, indeed, what he says of himself in his moments of frustrated self-contempt, 'a ludicrous figure, acting as a pennyboy for his aunts, a nervous, well-meaning sentimentalist, orating to vulgarians and idealizing his own clownish lusts'; he has never truly loved Gretta and is as hopeless a Dubliner as any other sufferer from physical or emotional paralysis.

To take this view involves, in my view, flying in the face not only of Gabriel's memories of his married life with Gretta, which may of course be self-deception, but also of the things which she says both to and about him; it is also to fly in the face of our common experience of life, which includes the awareness that sometimes we may be made awkward by a social contretemps with the likes of Lily or Miss Ivors and that even in the happiest of marriages one partner does not always know what the other is thinking or feeling and may receive shocks. The arguments against this reading seem overwhelming in terms of psychological plausibility and of how we have seen the personages of the story behaving.

Those who take the view that Gabriel's plight represents the culmination of the study of Dublin's paralysis are supported by the fact that there are, throughout the volume, a substantial number of images, keywords, repetitions, which point to parallels, often of an arcane nature, and that these are continued into 'The Dead'. They are not the excogitations of over-ingenious critics; they are there and Joyce's own comments tend to draw attention to them. An example from 'The Sisters' should make clear the sort of ingenuity which I have in mind. The small boy accepts the sherry which one of the sisters offers him as they leave the bedroom where the priest lies dead and go into the room where he has always sat with him during his life; but he refuses the cream crackers because he thinks he will 'make too much noise eating them'. This detail functions superbly to evoke the silence of the room and the constraint of the boy. But, it has been pointed out, to drink the wine and not to eat the bread is to reject what the laity take and to accept what (before Vatican II) was reserved for the priest; appropriately, therefore, in 'Araby' a boy carries the thought of the girl with whom he is in love through the crowded streets and 'I imagined that I bore my chalice safely through a throng of foes'. The chalice which the priest has relinquished has been taken up by the priest of love or art, the seeker of Araby, the un-Irish splendours of the Orient.

It is perhaps possible to accept this addition to the story as an optional extra (though there is surely something forced about the boy's likening his feelings to a chalice), but the sheer weight of recondite allusion soon demands too much attention for us to have much sense of the autonomy of character and social relationship. So far as 'The Dead' is concerned, the more attention we concentrate on a dense reticulation of thematic images the more we are bound to feel that the last story is the culmination of the volume. We will then seize on Joyce's comments that the stories concern the paralysis of Dublin and that he chose brown as the appropriate colour for the city and pick up a cluster of brown references in 'The Dead'.[3] Gabriel carves a brown goose, he wonders whether or not to quote in his speech from Browning, and one of the guests is Mr Browne who, attentive to his hostesses, 'is everywhere'. Gabriel is thus quickly fitted into the pattern of paralysis, aided by the fact that the opening word of the story, the name of the servant, 'Lily', is Gabriel's emblem and is also a funereal flower.

The kind of elaboration which Joyce employs here may be characterized as cryptographic, in the sense that it requires us to decipher it and, moreover, it is usually unrelated to the experience of the characters. There is nothing new in exhibiting within a novel a pattern which the reader registers, though the characters do not; but such patterns are normally an organic outgrowth from their experiences. Put very simply, we may say that Dickens in *Little Dorrit* makes us see a pattern of many kinds of imprisonment and Conrad in *Nostromo* a series of variations on enslavement to the silver of the mine, but that, though only the writer and reader share that vision, it would be possible to point out to many of the characters that it is true. One could not point out to Gabriel Conroy that Mr Browne is at the party because only a man with that name would be appropriate.

We may feel – I certainly do – that there is something ineffectively mechanical in thus labelling Lily and Mr Browne in a story which elsewhere relies so triumphantly on the verisimilitude of detail; but the distortion which is imposed upon Gabriel especially in his relationship with Gretta and his aunts is far more significant. Either, it seems to me, we must seek out and respond to the thematic scheme and consequently deny both what Joyce makes us feel about the characters in their minute-by-minute activity and our experience of life, or we must choose not to concentrate attention on the scheme. To do this will no doubt deprive us of some effective moments and a number of jokes and it will certainly allow those who take the other path to patronize us as naïve readers. But the price of sophistication may be too high and if the choice is to be a common reader or a professor then the former is to be preferred. I am, of course, using these terms in their Pickwickian sense: real professors may choose to be common readers and common readers may aspire to the professoriate. I do not underrate the devotion and intelligence and wit of those critics with whom I disagree and some of whom I list in my Bibliography, but it seems important to save Joyce's works – and especially *Ulysses* – for the common reader and from the professional symposia.

To make this choice is to assert that Joyce is sometimes a victim of his own impulse towards cryptographic elaboration, and *A Portrait of the Artist as a Young Man*, whose publication followed *Dubliners* in 1916, though an earlier version, *Stephen Hero*, dates from considerably earlier, may provide some explanation of this characteristic. The novel is a *Bildungsroman* in the specific form of a *Künstlerroman*, the study of the development of an artist from infancy to the moment when, assured of his vocation and having rejected the claims of his country, his church and his family, he prepares to take flight from his native Ireland. What is most striking in his development is that he does not seem to be led to a theme or to any engrossing subject or even to a personal mood which he wishes to embody in words – save for an unconvincingly decadent villanelle – but to a concept of himself as an artist and to the need for a theory of art. It seems that, having abandoned the scholastic theology of an upbringing intended to turn him into a priest, he must needs heed the question of the dean of studies, 'When may we expect to have something from you on the esthetic question?' and, picking up that misquotation from Aquinas, *'pulcra sunt quae visa placent'*, which doubtless seems a good starting-point for the dean, develop a detailed aesthetics to Lynch.

It seems natural to Joyce that his artist hero cannot, with a good conscience, be a writer until he has constructed a theology of art which asserts something like the same degree of intellectual rigour as the theology in which he no longer believes, one moreover which will admit of casuistry (*'If a man hacking in fury at a block of wood . . . make there an image of a cow, is that image a work of art? If not, why not?'*), and which will inevitably respond to multiple forms of interpretation. Lynch points out that this approach 'has the true scholastic stink', just as Cranly tells him that his mind is 'supersaturated with the religion in which you say you disbelieve'. He concludes his exposition to Lynch with the description of the position of the artist in relation to his creation which has been so often quoted in discussion of the book:

> The artist, like the God of creation, remains within or
> behind or beyond or above his handiwork, invisible,
> refined out of existence, indifferent, paring his fingernails.

Though sometimes claimed as a proclamation of the basic moral neutrality of the artist, this, in context, clearly means that in the dramatic form the artist does not intrude his opinions, that all his beliefs are embodied within the work. It is, moreover, right that Stephen, poor, lice-ridden, lonely, should liken himself to the God of creation, just as he has started the discussion by the arrogant proclamation, 'Aristotle has not defined pity and terror. I have.' But it is surely significant also as proclaiming a view of a work of art as a world created by an artist which will stand any amount of scrutiny, any amount of poring over, any amount of interpretation, as often as not in terms which its inhabitants could not envisage. Joyce has commonly been discussed, and rightly in many ways, as one of the masters of Modernism, and in his use of, say, the stream of consciousness has been related to Proust, to Virginia Woolf, and, of course, to that writer from who he said he learnt his method of character presentation, Édouard Dujardin; yet it is equally true that his central concept of a work of art is profoundly medieval.[4] In saying this I am assuming that in this aesthetic definition Joyce is in agreement with Stephen. There are certainly many sections of the book where it can be argued that Joyce is detaching himself from his hero and even mocking him, agreeing perhaps with Cranly's affectionate jibe, 'You poor poet, you!' The scene at the end of Part 4 in which Stephen is assured of his vocation on the beach, sleeps, and wakes, faces us with the task of deciding whether the lush prose is intended to evoke a sense of revelation and wonder in us or whether we are to feel that Stephen's revelation is intensely adolescent. If we choose the latter in its most extreme form then a great deal of the book is undermined and presumably we will find an essentially critical pun in its penultimate sentence, where Stephen goes 'to forge in the smithy of my soul the uncreated conscience of my race'; the shadow of Shem the Penman, Joyce's forger shadow, will lie heavily over the entire novel. We shall also find much of the eloquent prose towards which the novel has developed from the childish language of the opening, through the schoolboy vocabulary, hollow. It seems probable to me that Joyce may mock affectionately, as Cranly does, but it is hard to read the whole book as an ironic performance. Consequently I would hold that Stephen's aesthetics are, broadly, Joyce's, though he may, as is appropriate in a novel, present them with some irony and with a pomposity which befits his hero. But whichever view one takes of Joyce's relationship with Stephen need make no difference to my argument about the significance of the theories in relation to Joyce's habit of mind; he takes it for granted that a young artist with his background and upbringing would be impelled to construct a theology of art; if it is to be taken ironically as an awful warning it is certainly a warning which he himself needs but which he strikingly did not heed.

There is, however, one way in which Joyce indubitably breaks his aesthetic rules; the practice of writing sequels surely conflicts with the principle of *integritas*. Yet *Ulysses* opens with the reappearance of Stephen Dedalus and in the course of the novel we meet with many of what an older generation would have called 'old friends': Leopold Bloom, for example, goes to Paddy Dignam's funeral in the company of Messrs Cunningham, Power, and Kernan who, in 'Grace', have washed the pot together. However important it may seem to the Stephen of *A Portrait of the Artist as a Young Man* that each work of art should be 'selfbounded and selfcontained' it is clear that Joyce's concept of fictional characters and their relationship with their surroundings is of a continuing identity extending beyond the bounds of any one book.

Eight of the first nine sections of *Ulysses* are basically a mixture of straight narrative and interior monologue (or stream of consciousness or whatever other term seems best) of either Stephen Dedalus, returned from his visit to Paris and two years older than at the end of *Portrait*, or Leopold Bloom. The focus of our interest is thus fixed initially on the feelings, actions, and relationships of the people of the book.

But in a number of the later sections (and to a limited extent as a result of revision in some of the earlier ones) he abandons this direct presentation of character in favour of techniques of parody, pastiche, symbolic fantasy, and narration by question and answer from an omniscient narrator. It has been shown by a number of critics that Joyce changed his mind about the novel as he was writing it and that this involved not only constructing the later sections in a different manner from the earlier ones but also revising with varying degrees of thoroughness the earlier parts to bring them into accommodation with what follows. The revisions involved the introduction of a vast number of references to mythical patterns (or supposed ones, since it has been shown that he used as source books sundry speculative and unreliable guides) and of key images for each scene. These insertions are those which Joyce describes in the 'schema' which he sent to Carlo Linati with an accompanying letter on 21 September 1920 in which he says that the book

> is also a kind of encyclopaedia. My intention is to
> transpose the myth *sub specie temporis nostri*. Each adventure
> (that is, every hour, every organ, every art being
> interconnected and interrelated in the structural scheme of
> the whole) should not only condition but even create its
> own technique. Each adventure is so to say one person
> although it is composed of persons – as Aquinas relates of
> the angelic hosts.[5]

Michael Groden, whose *Ulysses in Progress* documents the rewritings very thoroughly and lucidly, says of the change from internal monologue to the other devices that 'Joyce changes his focus of interest from his characters to his styles', and many critics would clearly agree with him.

But it is difficult to be clear as to what this means. If the styles are themselves the focus of interest they have little to offer but examples of manners; a series of questions and answers is in itself inert and a chapter of parodies is the stuff of literary parlour games.

If, however, we believe that the focus is still on the characters but that, having established those characters in depth, Joyce now goes on to show the variety of ways in which we can perceive or interpret them, the development of the book is in its larger scheme quite unproblematical. We may find some of the methods more effective than others and we may, as I do, regard much of the encyclopaedic insertion as inert or positively distracting, but the deeply moving effect of the apparently most detached section – the questions and answers of 'Ithaca' – is sufficient evidence of the wisdom of his choice of development.[6]

Throughout there is one simple sense in which the novel aims at the encyclopaedic. Joyce sees to it that there are few experiences of human life, major or minor, at which we are not present and it was for the presence of some of these activities and the indecorous words used to describe them that the book was banned in both Britain and the United States for a number of years. We are with the characters when they are eating, drinking, sleeping, arguing, bearing children, burying the dead, pissing, working, shitting, bathing, fornicating, singing, menstruating, quarrelling, remembering, grieving, masturbating, teaching, being snubbed, being inquisitive, compassionate, jealous, forgetful, reconciled, boastful, unsure, doing and being, in fact, nearly everything that men and women can do and be except what is noble, dignified, and heroic. The paradox of the book is that we are frequently on the edge of attributing to Leopold Bloom nobility, dignity, and heroism.

Bloom is, indeed, modelled upon the legendary hero who gives his name to the book. He is the Ulysses/Odysseus in a mock-heroic *Odyssey* with Stephen as a weaker Telemachus and Molly Bloom as a Penelope who does not resist all her suitors. Writing on 10 November 1922 to his aunt, Mrs Josephine Murray, whom he hoped would read the book, Joyce recommended her to read a translation of the *Odyssey* first or even Lamb's simplified *Adventures of Ulysses*, and repeated this advice in his Christmas letter.

Joyce chose not to attach to the published book the chapter titles which he gave to them in accounts to various friends and critics, but they have been commonly used and provide a convenient way of referring to the sections of the novel. The relationship is at times a loose one and an awareness of the parallels is far more rewarding in some sections than in others, but it is impossible to discuss the book without having some idea of the general parallel as well as a number of specific ones. The course of the novel, with the parallels, is:

1. *Telemachus:* Stephen Dedalus, living in a Martello tower with a medical student, Buck Mulligan, whom he sees as mocking him, and Haines, an Englishman, the representative (albeit one interested in Gaelic culture) of the imperial power, feels an exile in his own land.
2. *Nestor:* He goes to the school and talks with Mr Deasy, a schoolmaster for whom he works, a Nestor whose conversation is replete with innaccuracies.
3. *Proteus:* He walks along the beach, brooding on flux and uncertainty.
4. *Calypso:* Leopold Bloom, a Jewish advertisement canvasser, enthralled by his wife Molly, a singer, buys and prepares breakfast and takes it to her in bed with a letter from Blazes Boylan, her concert agent, with whom she is having an affair. He promises to bring her a pornographic novel and reads, while sitting on the lavatory, a story in *Tit-Bits* with which he wipes himself.

5. *Lotus Eaters:* He collects a letter from a woman with whom he is con-
ducting a flirtation by correspondence and visits the public baths.
6. *Hades:* He attends Paddy Dignam's funeral and thinks about death,
reminded (as we realize later) by a child's funeral of the death,
many years before, of his own son Rudy.
7. *Aeolus:* He visits the newspaper office to place an advertisement.
Stephen also appears, but they do not speak to one another.
8. *Lestrygonians:* Bloom walks through the streets and has lunch at
Davy Byrne's pub.
9. *Scylla and Charybdis:* In the public library Stephen presents to
Mulligan and sundry others his theory about Shakespeare (already
advertised by Mulligan as Stephen's party piece). Bloom passes
through and is seen but not spoken to.
10. *Wandering Rocks:* This consists of a series of brief scenes, some
standing on their own (Blazes Boylan's visit to a fruit and flower
shop, for example, and the sudden appearance of Molly's bare arm
at the window – for she, too, is preparing for his visit – throwing
a coin to a beggar), but many of them linked by the progress of
Father Conmee across the city and, at the end, of the vice-regal
cavalcade which is seen by many of the personages of the book.
11. *Sirens:* Bloom, drinking a glass of cider in the Ormond Hotel,
listens to Ben Dollard (a 'base barreltone') singing for a group of
friends which includes Stephen's father. Boylan drops in for a
drink, too, and then leaves in a jaunting car for his assignation
with Molly.
12. *Cyclops:* Bloom visits Barney Kiernan's pub and is there involved
in an argument with an anti-Semitic bigot, referred to as 'the
Citizen'. He makes his escape as the Citizen throws a biscuit tin
at him.
13. *Nausicaa:* Relaxing on the beach, Mr Bloom sees a young woman,
Gerty MacDowell, through whose parodically sentimental interior
monologue we perceive the first half of the chapter; he daydreams,
masturbates, and feels sorry for Gerty because he sees that she is
lame.
14. *Oxen of the Sun:* Stephen, Mulligan, and various friends go to the
lying-in hospital where Mrs Purefoy is having a difficult labour.
Bloom, too, is there and sits with them as they get drunk. They
leave for Burke's pub and Bloom accompanies them in the hope
of saving Stephen from harm. After more drinks Stephen, with
Bloom following, makes for the brothel district.
15. *Circe:* He does save Stephen who is involved in a fight with two
English soldiers, though not before, in by far the longest section
of the book, the buried hopes, fears, and guilts of both have been
projected in a nightmare inner drama.

16. *Eumaeus:* Bloom takes Stephen to a cabman's shelter and buys him a cup of coffee and a bun; they talk but make little real contact. Bloom invites Stephen home.
17. *Ithaca:* They go to Bloom's house and drink cocoa; Stephen refuses an invitation to spend the night and goes away. Bloom looks round his house, recognizes signs that Boylan has been there and retires to bed, kisses his wife's rump, gives her an edited account of his day and falls asleep.
18. *Penelope:* Molly, half asleep, ruminates over the doings of her day, particularly her adultery with Boylan in the afternoon, and of her life, especially her lovers and possible lovers, and ends, remembering Leopold's proposal and her acceptance.

Joyce is as anxious to show what his characters share in their environment as in showing their individuality. The 'Wandering Rocks' sequence is, from this point of view, something of an epitome of the whole book. Its cross-cutting indicates the simultaneity of the experiences of many people who are acquainted but at the moment separated and the account of the vice-regal procession, in a style which veers from the court circular to the tone of the successive spectators, fixes a whole string of characters in postures of watching. The whole book is filled with a sense of people meeting, passing, bumping into one another, and the effect is achieved as much by the reappearance of phrases and objects in different contexts as by the actual contact of people. The symbolic significance of such objects as the three-masted *Rosevean* or the sandwich-board carriers or the throwaway sheet proclaiming the coming of Elijah has been commented upon a good deal but it is arguable that they have the even more important function of adding to the sense of a densely populated novel about a crowded city which is still small enough for those in it to share a world of streets and hotels and libraries and hospitals and shops and, above all, pubs. 'Above all' not because the community of Joyce's novel is a drinking one (though it is) but even more because it is a talking one and it is in pubs that people talk. That astonishing skill at persuading the reader that he is hearing a speaking voice, whether angry, plaintive, mocking, or whatever which Joyce displays in the Christmas dinner scene in the *Portrait* is deployed at length in Ulysses, from the jocular blasphemy of Mulligan on the first page to Molly's excited recollection of saying 'Yes' on the last, to create a world which is very largely one of voices.

Pre-eminent among these are the internal voices of Stephen and Bloom and, in the last section, of Molly Bloom. The first three chapters are presented to us largely through the perceptions and reflections of Stephen and the next three through those of Bloom, though a third-person narrative plays a large part in several of them; in the funeral episode, for instance, we move away from Bloom's meditation on death to hear Mr Cunningham's whispered confidence to Mr Power about the suicide of Bloom's father, and the book starts with a brisk objectivity. In addition to these first six sections we are plunged into the mind of Bloom in 'Lestrygonians' and for parts of 'Aeolus', 'Sirens', and 'Nausicaa', and of Stephen for much of 'Aeolus' and of 'Scylla and Charybdis'.

These three characters, Bloom, Stephen, and Molly, the Odysseus, Telemachus, and Penelope of this comic epic, have very differently stocked minds and much of the effect of the book comes from the sense thus created of inevitable incomprehension between Bloom and Stephen and, in the case of Bloom and his wife, of great superficial differences coexisting with a basic continuing awareness of one another and, despite infidelities and evasions, respect.

Our first entry into Stephen's consciousness announces one of the central preoccupations, his guilt for refusing to pray with his dying mother:

> Stephen, an elbow rested on the jagged granite, leaned
> his palm against his brow and gazed at the fraying edge of
> his shiny black coat-sleeve. Pain, that was not yet the pain
> of love, fretted his heart. Silently, in a dream she had
> come to him after her death, her wasted body within its
> loose brown graveclothes giving off an odour of wax and
> rosewood, her breath, that had bent upon him, mute,
> reproachful, a faint odour of wetted ashes.

To this guilt at not having paid lip service to the religion in which he no longer believes, but in whose theology and terminology he is 'supersaturated', is added a general sense of disinheritance; the English rule Ireland, the Irish give allegiance to the Roman Catholic Church, and Buck Mulligan's mockery seems to usurp Stephen's own attempt at a mental kingdom, though readers are likely to find Stephen's casting of Mulligan as villain somewhat paranoid, even if the Buck's bawdry and blasphemy is not to their taste. Perhaps as the priest of art Stephen feels that as successor state he inherits heretics along with splendours.

Throughout the book Stephen's response to his insecurity and loss is an assertion of superiority manifested in an often frenetic cleverness, seen at its fullest development in his disquisition on *Hamlet*, which Mulligan has earlier described as a proof that Hamlet is the ghost of his own father. Nor is Stephen's showing-off confined to public appearances. His ruminations as he walks alone on Sandymount strand in 'Proteus' emerge as a farrago of reminiscences of theology, English literature, Irish folk history, snatches of French from his recent stay in Paris, Aristotelian philosophy, Italian opera, and so forth. This doubtless corresponds to what stocks the mind of a highly educated literary young man, but minds are not merely passive repositories and the dynamic at work here is surely the parading of erudition and multilingual name-dropping as a defence against a feeling of isolation and failure.

Bloom is as different from Stephen as a man could be, except that, as a Jew in a Gentile society, he, too, sometimes feels not altogether at home and for him, too, the memory of death is important – in his case the deaths of both his father and his only son, Rudy. He is tolerant, kind, long-suffering, ineffectively prurient, and above all curious – curious about elementary science and administration and how people make their living and, in most striking contrast to Stephen, about what other people may be feeling. Stephen's stream of consciousness is loaded with memories of philosophy and literature and the liturgy; Bloom's mind is full of what may be best described by the title of the magazine in which he reads a sentimental story and on which he wipes his arse – *Tit-Bits*.

His internal monologue is marked, as is Stephen's, by two characteristics which make a first reading difficult but, in the long run, add immensely to the depth of our knowledge of them and increase the feeling of immediacy. The first, which gives a sense that the moment of experience is merely the forward edge of a continuum, is the frequency of memories, often triggered off by a perception which we cannot immediately comprehend. The other, related to it, is the constant occurrence of half-finished sentences, snatches of phrases, often remembered scraps of past conversations, which give a striking impression of the speed of the flow of association and its often indirect and apparently illogical nature. Before going out to buy his breakfast, Leopold Bloom asks his wife whether she wants anything:

> A sleepy soft grunt answered:
> – Mn.
> No. She did not want anything. He heard then a warm heavy sigh, softer as she turned over and the loose brass quoits of the bedstead jingled. . . .
> His hand took his hat from the peg over his initialled heavy overcoat, and his lost property office secondhand waterproof. Stamps: sticky-back pictures. Daresay lots of officers are in the swim too. Course they do. The sweated legend in the crown of his hat told him mutely: Plasto's high grade ha. He peeped quickly inside the leather headband. White slip of paper. Quite safe.

There are several things here which we will only understand later, notably that the slip of paper in his hat carries the false name which he uses to claim at the post office the letter from Martha Clifford (which also sounds like a false name) with whom he is carrying on a rather squalid postal flirtation. There is also the beginning of a train of associations which will develop largely through the book, for just as he is picking up old associations he is also still making them. The jingling of Molly's bed, repeated a few pages further on – 'She set the brasses jingling as she raised herself briskly, an elbow on the pillow' – is echoed several times by Blazes Boylan's jaunting car.

In 'Sirens' we find:

> Jingle a tinkle jaunted.
> Bloom heard a jing, a little sound. He's off. Light sob
> of breath Bloom sighed on the silent bluehued flowers.
> Jingling. He's gone. Jingle. Hear.

Bloom knows, as we do, that Boylan is on his way to set the loose brass quoits of the bed jingling, too, and he winces away from the knowledge.

But Joyce did not choose to write the whole book in those styles in which he first establishes his characters and their society; one of the assertions which emerges from the book is that not only can all human experience be seen, in essence, in eighteen hours of a Dublin day, but also that it can be discussed in any number of ways. We have already, quite early in the book, had in 'Aeolus' the comic and appropriate device of the insertion of newspaper headlines, ranging from the traditionally periphrastic IN THE HEART OF THE HIBERNIAN METROPOLIS to the demotic of the yellow press, where the windiness of the headlines goes along with the conversation. But the latter two-thirds of the book consists very largely of observations of the personages in sundry modes; this includes the five longest sections – 'Circe', 'Cyclops', 'Ithaca', 'Eumaeus', and 'Oxen of the Sun' – all of which are stylistically elaborated and which together take up slightly more than half the length of the entire novel. Expansion into parody, pastiche, question-and-answer linguistic fantasy is very natural in this mock-*Odyssey*, for the essence of the mock-heroic lies in the application of apparently inappropriate styles. Moreover, as in traditional mock-heroic, Joyce's stylistic choices usually have the effect of commenting upon the subject.

The simplest example – hardly more than the addition of yet another internal monologue – is the presentation of Gerty McDowell in the idiom of the sentimentally romantic and pious magazine. The section is relatively brief – twenty-one pages before we move into Mr

Bloom's mind – and it strikes hard at two of Joyce's pet targets, the namby-pamby mingling of sexual feeling and pretensions to elegance, and that religiosity which, in its masculine form, he has so satisfactorily dissected in 'Grace'. Gerty exposes herself to Bloom by leaning back and showing her good leg and thus provoking to masturbation that stranger whom she sees as a foreigner with 'his dark eyes and his pale intellectual face'; to the reader she exposes herself and that type to which she belongs by the style of her stream of consciousness.

By contrast the other exercise in parody (or pastiche; it is hard to know which is the correct description), 'Oxen of the Sun', seems to me to be the least successful of all the sections of the book. It follows the increasingly drunken conversation of Stephen, Mulligan, and some of their friends in the Holles Street lying-in hospital while the medical students await the birth of a child to Mrs Purefoy and Bloom watches them and decides to follow Stephen at the end to try to stop him getting into trouble. It is narrated in the form of a series of imitations of English prose, developing over about nine hundred years, for which Joyce pillages a number of standard works on English prose. This development is intended, according to Joyce's own account, to parallel the embryonic development of the baby; he also said, in a letter of 13 March 1920 to his friend Frank Budgen that 'Bloom is the spermatozoon, the hospital the womb, the nurse the ovum, Stephen the embryo'. Some of the parodies are good of their kind – the obvious Dickens, for example – but many seem flat and there are not a few places where the prose has the deadness which we shall later meet, used to deliberate effect, in 'Eumaeus'. This impression of labouredness comes about because, by contrast with the depiction of Gerty MacDowell, Joyce has no target for his parody, no characteristic to which each particular style is peculiarly appropriate. The imposition of a succession of styles is mechanical and inorganic. It is only at a highly rarefied level that we can equate the baby with the word and the effort to do so and to follow through the symbolic allusions with which the section is loaded cannot but take attention away from all the characters and from the social environment in which they move.

A similar objection can be made to the opening of what is, through most of its length, one of the most successful of all the episodes – 'Sirens'. Joyce said that it was written in the form of a *fuga per canonem* and it not only tells of singing and thinking about music but also mimics music in a number of effective verbal coinages – the splendid operatic cadence, for example, of 'Her wavyavyeavyheavyeavyevyevy hair un comb: 'd.' It is also loaded with supposedly verbal equivalents of a very large number of musical techniques. The insistently musical nature of the imagery is shared by the authorial narrator, Bloom, and all the other persons who visit the Ormond Hotel, and the jingle of

Boylan's jaunting car provides the lighter components of the percussion section. Simon Dedalus plays the newly tuned piano and later sings an aria from Flotow's *Martha*, Richie Goulding whistles a tune from Bellini's *La Sonnambula* and sets Bloom thinking of the plight of sleep-walking women, Fr Cowley plays an arrangement from *Don Giovanni*, Ben Dollard sings *The Croppy Boy*, and Miss Douce, the barmaid, to appreciative cries of 'sonnez la cloche', pings her elastic garter against her thigh. The easy, undemanding, and shared musical culture of Dublin fills the whole section, amid which Bloom thinks of the sexual power of the music, its way of articulating his own feelings and, since he is always the critical and thinking man, the way in which they are all swept away by it. An astonishing number of the central themes of the book and of the preoccupations of Bloom are set going in this section and carried to and fro on the tide of music.

But Joyce's urge to load every rift with significance made him conceive of the structure as being not merely about music but music itself. It is unlikely that any reader will actually identify and respond to the detail of the fugal pattern (it is, in any case, not possible to reproduce in a unilinear stream of words a genuinely contrapuntal effect), though we recognize a pattern of repetition and an indication of overlapping. But we are presented at the opening with a passage which can only have meaning as part of a pattern; it consists of fifty-nine snatches of what is to come later, mostly of less than a line in length. It has been suggested by some critics that this is an overture (though the addition of an overture to a *fuga per canonem* suggests an unsteady grasp of musical form) or, alternatively, that it represents the orchestra tuning up. There are objections to either of these if we are to think in terms of imitative form. Overtures, though they frequently contain themes from a work, are not thus constructed from incomprehensible fragments, and orchestral players, though they can often be heard practising a few bars of what they are to play, do not play sequential scraps of the whole work. Perhaps the opening can be taken as a very, very comprehensive programme note, the indication in words (incomprehensible as such notes may be) of what is to follow in another medium (here comprehensible words suggesting music). Whatever we decide, it seems to me an example of the kind of inert ingenuity which deflects attention from the real substance of the section – the pub culture of Dublin and Bloom's consciousness – to an idea of a self-subsisting technique. Moreover this is its effect whether one praises its inventive originality or, as seems equally justified, registers the objection that whatever the opening may represent it emphatically does not suggest the unity and logical economy of a fugue.

'Cyclops', the episode which follows 'Sirens', is one of the longest in the book and breaks just as radically with any kind of straightforward narrative form, whether authorial or interior monologue, but it does so in a manner which is wholly organic. Set into a vulgarly demotic account of how a boastful and anti–Semitic xenophobe known as 'the Citizen' holds forth in a pub, quarrels with Bloom, and drives him out, there is a succession of parodies of a variety of public styles. The significant difference between these parodies and those in 'Oxen of the Sun' is that these have a direct and criticizing relevance to the action in which they are interspersed. There are just over thirty parodies and the majority are of epics, medieval romances, journalistic accounts of such ceremonies as weddings, state visits, nationalist celebrations, parliamentary sessions, and rituals, but there are also sections mimicking legal terminology, a children's story, stilted literary dialogue, medical technicalities, the Bible, and a parody of the Creed. This is one of the episodes in the book in which the parallel with the *Odyssey* is clearest and most rewarding. The blinkered Citizen is the one-eyed giant Polyphemus, and Bloom, smoking a 'knockmedown cigar' which he has accepted rather than a drink, is able at the end to escape from the cave of the pub, but not before he has – ineffectively, given his audience – spoken against persecution and hatred and for love, proclaimed himself an Irishman and finally, by asserting that 'Christ was a jew like me', driven the Citizen to hurling after him the biscuit tin which stands in here for the rock which Polyphemus hurls in Homer's epic.

Most of the early parodies are of epic and romance and they are intercut with the tittle-tattle and patriotic assertions of the Citizen and his acquaintances in a manner which reminds us of, and at the same time deflates, the traditional praise of Ireland as the home of saints and heroes. When the hostility of the Citizen to Bloom first begins to manifest itself, while Bloom is still engaged in the hopeless task of trying to converse rationally about Ireland's heroes, the narrator jeers at 'his *but don't you see?* and *but on the other hand*' and, raising his glass:

> – *Sinn Fein!* says the citizen. *Sinn Fein amhain!* The
> friends we love are by our side and the foes we hate
> before us.

Immediately and appropriately there follows:

> The last funeral was affecting in the extreme. From the
> belfries far and near the funereal deathbell tolled
> unceasingly while all around the gloomy precincts rolled
> the ominous warning of a hundred muffled drums
> punctuated by the hollow booming of pieces of ordinance.

This episode comes closest in method to the traditional mock-heroic. The mundane doings of daily Dublin and the preoccupations of the drinkers who utter the patriotic pieties are mocked by likening them to the deeds of the heroes of epics or the newspapers, and Bloom, making his somewhat ignominious exit, is assimilated to Elijah (whom we have previously met several times on the handbill of the evangelist which asserts that 'Elijah is coming'), and the episode ends with a biblical assurance that crumbles in the last phrase into the vulgar!

> And there came a voice out of heaven, calling *Elijah!*
> *Elijah!* And he answered with a main cry: *Abba! Adonai!*
> And they beheld Him even Him, ben Bloom Elijah, amid
> clouds of angels ascend to the glory of the brightness at an
> angle of fortyfive degrees over Donohoe's in Little Green
> Street like a shot off a shovel.

But the effect is reciprocal. When one of the drinkers orders one more drink and says, rapping for his glass, 'God bless all here is my prayer' this meaningless piety provokes a solemn change of key: 'And at the sound of the sacring bell, headed by a crucifer with acolytes, thurifer, boatbearers, readers.' But this goes on with a list of saints, among whom coyly hides 'S. Marion Calpensis' – that is, Saint Molly Bloom of Gibraltar – which makes it hard for us to be impressed by the acolytes and thurifers. Bloom's transmogrification into Herr Professor Luitpold Blumenduft so that he can explain, in terms of 'a violent ganglionic stimulus of the nerve centres, causing the pores of the *corpora cavernosa* to rapidly dilate', why *in articulo mortis per diminutionem capitis* the hanged man may have an erection pokes fun not only at Bloom's addiction to tit-bits of popular science but also at the ponderous and self-important terminology which explains a phenomenon which the drinkers describe somewhat more vividly.

The impression created throughout this chapter is one of sprawling improvisation; the burlesques seem constantly in danger of running out of control and sometimes achieve an effect of manic monotony, especially in the lists (whether plausible or grotesquely implausible) of heroes and heroines of Irish antiquity, mourning dignitaries, priests attending a nationalist meeting, wedding guests with the names of trees, Irish beauty spots and saints. The effect of a list of thirty names in the nature of 'Miss Virginia Creeper, Miss Gladys Beech, Miss Olive Garth, Miss Blanche Maple, Mrs Maud Mahogany . . .' is not so much a parody of a newspaper list of wedding guests as of the act of producing such a symbolic parody itself.[7]

But it is inherent in the effect of such burlesques that we should feel that local bravura is in danger of disrupting the whole; the apprehension that an endless list of names may pour on for ever mixes the pedantic and the unnerving and the tension generated between the local spasm and our attempt to hold on to a sense of progression is what generates energy. The final effect of the episode is one of farcical high spirits and zany irresponsibility which not infrequently reminds us of Buck Mulligan's treatment of the preoccupations of his fellow countrymen; and in the midst of this explosion of exaggeration is the voice of Bloom, rather incompetently proclaiming those values which neither the drinkers in Barney Kiernan's nor the public voices will or can express.

In the schema which Gilbert published with Joyce's permission, the technique of 'Cyclops' is given, naturally enough, as 'gigantism'. 'Circe', too, might lay claim to this, though Joyce said that its technique was 'hallucination'. Its rhetoric, too, has much to remind us of Buck Mulligan's habit of speech and supports the view that he is closer to the authorial persona than his reputation as usurper suggests. Drunk, Stephen goes to Bella Cohen's brothel, followed by Bloom who hopes to keep him out of trouble. Joyce's technique for presenting his version of the story of the enchantress who turns men into swine is a fantasy play in which the hidden fears and suppressed urges of Bloom and Stephen are acted out in a grotesque medley of incidents from the Dublin day which we have seen and their own memories and imaginings. Stephen's mother rises from the dead to reproach him; Bloom's first hallucination is of his dead father and his last, at the point at which he bends over Stephen, is of his dead son, Rudy. There is a great deal which is deliberately disgusting or horrifying and much shameful self-glorification; but it is in the mode of farce, whether Bloom, transmogrified into a woman, is publicly degraded by Mrs Cohen, transformed into a man, or, anointed Leopold I, founds 'the new Bloomusalem in the Nova Hibernia of the future'.

In such a scene of evil enchantment the frightening and the disgusting and the grotesque are to be expected; what is not to be expected after mention of Antichrist and the last day is:

THE END OF THE WORLD
(*With a Scotch accent.*) Wha'll dance the keel row, the keel row, the keel row?

The deaf-mute idiot and stunted men and women of the opening, the sense of hunger and deformity and disease and violence are horrifying, but the explicit and stereotyped gratification of deeds previously without a name and the instant acting out of hidden fears emerge as slapstick. When Bloom is about to suffer the delicious pain of flogging by a voluptuous and high-born woman, egged on by two more of the same kind, his actual humiliation is enforced by the voices of inanimate objects:

THE TIMEPIECE

(*Unportalling*)

Cuckoo.

Cuckoo.

Cuckoo.

(*The brass quoits of a bed are heard to jingle.*)

THE QUOITS

Jigjag, Jigajiga. Jigjag.

When the English soldier, Private Carr, wants to fight Stephen the spectators greet it with the standard mock-heroic device of inappropriate language:

CISSY CAFFREY

They're going to fight. For me!

CUNTY KATE

The brave and the fair.

BIDDY THE CLAP

Methinks yon sable knight will joust it with the best.

CUNTY KATE

(*Blushing deeply.*) Nay, Madam. The gules doublet and merry Saint George for me!

As in 'Cyclops' the effect is one of excess and the struggle to reconcile this excess with the theme of the book and its narrative progress; the material is horrific enough but the technique simultaneously makes matters more vivid and, by its unstoppable outpouring of farcical specificity, obliges us to see the most unlikely matters within a comic vision. Again, as in 'Cyclops' the technical method is reciprocal in its operation: it asserts that Bloom's furtive sexuality is a manifestation of a gigantic perversity and also makes us regard gigantic perversity as being on a level with Bloom's little fantasies. The whores and the whoremistress are creatures from a diabolical underworld of the unconscious, but at the same time that sulphurous underworld is Bella trying to get Bloom to pay too much for a broken lamp and having as a regular customer a vet who pays her son's fees at Oxford. The episode ends rather as 'Cyclops' does, with a good deed from Bloom; but just as his definition of love to the Citizen is not very effective, so, here, his befriending of Stephen involves a good deal of man-of-the-world deviousness with the watch and the vision of his dead son, Rudy, which rewards him as he bends over Stephen, is subdued to the prevailing tone of burlesque – 'In his free left hand he holds a slim ivory cane with a violet bowknot. A white lambkin peeps out of his waistcoat pocket.'

The opening of 'Eumaeus', which recounts how Bloom takes Stephen to the cabman's shelter kept by a man reputed to be 'Skin-the-Goat', one of the Invincibles, buys him a cup of coffee and a bun, and then takes him home, declares its technique:

> Preparatory to anything else Mr Bloom brushed off the greater bulk of the shavings and handed Stephen the hat and ashplant and bucked him up generally in orthodox Samaritan fashion, which he very badly needed.

Joyce claimed to have written *Dubliners* 'for the most part in a style of scrupulous meanness' and this defines very well the prose of 'Eumaeus'. The rambling syntax and proliferation of hackneyed phrases project the boring stories of the sailor to which Bloom and Stephen listen, the weary gossip of nationalist derring-do, the reaction which has set in after the excitements and dangers of the brothel and the understandable tiredness of them both.

'Ithaca', which follows and tells of their journey to Bloom's home, their conversation and parting, and Bloom's retirement to bed, appears at first to be, if anything, even flatter. It is in a question-and-answer form which is the furthest from what one might expect of 'fiction'. Joyce once said that it was the 'ugly duckling' of the book and initially it appears to offer little to enjoy except an excess of documentation akin to some of the excesses of the preceding chapters. But it shows itself before the end to be a swan. The catechism is a pedantic and apparently reductive one, full of the kind of facts which Bloom loves – the way in which water is brought from the reservoir to the tap, for example, or the recital of strange coincidences concerning the results of the horse-race. But the severely factual nature of the answers, combining with our previous knowledge or partial knowledge of the matters dealt with, soon shows a surprising power to bring us unexpectedly close to the two men. There is one striking example of this near the beginning which takes us back not only through this book, but through *A Portrait of the Artist as a Young Man*, too. Bloom kneels down to light the fire and to the question 'Of what similar apparitions did Stephen think?' the answer is:

> Of others elsewhere in other times who, kneeling on one knee or on two, had kindled fires for him, of Brother Michael in the infirmary of the college of the Society of Jesus at Clongowes Wood, Sallins, in the county of

> Kildare: of his father, Simon Dedalus . . . his godmother
> Miss Kate Morkan . . . of his mother Mary, wife of
> Simon Dedalus, in the kitchen of number twelve North
> Richmond Street on the morning of the feast of Saint
> Francis-Xavier 1898.

Through most of the book, and most recently in 'Circe', Stephen's mother has been a fixed, raw-head-and-bloody-bones symbol of guilt and suffering; to find her here, lighting a fire six years before, caught in Stephen's memory before he has turned her into anything, is astonishingly moving; she is transformed from a symbol into a person.

Bloom's dead friends, of whom he is reminded when he parts from Stephen, 'companions now in various manners in different places defunct: Percy Apjohn (killed in action, Modder River), Philip Gilligan (phthisis, Jervis Street hospital) . . . Patrick Dignam (apoplexy, Sandymount)' have less need to be rescued, for, though Joyce may encourage us to think of Bloom's world as mythical and symbolic, this is not Bloom's own habit of mind.

One of the ways in which we are brought close to Bloom is by having revealed to us not, as we have throughout the book, the fluctuating contents of his mind and his momentary impulses and evasions, but the contents, the furniture, of his house – fixed, determined, and determining.

As we move towards the end of Bloom's story, we reach the most revealing, and therefore, locked drawers, in the first of which he will deposit the latest letter from Martha Clifford. The other contents of the first drawer are the higgledy-piggledy of a life: a drawing of him done by his daughter Milly as a child, an old Christmas card, a bazaar ticket, a magnifying glass, two dirty postcards, a cameo brooch of his mother's. The second drawer contains an insurance policy in Milly's favour, a record of his own savings, a docket for a grave-plot, a notice of his father's change of name by deed poll and sundry memorials of his father, including his last letter. Bloom regrets that he had once been disrespectful to the practices of Judaism and the question and its answer which follow seem to me to sum up a great deal of the realism and tolerance which make Bloom the hero of this book. In the face of all the large claims and the big words – not least those of Stephen when he parrots the theology in which he no longer believes – Bloom's conclusion, expressed with the linguistic spareness to which this episode has accustomed us, seems the epitome of sober wisdom:

> How did these beliefs and practices now appear to him?
> Not more rational than they had then appeared, not less
> rational than other beliefs and practices now appeared.

The wandering Bloom has returned to his household gods, but the wanderer Odysseus's return is enacted, too, in the mode of the comic and the muddled and the humane. And if the suitors of his Penelope are not to be put to flight and slain, then they must be put to flight by being tolerated by a man who does not wish to kill them, more because he lacks heroic vices than heroic virtues.

So, with a parody of Jewish festivals equated with his recollections of his day's doings ('The preparation of breakfast (burnt offering): intestinal congestion and premeditative defecation (holy of holies): the bath (rite of John): the funeral (rite of Samuel) . . .'), he retires to bed and the conquest of jealousy. The conquest is achieved by a number of reflections, some ignoble – that he and Boylan will share the proceeds of Molly's musical tour – some resigned – adultery is 'not more abnormal than all other altered processes of adaptation to altered conditions of existence' – and his last conviction – 'the futility of triumph or protest or vindication: the inanity of extolled virtue: the lethargy of nescient matter: the apathy of the stars'. With which he kisses Molly's rump, gives her a carefully edited account of his day's doings and sleeps – 'He rests. He has travelled.'

Having routed the suitors by tolerating them and offered paternal help to Stephen, who probably, though not certainly, will never return under his roof, Bloom must be reunited with his wife. For this Joyce returns to the internal monologue in what, in a letter of spring 1921 to Claud Sykes he called the 'amplitudinously curvilinear episode Penelope'. Molly Bloom's virtually uninterrupted and unpunctuated drowsy monologue ends in affirmation as she remembers accepting Bloom's proposal on the hill of Howth. But her preference for him can only come after she has remembered both her dissatisfactions with him and her pleasures, imaginary or actual, with others. Joyce made it clear that she is to be thought of not only as Penelope, unweaving at night what she has woven during the day, but also as an earth goddess affirming the female principle, and it is normally thus that she is discussed. Rightly so, in terms of much of the effect produced; but it should be noted that she is a strange choice for a fertility deity.

She has had two children. Of her daughter Milly she is more than a little jealous and her son Rudy is dead; since his death she has had no full conjugal relations with her husband. Various characters in the book think of her and gossip about her as a plumply provocative woman but, apart from a few furtive squeezes, she has until this afternoon's vigorous adultery with Boylan led a very unfleshly life. In 'Ithaca' we are given a list of twenty-five lovers, but her memories deny some of these and many are obviously farcical implausibilities. Even the most optimistic estimate suggests that she has endured months and very probably years on end of abstinence.

I suspect that the acceptance of her as a sexual goddess without noting this paradox came about originally because at the date of publication it was a welcome surprise to have sexual acts described and sexual words used. Molly's frankness to herself about her sensations came to be seen as the expression of a rich and fulfilled sexuality. Rich in potential it may be, but fulfilled it is not. After a Nestor who is Mr Deasy, a tedious schoolmaster, Sirens who are the barmaids of the Ormond Hotel, a Circe who is Bella Cohen, a Telemachus who is Stephen unable to accept the invitation to stay in Ithaca, and an Odysseus/Bloom who takes possession of his wife by kissing her behind and then falling asleep in the foetal position, it is right that Molly/Penelope, presented symbolically as an *Erdgeist*, should prove to experience her sexual urges nearly always in daydreams. I am not suggesting that we have no sense of her as the eternal female, but that the correspondences work both ways and that part of the effect of the last episode is of her symbolic function being subverted by her human nature and the restrictions of the Dublin society in which she lives.

Appropriately, this ending is in tune with the effect of the book as a whole. *Ulysses* is a novel in which the characters become symbolic and then assert themselves over that symbolism. Molly is far more interesting than Gea Tellus, Bloom than Everyman, Stephen than the alienated Son. Joyce's quasi-medieval desire to produce a work which could be interpreted endlessly in the way in which the theology in which he had ceased to believe could endlessly interpret the works of God comes close at times to replacing created life by the interpretation of it. Sometimes it seems that the novel is triumphant not because of, but in spite of, the conscious intentions of the author in the later phase of its writing. But, though the danger of excess is often there, the proliferation of cryptological features cannot, as it does in *Finnegans Wake*, overwhelm an interest in the human, removing the book from the grasp of the reader and consigning it to the professional student. *Ulysses* remains readable, a celebration of the daily, the mundane, the ordinary. Bloom, its hero, concerns us not because he is Odysseus or Everyman and is so identified by a multitude of hidden clues, but because he is a man. He matters not because of what he stands for or may be thought to prefigure but because the book engages our interest in an undistinguished member of our own kind, the fit hero for a great, sceptical, humane masterpiece.

Notes

1. The elementary lure of puzzles is not, of course, always easy to resist. I must confess that I am intrigued by one which, to the best of my knowledge, has not been solved. Stephen's favourite prostitute is Georgina Johnson, 'the clergyman's daughter'. She is referred to three times, on the last occasion as being 'dead and married'. She seems an odd companion for Biddy the Clap and Cunty Kate and it is difficult not to believe that there is more to her than meets the eye. But what?

2. See Richard Ellmann, *James Joyce* (1959), pp. 316–19 for a good discussion of this.

3. See, as one such comment among many, his letter of 1904 to C. P. Curran; *Letters of James Joyce*, edited by Stuart Gilbert (1957), I.

4. Few modern writers have resembled Joyce in thus writing works which encourage a kind of deciphering, but it is interesting that one great novelist of our time, Thomas Mann, should have done something of the same sort in burying clues about Frau von Tolna in *Dr. Faustus*, a work which aims to re-create in many of its aspects a late medieval outlook. See Victor A. Oswald Jr, 'Thomas Mann's *Doktor Faustus*: The Enigma of Frau von Tolna', *The Germanic Review*, 23 (December 1948), 249–53.

5. See *Letters of James Joyce*, pp. 146–47.

6. I should make clear that in imputing motives to Joyce I am imputing them to 'the consciousness behind the book at the point at which its final version was published'. It may well be that Joyce did, as has been suggested, bring his revision to a premature conclusion and would have wished, under ideal conditions, to rewrite the first sections more extensively so as to bring them into line with later ones. But this is a hypothetical speculation. He might (though it would seem unlikely), given enough time, have decided to burn the manuscript and narrate the whole book in yet another way. But we must discuss the book as it is and, as it is, it is one in which the characters are at the outset too thoroughly established as a focus of interest for anything to dethrone them.

7. I would emphasize that I am discussing the effect actually produced by the book. I think it likely, so far as one can judge Joyce's intentions, that as he elaborated this section he was thinking of the list in terms of wedding-guests-as-trees because the Citizen has spoken of the vanishing forests of Ireland and because the stake which blinds Polyphemus is made of wood and that there was, indeed, something obsessive in his revision, so that he did not think of the parody as parodying itself. But the list *is* laboriously facetious and the technique *does* subvert itself.

Chapter 11
The Reading Public and the Rise of a Profession

During this century two changes have taken place in the relationship assumed between writers and readers. The first is summed up in the concept of what was called by F. R. Leavis 'mass civilization and minority culture'; the second is the rise of literary studies as an academic profession. Though a number of those who believed most fervently that mass literacy was culturally disastrous were professional teachers of literature, the two tendencies were only loosely related. They have both affected ways of looking at literature and these effects have some similarities, but the impulses and beliefs which lie behind them are often very different.[1]

It is difficult to know how far, in this period, the readership of serious fiction changed either in its personnel or in its conception of itself in relation to the rest of the population. Those who believe that it did can certainly point out that many writers must have seen themselves in a different relationship with their public and with the larger society. Conrad was happy to be published in *Blackwood's Magazine* alongside popular writing of many kinds; Hardy saw himself as addressing a large public and was prepared, albeit reluctantly, to tailor his serial publications to the tastes of his readers and publishers; Bennett believed that he could do good critical work in his essays while boiling the pot at the same time. They all, in one way or another, thought of themselves as addressing the same general public as George Eliot or Trollope. They were often disappointed at being less successful than they hoped but it is notable that even James, though he often complained about being overlooked, did not seem to think in terms of there being a minority of specialized readers whom he was failing to find. By contrast, in the next generation, *Ulysses* first appeared in *The Little Review*, Virginia Woolf's novels were printed on her own small private press, and Lawrence's early work was published in 1910 in Ford Madox Ford's *English Review* by that editor of genius who certainly thought of his readers as a literary élite.

Such changes as this have often been interpreted as signs of a disastrous cultural decline and the consequent alienation of many writers and readers in the face of mass triviality. Forster's Education Act of 1870, it is said, created a reading public which demanded easy satisfactions and this was provided by such immensely successful organs as *Tit-Bits*, founded in 1880, and the *Daily Mail*, which first appeared in 1896. A cultural Gresham's Law began to operate, whereby bad intellectual currency drove out good.

This interpretation seems excessively simplified; it omits a great deal of the evidence and those propounding it normally use it to support strong and often unavowed political assumptions either about the striking wickedness of newspaper magnates who debauch public taste or about the inherent debauchability of the populace. The appetite for sensational triviality was certainly profoundly disheartening for those who had hoped that when literacy became the norm the reading tastes of the majority would be as serious as those of working people who had, against the odds, succeeded in acquiring education in previous centuries. But this was always an unreal expectation and the presence throughout the nineteenth century of popular trash should have warned such optimists. James Catnash, who sold the sensational 'dying confessions' of criminals by the million, was only the most successful of many, and G. W. M. Reynolds's *Mysteries of London* and *Mysteries of the Court of London* ran for 624 penny numbers.[2] Reynolds's scabrous republicanism is stirring stuff, but it would be hard to suggest that the millions who read his works were responding at a more refined level than the readers of *Tit-Bits*.[3]

Nor is the evidence for the taste of the public at the turn of the century uniformly gloomy. The decades after Forster's Act saw the end of the expensive three-decker library novel and the general spread of cheaper fiction, both good and bad, with large circulations, as well as the proliferation of cheap reprint series, of which the best known is probably the Everyman's Library, founded in 1906. The concept of a saving remnant holding out for a while as the tide of rubbish rises about them will hardly survive such facts or a scrutiny of the figures for sales of serious fiction. Most of the writers with whom I am concerned in this study were published by commercial firms and achieved sales which enabled them to live by the pen.

But a concept of the serious writer and his readers as a conscious minority in a debased cultural situation certainly existed for many and has a cultural significance whether or not it rested on an accurate sociological analysis, not least because it has figured so largely in later accounts. By the time of the publication of *Ulysses* in 1922, say, a number of individuals and groups saw themselves as supporters of genius against philistinism, whether this philistinism was the indifference of the Boots' Lending Library public or the repressive habits of Home Secretaries. Though it seems to me unlikely that there was in reality a greater gap between the reader of serious literature and the mass of the population in 1920 than there had been a hundred or two hundred years before, yet there was one striking difference: the tastes of the readers of the popular press were obvious and undeniable. In the past it had always been possible to hope that education would produce a larger informed reading public and critics were bound to be disheartened, even if the actual public for serious works of literature was larger, to see that it was now a smaller proportion of those who could read.

The sense of alienation of the writer and the serious reader from society extends, of course, far beyond strictly literary matters; there is a natural tendency for those whose main concern is literature to think that literary taste is a reliable index of emotional and moral life. The deplorable literary tastes of a large number of their fellow citizens appeared to many as an indication of a general emotional and social degradation, though in fact it is observable that readers of *Tit-Bits* and the romances published by Messrs Mills and Boon are every bit as able to manifest decency and even subtlety and refinement in their personal lives as their literary betters. What we see developing from about the 1920s onwards, though it can be traced back at least as far as Ruskin, is the concept of a vanished golden age, a harmonious society of men and women whose work had a meaning for them and whose folk culture embodied permanent values, and its replacement by a rootless, half-educated proletariat which was progressively debased by industrial changes and the machinations of greedy newspaper magnates and the pulp fiction industry. Leavis propounds this view in *Mass Civilization and Minority Culture* (1930) and it underlies much of his criticism; it can be seen in a more specifically political form in such writings of T. S. Eliot as *Notes Towards the Definition of Culture* (1948), and it is to this, I think, that one can trace the sometimes grotesque overvaluation of D. H. Lawrence not as a novelist but as a diagnostician of the ills of the modern world.

There is one striking change in the periodicals in which literary works were discussed and new works published which suggests a change not in the mass public but in the élite one; the great journals of the nineteenth century discussed literature alongside politics, economics, and social comment; many of the significant periodicals of the new century tended to be more specifically literary. Though other matters were not totally absent in such magazines as Ford's *English Review*, Eliot's *Criterion*, Middleton Murry's *Adelphi*, and Harriet Weaver's *The Egoist* (in which *A Portrait of the Artist as a Young Man* first appeared) they were addressed primarily to a literary public. Many of them were conceived as proselytizing organs and, so far as they concerned themselves with social issues, did so with literary and especially with new and experimental literary works as their starting-point. Increasingly, too, as the academic study of English grew, this specialized public came to be associated with the universities. This can be seen very clearly in one of the most influential of all the journals, *Scrutiny*, founded in 1932, which lasted until 1953 and which provided the chief forum for the ideas of F. R. Leavis and those associated with him. Unlike earlier magazines, it was not only edited by academics but also addressed to those for whom the study of literature was a primary occupation.

The rise of the discipline of English in universities happened surprisingly late. Cambridge University did not have a professor of English until 1911, though Oxford, buttressing the new subject with linguistic claims, had set up an English Honours School in 1893.[4] But by 1940 English studies were firmly established in this country and in the United States. There was thus a far greater chance in 1940 than at the beginning of the century that a man or woman introducing a new book to the public was a professional academic. The writer of a book about some established figure of the past was almost certain to be a professional. This tendency has increased vastly since 1940 and it is now true to say that virtually every book which I mention in this study is a set text. More significantly, many of their readers will have first encountered them as set texts. Nor, though I wish to draw attention to some of the disadvantages of the professionalization of literary studies, can I deny that I am an academic writing a book for a public which will be to some extent an academic one.

The terms of literary discussion in 1890 tended to be those of a confident ruling class, for whom literature was one interest among many, even if the personal status of many literary journalists was not actually what the tone implied. At its best this situation produced well-informed, shrewd judgements of literature, alongside similar judgements about public affairs; at its worst it produced book chat of an excruciatingly self-indulgent and cosy kind. By contrast discussion now suggests that literary study is a communal enterprise, moving forward on a broad front and engaged in by trained professionals. This was neatly exemplified by an article in a recent journal which compared the number of critical studies devoted to six modern novelists and noted that 'Woolf criticism and scholarship has shown a 25.59% increase in the 1980s; it may be a surprise, even a shock, to Conradians to note that Conrad items have decreased 17.63%'.[5]

The gains are obvious; we can, for almost all writers, take good editions for granted, together with an abundance of such supplementary matter as letters and biographies; factual accuracy and a sense of responsibility before the text can normally be taken for granted; a greater sophistication in distinguishing connotative and denotative factors (the stated and the implied, the text and the subtext) and a greater understanding of the implications of genre and of the nature of literary tradition are widespread. Not least, a number of good critics have been put in a position to spend their time at a job for which they are suited and this has been of particular importance in making accessible new and difficult works.

But when we consider the two chief ways in which the literary profession has affected our approach to literature – the determination of a canon and the establishment of an appropriate critical approach to individual works – we see that there have been substantial disadvantages which are rooted in the nature of a profession. It is a popular truism that all professions are conspiracies against the public; one does not need to go as far as this to recognize that they are inevitably exclusive; the academic literary one is no different from others in feeling the need to distance itself from the claims of non-members to know how to do the job. This natural tendency has, I think, been exacerbated because literary critics are always in danger of feeling that their skills are not immediately apparent. They must all, at one time or another, have had the experience of finding that nuclear physicists, say, can talk to them intelligently about novels while they are quite unable to reciprocate by sensible comments about quantum mechanics. This fact has surely not been without influence in the tendency of some critics to elaborate a methodology and its accompanying technical vocabulary which implies that the uninitiated are not able properly to understand works of literature until they put themselves to school to the critics. In extreme cases we see books processed as part of a critical argument, with the implication – and sometimes even the proclamation – that this argument is in itself as important as the books which it uses as raw material for its generalizations.[6]

The most obvious way in which professionalization has served readers ill is its tendency to overvalue those elements in works which give the critic something to do; normally this means either the explication of difficulties or the reinterpretation of works away from their apparent meaning. Most common readers (readers, that is to say, whose immediate reaction to liking a novel is to procure another book by the same writer rather than to read a critic or write a dissertation) are very interested in the characters in books. They tend to talk as if they were real people, though they are not such fools as to believe that they are; it is simply that this is the obvious way of talking about them and they do not feel obliged to mince their words for fear of accusations of naïve mimeticism. They are also concerned if not with the plot (though some often are), then with a sense of some forward movement through the book. These are among the most elementary elements in fiction and in their liking for them common readers resemble the authors of practically every novel written in any language whatever and virtually every critic and commentator until very recent times. Yet, as I have said in the previous chapter, a vast amount of critical discussion of Joyce passes by questions of character and happening in favour of quasi-cryptographic devices of a mechanical but explicable kind. A discussion of the works of Conrad as self-referential metafictions is of the same nature.

The emphasis on that which needs elucidation or on the need to reinterpret works into new categories draws support very often from a misleading metaphor of surface and depth, with its implication that what we can all see is superficial and thus not worthy of discussion, while what is only to be found by excavation is profound and hence the proper subject for scholarly activity. It is, alas, not unusual for innocent readers of major works like *Tess of the d'Urbervilles, The Rainbow*, or *The Secret Agent* to seek help from readily available and often widely recommended critical anthologies and to come away either with a baffled sense that they must be stupid not to have noticed hidden significances brought up from the depths by critics busy scraping the barrel, or with a sense that no critics are worth reading because they are not interested in the central features of the novel. Either reaction is deplorable but my preference must be for the latter.

The establishment of a canon is clearly affected by the professionalization of literary studies; it could, indeed, be said to be one of its purposes.[7] Moreover a canon enshrined in syllabuses is not easy to change. It seems to be agreed among publishers, for example, that it is very hard to revive minor writers of the inter-war years and to keep them in print unless they find a place on a syllabus. Nor will theoretically based efforts to overturn a canon lead to much greater freedom of choice for the ordinary reader.

The canon of modern literature differs from that of the past in that it has been established in part by the efforts of academic critics. Our estimate of Fielding or Dickens may differ from that of our predecessors, but they were firmly established as major writers long before the rise of English departments. The status of our modern classics owes much to academia. One of the tasks of critics throughout the earlier part of this century, for example, was the valuable one of helping to create the taste for works which broke with established tradition. This involved emphasizing – sometimes polemically overemphasizing – the importance and effectiveness of what was new or experimental in these works with a consequent taking for granted of what was not. But what is taken for granted can easily come to seem unimportant. Once the task was achieved, therefore, and writers such as Joyce, Lawrence, and Virginia Woolf were accepted, the natural tendency of critics to concentrate attention upon what they themselves can do and what the general reader cannot had the effect of making the tradition of Modernism seem not merely one tendency among a number but the only one. The persistent undervaluation of Bennett and the neglect of such writers as Henry Handel Richardson has been brought about in part because they do not fit in with the generalizations which were constructed primarily to link together a number of difficult works.[8] One paradoxical effect of this has been to make Bennett, for example, seem not only less important but also much simpler than is justified. He is often a subtle novelist but his works do not lend themselves easily to the critical procedures which emphasize the spatial as against the temporal aspects of the books and which seek symbolically thematic elements as the chief carriers of meaning. It is not that such elements are not present, but they are not dominant and we have paid less attention to matters of narrative dynamics, variations of pace and intensity, and manœuvres to do with suspense, than they deserve.

Ford Madox Ford, by contrast, seems to me to be a writer who has benefited unduly from the preoccupations of criticism. He was an editor of genius; Lawrence was only one of the writers who owed him much. He was very interested in literary techniques; there seems no doubt that he had for a time a very great influence on Conrad and gave him much help in discussion of the need for the *mot juste* and the potentialities of what he called *progression d'effet*. The manipulation of time which plays so large a part in Conrad's works was probably encouraged by Ford and, in so far as Conrad thought of himself as a beginner in an art in which Ford was already an established performer, he must have been a great liberator. As what he would certainly have been happy to call *un homme de lettres* he has an undoubted importance which is not diminished by the fame of his creative memory of various notable figures and his appearances under a thin disguise in Hemingway's *The Sun Also Rises (Fiesta)*.

But in his novels very real abilities are vitiated by central flaws; the abilities are mostly ones which, in their eschewing of the obvious, require analysis; the flaws are elementary but basic. He wrote thirty novels but by general consent his claims to serious consideration must rest on the tetralogy *Parade's End*[9] and *The Good Soldier* (1915). He is often astonishingly good at evoking a scene or a face or a snatch of conversation and at moving the reader from scene to scene so as to achieve unusual perspectives and juxtapositions. But the central personages and the issues of human feelings are very often totally implausible. Christopher Tietjens, the central character of *Parade's End* – central enough for it often to be referred to as 'the Tietjens tetralogy' – is presented as the last English squire, the last Tory, the represent-ative of all those traditional values which are under threat from the Great War and a general moral collapse.[10] Persecuted at the hands of an unspeakably selfish and unfaithful wife, aided by a collection of time-servers, he behaves according to Ford's concept of the ideal code of a country gentleman, failing to understand a good deal of what is going on around him and remaining quixotically chaste in his relations with a young woman who loves him. It would be possible to make a comic novel from the discrepancies between his conception of how he should behave and the consequence of his behaviour on other people. But Ford remains deadly serious, which has the effect of turning Tietjens into a monster of bumbling self-regard.

The case is even clearer in *The Good Soldier*. This is a rather Jamesian work, narrated by a rich and cultured American, in which Ford shows extraordinary dexterity in working over and over the relationships of the narrator, his wife, and a married couple who are their friends and close companions at various watering places. By first concealing matters from us and then revealing them he makes us constantly reassess what we have taken as reliable perceptions. But he requires us to take seriously this narrator whose wife has, by claiming that her heart has been strained by a rough transatlantic crossing, persuaded him not to consummate their marriage for twelve years while cuckolding him for a good deal of this time with his best friend, whose wife is well aware of her husband's numerous infidelities. Only a complete fool, one feels, could have lived in this *ménage à quatre* and retained illusions about the lecherous good soldier of the title, but Ford presents him as a thoughtful man whose judgement we must often respect. In concentrating on the technical legerdemain he forgets the actual possibilities of human feelings.

It seems to me obvious that we can only take Ford as a significant novelist if we give all our attention to the elaborate narrative strategies and the subtle effects of echoes and repeated symbols while dismissing as too elementary for discussion questions of psychological plausibility and consequent moral judgements about the results of our actions, including our stupidities.

Belief in a chosen few writers as part of an intellectual and spiritual élite in a world of mass shoddiness is less popular now than it was; it can still be found but its heyday was in the years between the wars and for some little time thereafter. The professionalization of literary studies, on the contrary, shows no decline. The former appears to have influenced a few writers and a number of influential critics. The latter influenced no writers (with the possible exception of Joyce) in the period with which I am concerned in this study, but the situation now is far different. There are writers still in mid-career who know that they are the subject of theses, critical works, and bibliographies and that their novels figure in academic syllabuses. It is difficult to believe that they can all be totally unaffected by this when they envisage their likely readers.

Belief in an élite had far more political implications and could easily include a distaste for the professionalization of study. This professionalization can be political, but usually it is not except at a highly theoretical level; indeed it frequently discusses novels in a manner which removes them altogether from the daily world of action. What both tendencies do is imply the unimportance of the common reader, whether because he is assumed to be tainted by shoddiness or because he is academically untrained. Since it is easier to overawe people by saying that they lack specialized knowledge than by telling them that they are emotionally inferior, academia can probably do more harm than claims for the minority against the mass. Nobody can feel happy about this situation except those who wish literary criticism to be a purely minority pursuit in which professionals talk to professionals about theories, while those outside the walls get on with reading novels. There are those who take this view of the critic's function but they would find it hard to explain it to the novelists about whom they write.

Notes

1. Not the least of the differences between them is that the concept of mass civilization and minority culture now seems a historical phenomenon whose heyday is over, whereas the vast increase in the academic profession has occurred since the Second World War. Though this is outside the period with which this book deals it seems important to discuss it since I and my readers, looking back, are not unaffected by present circumstances.

2. A good account of the popular cheap fiction of the nineteenth century is given in Richard D. Altick's *The English Common Reader* (1957). See bibliography for further discussions of publishing and popular taste.

3. There is some reason to believe that one of the readers of this much-despised periodical was Joseph Conrad. It is possible that his short story 'The Black Mate' was originally written for a competition in it. See Z. Najder, *Joseph Conrad, A Chronicle* (1983), pp. 114 and 339, and J. Baines, *Joseph Conrad, a Critical Biography* (1960), pp. 84–85.

4. There is a very interesting and often entertaining account of the struggles to found or to prevent the foundations of departments of English and also of the nature of such departments in John Gross's *The Rise and Fall of the Man of Letters* (1969).

5. David Leon Higdon, 'Conrad in the Eighties: A Bibliography and some Observations', *Conradiana*, 17 (1985), 214–49. It is fair to say that in taking calculations to two places of decimals Higdon is not unaware of what is comic in an issue which should be taken seriously.

6. There are, of course, circumstances in which literary works can provide evidence for doctrines or systems which take the reader into account only as a factor in the total situation. Some sociological studies, for example, are of this nature, though it is interesting that they are usually most enlightening when dealing with very elementary works. But this is irrelevant to any claim that they can enlighten the reader concerning the meaning or value of the works.

7. There is a good account of the concept of 'institutionalized competence' and its role in establishing a canon in Frank Kermode's 'Can We Say Absolutely Anything We Like?' and 'Institutional Control of Interpretation', reprinted in his *Essays on Fiction* (1983).

8. Richardson's work is, of course, well recognized in her native Australia, but see Karen McLeod's *Henry Handel Richardson, a Critical Study* (Cambridge, 1985), for the presentation of the case for regarding her as a significant English novelist.

9. Ford referred to the tetralogy by this name, though it does not appear on the original editions. The volumes are *Some Do Not . . .* (1924), *No More Parades* (1925), *A Man Could Stand Up* (1926), and *Last Post* (1928). Ford later said that he regretted the last volume and the most recent edition from the Bodley Head omits it and Graham Greene, in the introduction to that edition, claims that this is the first publication of the trilogy which Ford wanted.

10. The resemblance to him of Guy Crouchback, the hero of Evelyn Waugh's war trilogy, is extraordinarily close; they share good blood, bumbling inefficiency, vicious wives, a belief that standards are crumbling, and the virtually uncritical adoration of their creators.

Chapter 12

D. H. Lawrence: Our Bert versus Our Lorenzo

D. H. Lawrence was an immensely productive writer whose labours, pursued over years of ill health and, indeed, years of slow dying of tuberculosis, can only be called heroic. He was also an extremely uneven one. Had he written always at his best, as in the finest parts of *Sons and Lovers* (1913), *The Rainbow* (1915), *Women in Love* (1920), and many of his short stories, it could be argued that he is the greatest of twentieth-century novelists. Had he written always at his worst, as in, for example, *The Plumed Serpent* (1926), he would be not merely a bad but a deplorable writer. The reason why I use the word 'deplorable' is because, unlike Bennett or Joyce or Conrad but rather like Kipling, he is a writer who sees his task as that of a man with a mission to diagnose the evils of society and suggest cures, and his rhetoric is one which seeks to involve us in his mission.[1] We cannot dissociate ourselves from his struggles to change human consciousness so that we are likely to feel that we cannot merely dislike *The Plumed Serpent*; it is our duty to oppose it.

It is not a matter of chance that the prosecution in 1960 of his last novel, *Lady Chatterley's Lover* (1928), was the crucial test of what was to be acceptable in the fictional treatment of sexual feelings and actions (though it must be said that the advantage which has since been taken of the freedom won by that defence would mostly have horrified him). He wrote the book three times and his letters make it clear that one of the purposes of the last version was to make it impossible for readers to overlook his passionate conviction that sexual love is not merely one of the most important of human feelings but also an index of the health of both the individual and society and that this cannot be made clear until the writer is freed from restraints as to what he can describe and the language in which he can describe it.[2]

The task of the critic confronted by Lawrence's works seems to me a particularly difficult one. The moral and political questions which he addresses are central ones and he has been a guru to many; his beliefs are sometimes embodied in the novels and stories but sometimes seem to be superimposed on them so that one has the sense of frenzied rhetoric from a soap-box. Sometimes these beliefs and perceptions seem to me to be profoundly true and sometimes perversely false. In some of the novels – particularly *Women in Love* – the critic sometimes feels that he is digging out a great novel from a mass of inferior matter in which the novelist has buried it. This runs the risk not merely of encouraging arrogance in the critic but also of presenting a more obviously palatable but shallower and less complex work.

By general consent Lawrence's first major novel is the autobiographical *Sons and Lovers*. The accuracy or otherwise of this as autobiography does not seem important; what is significant is that we have in it a sense of someone writing about a society from the middle of it and creating what at the time must have seemed very new – a picture of a mining community from the point of view of a miner's family, not conceived as a sociological explanation but as a depiction of what is taken for granted. In this the book is in sharp contrast to many of his later works; even in his next novel, *The Rainbow*, he writes about the Nottinghamshire mining communities as if he is looking at them from the outside and finding them, as Ursula Brangwen perceives Wiggiston, 'like a skin disease' (12).

Lawrence's own conception of the novel is given in a well-known letter of 19 November 1912 to Edward Garnett:

> a woman of character and refinement goes into the lower class, and has no satisfaction in her own life. She has a passion for her husband, so the children are born of passion, and have heaps of vitality. But as her sons grow up she selects them as lovers – first the eldest, then the second. These sons are *urged* into life by their reciprocal love of their mother – urged on and on. But when they come to manhood, they can't love, because their mother is the strongest power in their lives, and holds them. – It's rather like Goethe and his mother and Frau von Stein and Christiana – . As soon as the young men come into contact with women, there's a split. William gives his sex to a fribble, and his mother holds his soul. But the split kills him, because he doesn't know where he is. The next son gets a woman who fights for his soul – fights his mother. The son loves the mother – all sons hate and are jealous of the father. The battle goes on between the mother and the girl, with the son as object. The mother gradually proves stronger, because of the tie of blood. The son decides to leave his soul in his mother's hands, and, like his elder brother, go for passion. He gets passion. Then the split begins to tell again. But, almost

unconsciously, the mother realises what is the matter, and begins to die. The son casts off his mistress, attends to his mother dying. He is left in the end naked of everything, with the drift towards death.[3]

The relationship between the mother and the father, Mr and Mrs Morel, is the focus of interest for the first third of the novel, and what is striking about it is the way in which Lawrence makes our sympathies ebb and flow between the two. Morel is physically stronger than his wife, he has control over the family's money because he earns it and he can drink it away in the pub and leave his wife short of cash for necessities. Mrs Morel appears to be in a weak position, yet what we see is a steady erosion of her husband, turning him into something more brutal, more clumsy, and more worthy of contempt. But he is a man who can recognize contempt when it is directed against him, and this part of the book, and, indeed, those passages later in the work in which he plays a part are filled with a sense of loss and of the spoiling of two people through their incompatibility.

The technical method which Lawrence employs in the first part of the book seems basically the traditional one of combining dramatic scenes with an authorial commentary. The scenes often culminate in very vivid and sharply observed descriptions of natural objects which seem to sum up or embody the emotional states of the characters. There is a particularly fine example in the second chapter. After a scene of mingled embarrassment, humiliation, and hostility in which Morel comes home and spoils Mrs Morel's tea with the visiting parson, in which we feel some sympathy for the hard-working man who finds himself merely a disturbance in the midst of this elegance from which he is shut out but where we also see that he is self-pitying, Mrs Morel goes for a walk. The calming of her mind as she watches children playing on the cricket field is conveyed with great precision:

Children played in the bluish shadow of the pavilion.
Many rooks, high up, came cawing home across the
softly-woven sky. They stooped in a long curve down
into the golden glow, concentrating, cawing, wheeling,
like black flakes on a slow vortex, over a tree-clump that
made a dark boss among the pasture.   (2)

The authorial commentary is more problematical; it often appears at first sight to combine extreme dogmatism with arbitrariness, yet it is clearly central to the whole way in which Lawrence conceives of human character and relationships. There is, for example, in Chapter 4 a description of young Paul telling his father that he has won a prize in a painting competition; the conversation dies away and Lawrence comments: 'And that was all. Conversation was impossible between the father and any other member of the family. He was an outsider. He had denied the God in him.' If we are to understand what Lawrence is saying in such a passage as this we must bear in mind that throughout – and this includes authorial commentary – Lawrence is insisting that spontaneous shifts of feeling are fundamental to our experience. The quality of our lives is to be measured not necessarily by our long-term conclusions but by our moment-by-moment experiences. But this does not imply any element of the tentative in the way in which perceptions are registered. Lawrence rarely writes a scene which leaves us with the feeling that he does not altogether understand what his characters' experiences mean and that he, like the reader, is exploring them. Such an effect is common in, for example, Arnold Bennett; we are shown the interaction between the sisters in *The Old Wives' Tale* and we have to decide what is implied in some of the scenes; Bennett, we are made to feel, knows no more than we do. But Lawrence always gives the impression that he knows. It is not in his nature to state or to imply an uncertainty; he wants to get as close as he can to the moment of lived experience and he obviously feels that when we live through an experience we know what is happening to us. But shortly afterwards a new stimulus may present itself, a new mood overcome us and we feel something totally different. We must be prepared, then, for successive contradictory dogmatic statements.

This applies to Lawrence's own commentary as much as to the registration of the responses of characters. We normally expect authorial statements to present general conclusions by the writer, but in Lawrence they represent an immediate response. Lawrence's attitude to his characters is not fixed and his commentary is not static but dynamic. This is one of the more obvious reasons why it is misleading to extract any comment from a work and claim that it expresses Lawrence's conclusion. The strength of this method is its astonishing ability, when combined with sharply realized scenes, to involve us in the warring contradictions in the minds of his characters – in the awareness in *Sons and Lovers*, for example, that we are trapped not by what we hate but by what we love. Its weakness is that we sometimes have the sense that there is an unavowed basis of judgement, that Lawrence is implying a theory which he does not substantiate, which, indeed, he cannot substantiate in terms of action.

The theme which Lawrence set out in the letter to Garnett which I have quoted is followed through for the latter two-thirds of the novel in Paul Morel's search for a relationship first with Miriam Leivers, the daughter of a local farmer, a girl who is temperamentally akin to his mother, and also with Clara Dawes, with whom he achieves physical fulfilment but from whom he separates. But another theme comes to the fore as the book proceeds, a theme which is to recur in Lawrence's later novels: the search by the protagonist for some relationship which is large enough to take him out of himself, something large enough to give importance to personal feelings but which will transcend them. At one point in what Lawrence calls Paul's courtship of Miriam, though it as often as not presents itself as a desperate struggle, he feels:

> Never any relaxing, never any leaving himself to the
> great hunger and impersonality of passion; he must be
> brought back to a deliberate, reflective creature. As if from
> a swoon of passion she called him back to the littleness,
> the personal relationship. He could not bear it. 'Leave me
> alone – leave me alone!' he wanted to cry; but she wanted
> him to look at her with eyes full of love. His eyes, full of
> the dark impersonal fire of desire, did not belong to
> her.   (11)

We may well feel that Paul is blaming Miriam for what, in terms of the theme of the book, is his own incapacity, but by this stage in the story Lawrence seems at times so close to Paul that he accepts his judgement. If the latter part of the novel seems thus distorted it is surely because by the time he was writing it Lawrence was already set on the quest for a belief or a way of feeling or a doctrine which was to preoccupy him for the rest of his life.

His next novel, *The Rainbow*, starts with a series of generalizations about the men and women of the Brangwen family, whose history through a number of generations is the subject of the book. Lawrence talks about the people as if they have some kind of racial consciousness, some common perceptions which assimilate them to shared life and though in the first section of the first chapter he identifies a named character, Tom Brangwen, yet he continues to make general statements about 'the mother' and 'the Brangwen wife of the Marsh' which cannot refer to any specific peson. This opening, with its highly quotable rhetoric – 'They took the udders of the cows, the cows yielded milk and pulsed against the hands of the men, the pulse of the blood of the teats of the cows beat into the pulse of the hands of the men' – has often been cited as a key to the theme of the book; but in fact the generalizations of the first part are not fulfilled later. They are not, indeed, even fulfilled quite early. After telling us that it is the women who look outwards to the aristocratic and the educated, we find that it is in fact Tom, after one of his jaunts into the town, who 'dreamed day and night, absorbedly, of a voluptuous woman and of the meeting with a small withered foreigner of ancient breeding'. Once Lawrence is creatively engaged with an individual character the theories and the generalizations fall away.

The Rainbow is basically a family chronicle of three generations or, if one includes the very short passage at the beginning about Tom's father, Alfred, and his unnamed wife, four. In each generation life becomes more complicated in that the people have more intellectual development and more interaction with the outside world which they must bring into harmony with their basic impulses.

Tom, a farmer, marries Lydia Lensky, the widow of a Polish refugee. The tides of feeling which flow between Tom and Lydia and within the family, towards and from the children, are deep and intense, but they are not usually articulated by them, and Lawrence certainly wants us to believe that issues of social affairs and politics, which bulk fairly large later in the book, are not for them of any particular concern. Lydia's daughter, Anna, who has become Tom's particular favourite, more indeed than any of his own immediate children, forms the representative second generation. She marries her cousin Will, and though their feelings are frequently difficult to articulate and akin to those of the older generation, yet Will is concerned with his community, and his job is one which is not given to him in the sense that Tom's is, but which he has to find. His abilities at wood-carving and music are an important part of his life, and a part of the struggle between him and Anna is concerned with the relationship between those impulses in him which go out to such public activities and his feelings within the family. In the third generation, their daughter Ursula is in many ways the New Woman, about whom so many people at the time were writing, and who was so important a kind of person for Lawrence. Her race is indeed only half-run by the end of this novel, and it continues, though her character has changed a good deal so that the whole conception of her is a little inconsistent, in Women in Love. She comes into contact with the Women's Movement, works as a teacher, goes to the University and endeavours to come to terms with most of the issues current at the time.

It is a long novel and in general its pace seems slow, so that some of the most impressive parts emerge naturally as an effect of the passage of time and the gradual shifts of feeling. As Anna moves towards the man she is going to marry her stepfather becomes jealous. This is not presented in a single scene; we are given a sense of a growing, reluctant recognition on his part that his feelings are not as he would wish them to be. Again, in Chapter 9, after Tom has been drowned in the flood on his way back to the farm from the town, there is a superb passage when Lydia answers the questions of the small girl, Ursula, about her two grandfathers and Lydia remembers, with mixed feelings, her first husband. The sudden surging back of vivid memories and feelings which have not, for a long time, been present in Lydia's mind depends upon the sense that Lawrence has given us of the slow accretion of experience which creates a person and which can, until the crucial moment comes, seemingly obscure parts of the past.

The provisional title for an early version of the novel, while he was still engaged in the task of separating it off from that combination of this book and *Women in Love* which he called *The Sisters*, was *The Wedding Ring*, and it is clear that the discovering of one's mate is for all the people in the book far and away the most important issue in life. But Lawrence makes no distinction between sexual and other feelings in the sense that he sees the quality of feelings in one sphere of life as being an index of feelings in all others – feelings to do with childhood and parenthood, naturally enough, but also about work and politics and art. If Tom and Lydia, after a period of estrangement, come back together, this, we are meant to feel, is because something has come right in them, not only in terms of a flaring up of attraction or a swallowing of resentment but because they are better in all ways. All the characters for whom we are meant to care seek perfection in their marital relationships because this implies the nearest which human beings can come to general perfection.

Nor does his language leave one in any doubt that he conceives of the most fundamental human feelings as being in some way religious. The early married life of Anna and Will is a stormy one. It is not, as we would expect in some other novels, that they have specific quarrels about specific things, but rather that their feelings ebb and flow, and, being the kind of people for whom these feelings are more fundamental than anything else which they can conceive in life, they are frequently in a condition of extremity. When they are, the language is not only highly rhetorical, but unequivocally religious. Of Will Lawrence says: 'Then as if his soul had six wings of bliss he stood absorbed in praise, feeling the radiance from the Almighty beat through him like a pulse, as he stook in the upright flame of praise, transmitting the pulse of Creation' and of Anna: 'She was subject to him as to the Angel of the Presence.'

Ursula, in her turn, expresses her quickening sexual feelings in terms of the religion by which she is, at the time, preoccupied, terms which are to be taken up very strikingly and importantly in *Women in Love*: 'So utterly did she desire the Sons of God should come to the daughters of men; and she believed more in her desire and its fulfilment than in the obvious facts of life.'

But there is a paradox at the heart of Lawrence's method in this book. It is akin to the difficulties which I have described in *Sons and Lovers*: Lawrence's dynamic and apparently dogmatic commentary on the fluctuating moods of his characters. But the problem is more acute in *The Rainbow* because the issues with which the book deals are so much wider and are often, particularly in the sections concerned with Ursula, matters of general social principles or public debate about which the reader may have beliefs and judgements.

Lawrence is concerned with the most intimate feelings, those which it is hardest to put into words and for which no established categories or phraseologies exist, and he believes that these feelings cannot be separated from the practicalities, even the political and social principles of mundane life. Yet he often endeavours to make those feelings clear by apparently unambiguous and often lengthy statements. The consequence is that though he persuades us that the tides of feeling are more mysterious than previous writers have usually suggested, that logical cause and effect are often ineffective as explanation, that moments of sensation are more violent than they seem in retrospect, yet because the voice which is telling us this seems to be Lawrence's voice we tend to feel that too much is being asserted and asserted too frenetically.

When he produces a scene in which we are sure that the feelings are, without doubt, the local and individual ones of that person at that time, the effect is convincing. There is, for example, a passage in Chapter 13 which deals with one of the crucial experiences of Ursula when she is a schoolteacher, her beating of the boy Williams. As she leaves school her hand is bruised by a potato thrown at her by one of the groups of boys. She waits for the tram, giving no sign that she has been hurt, and we are told:

> She was afraid and strange. It was to her quite strange and
> ugly, like some dream where she was degraded. She
> would have died rather than admit it to anyone. She could
> not look at her swollen hand. Something had broken in
> her; she had passed a crisis. Williams was beaten, but at a
> cost.

The language is, indeed, extreme, but it is the extremity of a recognizable moment, not a general judgement about her nature. It is related to a complex situation in which her feelings about the schoolmaster who seems to despise her, an intense dislike of the boy, her awareness that if she is to survive as a teacher she cannot yield and her repugnance at brutality, including her own, are all simultaneously present.

It is not an accident that most critics single out certain passages in the book as particularly effective, for these are the ones where, most strikingly, Lawrence discovers the physical happenings and objects which give an external equivalent for the feelings which he is presenting. Two examples should make this clear. The first is the latter part of Chapter 2 in which Tom takes his stepchild Anna to feed the cows while her mother is in childbirth. His action seems unforced to us not only because it is in his nature but because we recognize in it what we all share. It is all very logical; the child must be distracted; she goes on screaming 'I want my mother', and nobody can do anything with her. Under these circumstances one distracts a child, and Tom does distract her. He takes her away from the servant, Tilly, and out into the barn and the description brings us, the readers, as well as Anna, into a new relationship with Tom. The routine of fetching fodder quiets them both until:

> the two sat still listening to the snuffing and breathing of
> cows feeding in the sheds communicating with this small
> barn. The lantern shed a soft, steady light from one wall.
> All outside was still in the rain. He looked down at the
> silky folds of the paisley shawl. It reminded him of his
> mother. She used to go to church in it. He was back again
> in the old irresponsibility and security, a boy at home.

We have moved away from our preoccupation with the situation of Lydia, have been distracted, because it is a revelation that Tom is recovering something, not merely feeling very close to Anna but also remembering things about himself as a child.

My second example is from Chapter 4 when Anna and Will come together while piling up the sheaves of oats. Before this they have been self-conscious and awkward. Anna suggests that they should put up some sheaves and they begin to work together. Clearly this can be seen as part of the general biblical symbolism of the work and doubtless is intended as such, but the more striking immediate effect is that they submit themselves to a rhythm of work and are brought together by a force seemingly outside themselves.

> They worked together, coming and going, in a rhythm,
> which carried their feet and their bodies in tune. She
> stooped, she lifted the burden of the sheaves, she turned
> her face to the dimness where he was, and went with her
> burden over the stubble. She hesitated, set down her
> sheaves, there was a swish and hiss of mingling oats, he
> was drawing near and she must turn again.

The self-consciousness fades until

> There was only the moving to and fro in the moonlight,
> engrossed, the swinging in the silence, that was marked

only by the splash of sheaves, and silence, and a splash of
sheaves. And ever the splash of his sheaves broke swifter,
beating up to hers, and ever the splash of sheaves recurred
monotonously, unchanging, and ever the splash of his
sheaves beat nearer.

The incantatory repetitions are justified by the monotony of the
actions, which function as a metaphor for the inevitability of their
union.

But when Lawrence's accounts of his characters are not tied down
to specific happenings and objects which provoke and articulate the
feelings, he too often appears arbitrary, and, as I have suggested, the
risk is greater in this novel than in *Sons and Lovers* because his characters are far more often caught up in public issues about which
Lawrence has strong feelings and about which he wishes to convince
us. Perhaps the most striking example is the treatment of Winifred
Inger and Ursula's Uncle Tom, and this is, I think, because Lawrence
is using them to put forward some of his growing convictions about
the social and political tendencies of the time.

Ursula, one might trivially say, has a crush on her teacher, Winifred
Inger, and they have a rather quiet, more or less lesbian relationship.
This is very effectively presented, from the cold, clear moment when
they swim together and Winifred carries Ursula into the water,
through Ursula's involvement in her teacher's ideas and activities, to
the beginning of revulsion. Here, however, Lawrence moves into a
language which is not related to any clear individuality of happening
and in a prose which drops into the banal: 'The fine unquenchable
flame of the younger girl would consent no more to mingle with the
perverted life of the older woman.' Ursula resolves to bring Winifred
together with her Uncle Tom, marrying one corruption to another,
for Tom, who has been described earlier in the book as having a
'bestial' way of laughing, is also marked with arbitrary evil:

> The fine beauty of his skin and his complexion, some
> almost waxen quality, hid the strange, repellent grossness
> of him, the slight sense of putrescence, the commonness
> which revealed itself in his rather fat thighs and
> loins.   (12)

Their union has an argumentative function in the book, for Tom
has become the manager of a large colliery; Ursula's horror of the
mining town, a horror which will recur at the very end of the novel
in her vision of an industrial world which is 'the expression of corruption triumphant and unopposed, corruption so pure that it is hard and

brittle', fixes itself on Tom and on Winifred. But it is hardly possible
to accept this simply as Ursula's judgement. We cannot but believe that
it is also Lawrence's when we read:

> His real mistress was the machine, and the real mistress of
> Winifred was the machine. She too, Winifred, worshipped
> the impure abstraction, the mechanisms of matter. There,
> there, in the machine, in service of the machine, was she
> free from the clog and degradation of human feeling.
> There, in the monstrous mechanism that held all matter,
> living or dead, in its service, did she achieve her
> consummation and her perfect unison, her
> immortality.   (12)

Nothing that we have seen in terms of her behaviour, nor, for that
matter, in Tom's, has justified this judgement nor are we shown a
concrete action which supports it. We are left with an arbitrary
assertion.

But here, as elsewhere, what is bad in Lawrence is closely akin to
what is good, for it must be said that in life many things do appear
to be arbitrary and Lawrence is often peculiarly good at showing this.
If we feel – as I think we do – that the image of Will as a bud which
never really opens is true, that though he has made a basically happy
marriage and performed useful tasks in society, yet he has never
fulfilled what lay in him, it is not because we can point to any obvious
moral or emotional inadequacies; he is simply as he is. In his perception
of characters who are inherently what they are and can be neither
praised nor blamed for it Lawrence is like very few English novelists.
Perhaps in this the one whom he most resembles is Emily Brontë, and
it is a view in him, as in her, which can be harsh and painful and which
leaves characters in a position in which they may be judged without
there being any possibility of appeal. What distinguishes the arbitrariness which we register as Lawrence imposing values upon his characters from the arbitrariness which we recognize as akin to our normal
awareness that some people are born more intelligent or more beautiful
or stronger than others is that the former emerges as part of a doctrinal
system. Tom is not merely shown to us as a man who affects people
as being rather brutal and at the same time defeated and whom
Lawrence in his dynamic interaction with his characters sees for the
moment as that; rather he has become part of an argument about the
progress of industrialization. Lawrence was appalled by the mechanical
and the dead; forgetting, it seems, what he knew in *Sons and Lovers*,
he equates this with the mining town and comes to believe that the
colliers themselves assent to their dehumanization and that those who

organize the business are evil. Tom and Winifred have wished on them the hatred which belongs to Lawrence's judgement about mechanization.

Lawrence did not take an exclusively aesthetic attitude towards his fiction; indeed, as he makes clear in his critical studies of such writers as Hardy, Galsworthy, Thomas Mann, and Melville, he sees literary works as an index to the quality of life and the writers as men with whom one should ally or whom it is one's duty to oppose. In writing *The Rainbow* he wanted to open people's eyes, to make them aware, in the long run to affect their conduct. Yet he is also the man who made the famous comment about always trusting the tale and never the artist, who asserted that most great novelists have a didactic purpose directly opposed to their passional inspiration.[4] In this novel some of the striking weaknesses are brought about by the intrusion of the artist. As might be expected these are usually matters which were central to Lawrence and they are marked by the deterioration of the prose and a shift of the focus from the characters towards argument. At the end of Chapter 10 the Christian year is described in terms of the participation of Ursula and the other children in decorating the church or going there on Good Friday but this ends in Lawrence's own protest against the separation of body and spirit:

> The Resurrection is to life, not to death. Shall I not see those who have risen again walk here among men perfect in body and spirit, whole and glad in the flesh, living in the flesh, loving in the flesh, begetting children in the flesh, arrived at last to wholeness, perfect without scar or blemish, healthy without fear of ill-health? Is this not the period of manhood and joy and fulfilment, after the Resurrection? Who shall be shadowed by Death and the Cross, being risen, and who shall fear the mystic, perfect flesh that belongs to heaven?

In Chapter 11, soon after a magnificently convincing quarrel between Ursula and Skrebensky in which, though she outrageously changes the terms of argument whenever it suits her attack on his conventional views about his duty as a citizen and a soldier, yet we are bound to sympathize with her, Lawrence presses the attack home *in propria persona*:

> The good of the greatest number was all that mattered.
> That which was the greatest good for them all,
> collectively, was the greatest good for the individual. And
> so, every man must give himself to support the state, and
> so labour for the greatest good of all. One might make

> improvements in the state, perhaps, but always with a
> view to preserving it intact. . . .
>
> He could not see, it was not born in him to see, that
> the highest good of the community as it stands is no
> longer the highest good of even the average individual.

The objection to such passages as these is not simply that they are inconceivable as what Ursula felt or what Skrebensky debated within himself, but that such dogmatic statements and rhetorical questions are a positive incitement to us to argue with the writer. But once we are in an argumentative frame of mind we may well be led to argue not only with this view of the Resurrection or this analysis of Skrebensky's beliefs but with the whole conception of Ursula's religious feelings or Skrebensky's character. Such a response would be destructive of any book but especially of one in which the characters are created, as we have seen, by a dynamic engagement of the writer with his creations which often appears dogmatic. That the book is not more damaged is striking proof of Lawrence's ability at his best to embody his convictions in sharply realized moments of experience.

Women in Love was originally conceived as forming, with *The Rainbow*, one novel, *The Sisters*, and its central preoccupation is that awareness of the desolation of industrialization and the destruction of spontaneous feeling with which Ursula is grappling at the end of the earlier novel, what in Chapter 27 of *Women in Love* is called by Birkin 'the slope of mechanical death'.

But it is a very different kind of novel from its predecessor; not only have some of the characters changed their natures a good deal, but the techniques which Lawrence employs are new. The pace is much quicker; instead of a small number of very long, continuous chapters, we have thirty-one chapters in a book which is only slightly longer. Some of these chapters are substantial but many are of only a few pages and in them Lawrence explores one idea after another from various points of view. In particular what we find here, unlike in *The Rainbow*, is great use of dialogue. The characters argue all the time and the central issues emerge from these clashes. In *The Rainbow* we have a sense of the slow unfolding of feelings and the ideas which come with them; here we see ideas hammered out in argument and often taking precedence of the feelings which accompany them.

It is not altogether easy to adjust ourselves to the dialogue. At times it is clearly intended to be realistic; the phraseology of the aristocratic Hermione is often one which registers her sense of belonging to a different class from some of the other persons and this can only be conveyed if we have recognized a realistic register. Elsewhere Lawrence wants his characters to explore complex ideas and for this they are given great eloquence and frequently a terminology which is related to a general train of imagery which runs through the book. There are times when we are not sure where we stand on this continuum from the colloquial to the apocalyptically rhetorical. There are substantial sections in which the language is pretentious and over-blown though it is worth noting that Lawrence can, and does, make fun of himself. In many of the arguments between Ursula and Birkin and sometimes between Gerald and Birkin the inflation of the rhetoric is under question as well as the ideas expressed in it.

The argument, expressed very often in hot disputes, centres on the relationships of the two sisters Ursula and Gudrun with Rupert Birkin, a schools' inspector, and Gerald Crich, the son of the mine-owner of the district. Each relationship has a third party. In the case of Ursula and Birkin it is Hermione Roddice with whom Birkin has had a protracted love affair, marked by possessiveness on her part and a neurotic and willed sensuality; in the case of Gudrun and Gerald it is the German painter, Loerke, for whom Gudrun in the end leaves Gerald. Hermione, one may say simply, is the wrong person for Birkin and his progress through the book is to leave her and move towards Ursula. Loerke, we might equally simply say, is shown as the right person for Gudrun; but he is right only in the sense that his strain of sado-masochistic destructiveness calls to the same impulse in her.

To describe the novel thus is to make it sound schematic and indeed it is, but throughout there is a conflict between Lawrence the system-seeking propagandist and Lawrence the novelist who works against the scheme, admitting much which does not fit the thesis and leaving us with far more freedom of response than seems at times likely.

Birkin's basic outlook is expressed early in Chapter 5, 'In the Train'. It is akin to the perceptions of Ursula at the end of *The Rainbow*, and it clearly has much in common with Lawrence's own views. The argument is presented here less apocalyptically than elsewhere but it is not different in its bearing. Birkin wants to reject 'this life that we've brought upon ourselves' because it is too corrupt to be reformed; chiefly he lacks faith in material improvement:

> we cover the earth with foulness; life is a blotch of labour,
> like insects scurrying in filth, so that your collier can have
> a pianoforte in his parlour, and you can have a butler and
> a motor car in your up-to-date house.

As often happens his opponent, although we are meant to think that in the long run he is wrong, is given a good argument, to such an extent that Birkin's contempt for the collier who wants a piano seems insensitive and arrogant. What we realize as they talk is that Birkin is

not merely contemptuous of those who do not share his views; he is
in a state approaching despair and can have faith in nothing but some
kind of individual love to make his life have meaning. He says:

> 'The old ideas are dead as nails – nothing there. It
> seems to me there remains only this perfect union with a
> woman – sort of ultimate marriage – and there isn't
> anything else.'
> 'And you mean if there isn't a woman, there's nothing?'
> said Gerald.
> 'Pretty well that – seeing there's no God.'

In his long struggle to come together with Ursula he has to take
account of a woman who loves him while being quite prepared to crit-
icize him and to see him as 'a prig of the stiffest type' (11) and who,
even as they are preparing to go away together, in Chapter 26, tells
him 'you can't *force* the flowers to come up'. But though she changes
him and he finds that with her he can find this 'sort of ultimate
marriage' he still despairs of society: 'I don't believe in the humanity
I pretend to be part of, I don't care a straw for the social ideals I live
by, I hate the dying organic form of social mankind – so it can't be
anything but trumpery to work at education.' His first action after they
have committed themselves to one another is to send in his resignation
from his job and to dictate to Ursula her own resignation. This he can
do because he has a private income of four hundred pounds a year. It
was presumably Lawrence's own total despair about England (and
especially the effect of the Great War, during which he was writing
the book) that made it possible for him not to realize that some readers
at least would detect here some evasiveness of the issues about which
he is writing.

The values which Birkin sees as destroying life are largely embodied
in Gerald Crich, who is both friend and adversary, personally loved
but representing death. He is the mine-owner, a masterful man,
admired by many and seemingly self-sufficient, and this is the nature
of his appeal to Gudrun. There is a strong element of the sado-
masochistic in their relationship. When, in Chapter 9, 'Coal-Dust', the
sisters watch him forcing a mare which he is riding to stand firm while
a train passes at the level-crossing, Gudrun's orgasmic reaction is very
different from Ursula's cold contempt for a man who is bullying an
animal. Later in Chapter 18, 'Rabbit', as they compare the gashes on
their arms made by the frantic animal, 'they were implicated with each
other in abhorrent mysteries'.

Gerald is in many ways a tragic figure. He has killed his brother
in an accident with a gun; when he is trying to rescue his sister from

drowning in Chapter 14, 'Water Party', he goes on diving again and again long after there is any chance of finding her, and his bleak utterance to Gudrun: 'There's room under that water for thousands' seems to express a deep yearning for oblivion.

It is oblivion which he seeks, too, in his relationship with Gudrun. At the risk of oversimplifying the relationship between Birkin and Ursula we could say that they are each highly individualized and that they move together through conflict, each insisting that they retain their identity and unite as individuals. But Gerald either wishes to remain detached, as in his insistence that after his night with Minette he should pay her off, or, as in Chapter 24, 'Death and Love', when he first comes to Gudrun's bed, plodding up the stairs with the mud from the graveyard where his father has been buried on his boots, he seeks a complete submergence of himself. Even here, though, when he leaves her in the morning, he has separated himself:

> His mind was beautifully still and thoughtless, like a still pool, with his body full and warm and rich. He went quickly along towards Shortlands in a grateful self-sufficiency.

But Gerald is not merely a man involved in a disastrous love-affair with Gudrun which can only end with that death with which he has so many affinities; he is also the chief representative of all those forces in society which Birkin, and Lawrence, too, detest. Chapter 17, 'The Industrial Magnate', in particular argues that he represents the forces of industrialization and intellectual control which are the causes of the destruction of life:

> He found his eternal and his infinite in the pure machine-principle of perfect co-ordination into one pure, complex, infinitely repeated motion, like the spinning of a wheel.

Not that he is a simple exploiter of labour. In accordance with that idea of necessity which causes Birkin to say that those who are murdered must in some sense wish to be murdered, he is a manifestation of a general and accepted tendency. The miners whose work he controls do not merely assent to what he is doing, they positively rejoice in it:

> The men were satisfied to belong to the great and wonderful machine, even whilst it destroyed them. It was what they wanted. It was the highest that man had produced, the most wonderful and superhuman. They were exalted by belonging to this great and superhuman

system which was beyond feeling or reason, something
really godlike. Their hearts died within them, but their
souls were satisfied.

Lawrence was writing the book during the Great War and if this
concept of the mass of men as welcoming their destruction seems
unconvincing as a picture of work it makes more sense if we think of
the ready volunteers for the Western Front. The most that Lawrence,
like Birkin, can hope for is the blending of a personal relationship of
sexual love with an apocalyptic sense of 'non-human mystery'. In the
concluding pages of the book Lawrence seems to bring back the God,
whom Birkin has previously denied, as a comforting mystery:

God can do without man. God could do without the
ichthyosauri and the mastodon. These monsters failed
creatively to develop, so God, the creative mystery,
dispensed with them. . . . The game was never up. The
mystery of creation was fathomless, infallible,
inexhaustible, for ever. Races came and went, species
passed away, but ever new species arose, more lovely, or
equally lovely, always surpassing wonder.

The paean, I imagine, convinces very few readers; its emphasis
serves most, perhaps, to register despair with society and a baffled
belief that the deepest human relationships must have some meaning
beyond the personal.

The arguments of the book, the theories which it expounds, are not
what convince, and it is an immense pity that they have often been
the focus of discussion. What gives us the immediate conviction of
great fiction is Lawrence's ability to create a sense of feelings and
relationships which persuade us of their importance without argument.
It is as true of this novel as of *The Rainbow* that those scenes in which
the feelings and the arguments are most closely tied to concrete and
specific acts and objects are by far the most successful.

Nowhere is this more clearly seen than in Chapter 23, 'Excurse'.
In it is recounted the definitive commitment to one another of Birkin
and Ursula and it contains some of the best and some of the worst of
Lawrence. Birkin (forgetting, one must suppose, his earlier expressed
contempt for motor cars) takes Ursula for a drive in a car and proposes
to return early in time to say goodbye to Hermione. Ursula, understandably irritated, reviles him; he stops the car, she gets out, they
continue their quarrel in the road. At the height of her rage a cyclist
approaches; despite saying that she doesn't care, Ursula suspends her
harangue while the cyclist passes. This is something rare in Lawrence,

a moment of pure comedy of situation, but it is extraordinarily effective in setting the extremity of her accusations and his contemptuous replies within a local context.

Their language to one another is loaded with violent generalizations – 'What you are is a foul, deathly thing, obscene, that's what you are, obscene and perverse' – and so is Lawrence's narration: as Ursula, having thrown in his face the rings which he has given her, walks away down the road:

> There was a darkness over his mind. The terrible knot of
> consciousness that had persisted there like an obsession
> was broken, gone, his life was dissolved in darkness over
> his limbs and his body.

But the violence, even the violent abstractions, are part of the violence of a moment. We can if we wish demonstrate that the feelings follow a logical, if bumpy, course, that Ursula's rage shows him how he affects her or that her disappearance along the road leaves him with nobody to answer but himself; but we are probably more likely to recognize that this is how quarrels between people who love one another proceed. She comes back along the road, 'desultorily', and shows him some heather which she has picked; they embrace and are 'at peace with each other'. Throughout the passage the movement of their feelings is linked with sharply realized objects: the spindleberries which Ursula tears and fastens in her coat, the rings from which Birkin unconsciously wipes the dirt of the road, the bell-heather against Ursula's 'over-sensitive' skin.

But Lawrence is not content with this. It is his purpose to try to define more precisely the nature of their feelings and this leads him on to some of the most unsatisfactory and most puzzling passages in the book. Ursula and Birkin drive on and go for high tea to the 'Saracen's Head' in Southwell and there follows a scene, apparently on the hearth rug of a public room in the inn, which begins with Ursula's recurring to the biblical imagery of *The Rainbow*:

> She recalled again the old magic of the Book of Genesis,
> where the sons of God saw the daughters of men, that
> they were fair. And he was one of these, one of these
> strange creatures from the beyond, looking down at her,
> and seeing she was fair.

She kneels before him 'tracing the back of his thighs, following some mysterious life flow there' and Lawrence insists, again and again, on the revelatory nature of this particular physical caress:

> She traced with her hands the line of his loins and thighs,
> at the back, and a living fire ran through her, from him,
> darkly. It was dark flood of electric passion she released
> from him, drew into herself.

The culmination of her experience emphasizes that they have broken through into some sensual experience beyond what she has ever known before:

> She had thought there was no source deeper than the
> phallic source. And now, behold, from the smitten rock of
> the man's body, from the strange marvellous flanks and
> thighs, deeper, further in mystery than the phallic source,
> came the floods of ineffable darkness and ineffable riches.

The incantatory prose rolls on, unrelated to any localizing reality, unless, indeed, we envisage the room and fear the (in all senses disruptive) entry of another customer.

It is tempting, when reading, to skim over the second half of this chapter and some similar passages in the book and to replace them by something more general, saying, for example, that Ursula and Birkin, embracing, have a sense of total intercommunion. But to do so would certainly be to resist what Lawrence wants of us, for he is clearly aiming for a unified view of human experience in which our physical passions are a central part of our moral lives and our social beings. He is not willing to say 'They made love' and leave it to each reader to take his or her own experience of love and apply it to the book. He insists that we know how they made love because their actions seem an index of the quality of their lives. This can be seen very neatly in Chapter 5 of *Lady Chatterley's Lover* where the premature ejaculation of Michaelis is not merely an unfortunate aberration or a condition requiring treatment or tact or regret but a sign of a weakness in his character and a central flaw in the whole society of which he is made a representative.

The rhetoric of the second half of 'Excurse' is often baffling but there is clearly a strong anal component in the sexual experience, so that we cannot but believe that there are for Lawrence forbidden mysteries which must be broken through if we are to achieve true erotic freedom.

Something of a similar problem confronts us when dealing with the indubitable emphasis placed by Birkin upon his love for Gerald. To say that there is a homosexual element in Birkin and, as has often been suggested, in his creator as well makes matters both too simple and too vulgar. But it is not quite enough to say that Birkin is asking for no more than deep friendship. When, at the end of the book, we are told that one of the reasons why Gerald is lost is that he has not accepted Birkin's offer, Lawrence is not merely asserting that if you cannot commit yourself in real friendship with a member of your own sex then you will not be able to commit yourself in a real marriage either. To that we could probably all agree without much difficulty, but there is too much emphasis upon the physical reality of Gerald's body in relation to Birkin's for us to believe that this is all there is to it. The description of their naked wrestling in Chapter 20, 'Gladiatorial', and Birkin's assertion at the very end of the book that though his love for Ursula is 'eternal' yet he also wanted 'eternal union with a man too', suggests that Lawrence would not thank us for translating his more puzzling and extreme passages into something more moderate.

The apocalyptic note was to sound more and more strongly in the later novels and they were to be more concerned with the proclamation of a gospel – or a series of gospels – and less with the exploration of those feelings and relationships which were rooted in his youth and early manhood. As a boy and young man he was often referred to as 'our Bert' – 'our' in the sense that he was related to or a neighbour of those speaking; later he was often claimed as 'our Lorenzo' – 'our' in the sense that disciples had chosen him as a guru. It is deeply saddening to watch, in works like 'St. Mawr' and *The Plumed Serpent* and *Kangaroo*, the triumph of our Lorenzo over our Bert.

Notes

1. It is typical of Lawrence that he introduces into *Lady Chatterley's Lover* his statement of faith in the supreme importance of fiction: 'And here lies the vast importance of the novel, properly handled. It can inform and lead into new places the flow of our sympathetic consciousness, and it can lead our sympathy away in recoil from things gone dead' (9).

2. This was not his only encounter with censorship. *The Rainbow* was banned and copies seized; a publisher could not be found for four years for *Women in Love*; an exhibition of his paintings in 1929 was closed and the police carried off numerous works; in the same year manuscripts of the poems, 'Pansies', were seized in the post and subsequently published only in an expurgated form.

3. *The Letters of D. H. Lawrence*, edited by James T. Boulton (1978), I, pp. 476–77.

4. The two comments are worth quoting at greater length. The first, from the
first chapter of *Studies in Classic American Literature*, runs:

> The artist usually sets out – or used to – to point a moral and adorn
> a tale. The tale, however, points the other way, as a rule. Two blankly
> opposing morals, the artist's and the tale's. Never trust the artist. Trust
> the tale. The proper function of a critic is to save the tale from the artist
> who created it.

The second is from his essay, 'The Novel':

> It is such a bore that nearly all great novelists have a didactic
> purpose, otherwise a philosophy, directly opposite to their passional
> inspiration. In their passional inspiration they are all phallic worshippers.
> From Balzac to Hardy, it is so. Nay, from Apuleius to E. M. Forster.
> Yet all of them, when it comes to their philosophy, or what they think-
> they-are, they are all crucified Jesuses. What a bore! And what a burden
> for the novel to carry!

Chapter 13
The 1930s: An Aftermath

Rarely can a contemporary view of a literary situation have been so different from a retrospective one as in the year of Lawrence's death, 1930. Looking back from half a century or so on, it seems to mark the end of a great period of English fiction, but at the time matters must have seemed otherwise. Conrad and Hardy, men of an older generation, had died in the previous decade, but there was no reason to believe that Forster would never write another novel nor to foresee that Virginia Woolf's best work was already done; Bennett was still alive and Joyce still writing and surely a younger generation would follow. Hardly a five-year period had passed between the publication of *Tess of the d'Urbervilles* in 1891 and *To the Lighthouse* in 1927 without the appearance of a masterpiece: *What Maisie Knew, Nostromo, The Old Wives' Tale, The Rainbow, Ulysses, A Passage to India* were merely some of the more striking and different ones. Most of them are books which make demands on the reader both in terms of the techniques employed and the sympathies demanded; many of them deal with large political, social, and moral issues and they all oblige us to come to terms with newly explored experiences. Ambition and confidence are the marks of the giants of early modern fiction. Was it not to be expected that such a tradition should continue?

Yet in retrospect the literary scene of the 1930s and for long thereafter displayed nothing in fiction of comparable scope to what had gone before. Joyce Cary, who was to establish his reputation later, published five novels in the 1930s and George Orwell began his literary career, though his talents were clearly not those of a novelist so much as a journalist and polemicist. But those novelists who established themselves in the late 1920s and 1930s and whose works are still read seem mostly to have chosen deliberately smaller subjects and to have turned their backs on technical innovation.

Ivy Compton-Burnett had one thing which she did marvellously well and clearly had no intention of moving away from it; Richard Hughes produced a short but memorable minor classic in *A High Wind in Jamaica*, Elizabeth Bowen published a number of delicate small-scale post-Jamesian studies, mostly of children and adolescent girls; Evelyn Waugh and Anthony Powell set themselves to produce works of wit within a very limited social and emotional range. Akin to these in many ways, but puzzlingly different in others, was Henry Green who, gifted as it seems with everything required for a serious and major novelist, resolutely refused to write anything but studiously small masterpieces.

This, like all such generalizations, is based upon judgements about a multitude of novels and must bear the marks of the critic who makes it. Admirers of J. C. Powys and Wyndham Lewis would make very different generalizations. The former – and perhaps his brother T. F. Powys – would be seen as strikingly original fabulists in a regional mode which owes something to Hardy, and the latter would certainly be seen as continuing the line of Modernism. Nobody can doubt that they make large demands for their importance and I refer my readers to the Bibliography for different views. Both are obviously gifted with many of the qualities which fiction demands and Lewis was undoubtedly a polemicist of great force and intermittent insight, but neither seems to me able so to organize his talents as to construct a major novel.

A great deal has been written about the social, philosophical, and political reasons for – or accompaniments to – the movement which we loosely call Modernism. Its surprisingly sudden end in England has attracted less attention. Perhaps it is felt that it is more normal not to have major novelists and that normality asks for no explanation. It has been suggested (by C. P. Snow, somewhat self-servingly, among others) that Modernism was a cosmopolitan intrusion into an English fictional tradition which runs from George Eliot through Hardy to certain post-Second World War social novelists, in this paralleling a similar case made for the development of English poetry which by-passes Yeats to reach Betjeman. This would perhaps be a more convincing argument if one could feel that the 1930s was a thin patch and that since then an English tradition has flowed strongly. Alas, I cannot believe this. Conrad, Joyce, and Lawrence are indubitably great writers who deal with great central issues; they are not aberrant intrusions except so far as genius is always an intrusion into run-of-the-mill normality. Moreover, as I have said, what is most significant about so many of those writers of the 1930s and 1940s whom we can still read with pleasure is not so much that they are minor novelists as that they appear to have turned their backs on the large issues and the ambitious structures of their predecessors. Instead they tend to deal wittily, allusively, quirkily, from rather unusual points of view, with the kind of material presented to them by a very limited social scene. In this they may be said to be provincial in a sense very different from Bennett or Hardy.

A partial explanation may lie in the experience which they had just missed but which must have shadowed their childhood – the Great War. The experience of the trenches produced a good deal of poetry and a number of novels, but for those born in the early years of the century it may be that the shock of the war, impinging on them in their adolescence, and the disillusion of the post-war years turned them against large claims and confident certainties and left them happier with the familiarities of domestic life and other in-groups. For it is of in-groups that many of them tend to write and Waugh and Powell in particular take up the tradition of the dandy which was so enthusiastically adopted by Ronald Firbank and continued by 'Saki' (H. H. Munro), who died on the Western Front.

If one begins to think about their self-imposed restrictions one cannot avoid speculating about the relative uniformity of social origins, background, and education of these writers; one also realizes that it was shared by such rising poets of the time as Auden, Spender, and MacNeice and by a large number of the editors and middlemen of literature. In this they differ from the major writers of the earlier part of the century, who had been marked by a great variety of back-grounds: Hardy was a countryman of lower-middle-class origins, Conrad a naturalized Pole of the minor gentry, Bennett came from a provincial family which was rising in the world from humble begin-nings, Lawrence's father was a miner, Virginia Woolf was educated in the library of her father, the great Sir Leslie Stephen, Forster progressed from an orthodox public school to King's College, Cambridge.

It is striking that Forster is the only one of these who speaks much of his education and, so far as the school part of it is concerned, totally unfavourably. The public school, he asserts, produces trained bodies, half-trained minds and untrained hearts; the Empire, so he says in *A Passage to India*, is run on public school lines; Sawston, based on his own school, Tonbridge, sums up all that is opposed to life and truth. By contrast Hardy does not seem to have been much preoccupied in his adult life by the British School in Dorchester nor Bennett by his school at Newcastle-under-Lyme nor Lawrence by Nottingham High School. Is it merely an idiosyncratic aberration that Forster suggests that his school and others like it were the determining factor in so much of English life? One might well take that view were it not that an astonishing number of writers of the period which I am discussing appear to agree with him, though they often rejoice in, rather than regret, their schools.

It is not surprising that they should have been educated at public boarding schools and, frequently, at Oxford or Cambridge, for most of them came from the professional or upper middle classes and such an education would have been taken for granted in their families. What may seem surprising is that the schools, and to a lesser extent the universities, should have continued to have such an importance for them. This can be explained, I think, by a consideration of the function which, over and above the teaching of academic subjects, was the characteristic of the public schools. The number of such schools grew so immensely during the nineteenth century because they were needed to produce an elite which could run a large Empire; some were overt in their aim – Kipling's school was one such – but those which did not proclaim the aim were equally devoted to producing disciplined and self-confident men who would form a ruling caste. In the process, and doubtless often against their will, the schools also helped to produce such self-confident literary castes as the members of the Bloomsbury Group and the dominant literary editors and reviewers of the inter-war years.

It is this sense of membership of a caste which is so striking in this period. The characters of Anthony Powell's early novels (and of his later ones, too) register their positions in relation to other people in terms of what schools they attended, what regiments they were in, to which houses they are invited. The subject of Waugh's first novel is the progress of his hero from Oxford, via a stint as schoolmaster in a parody school, back to Oxford. The fashionable young people of Green's *Party Going* are of the class that gets into the papers as they tread the round of parties at which everybody knows everybody else. Nor is this fixation confined to those who seem to have enjoyed membership of the dominant caste. The schoolboy adventure element in such temporarily Communist writers as Auden has often been noticed and it must seem astonishing to any Continental political thinker that Orwell's time at St Cyprian's and Eton has played such a part in discussion of his outlook.

The significant characteristic of a caste is that its members recognize one another as fellow-members, whether they like one another or not, and that they find it hard to conceive that those outside the caste can have much in common with them. In some cases this manifests itself in a cultivated snobbery, as in Waugh; in others, of whom Orwell is the most striking example, we see a writer trying rather unavailingly to put himself on a level with the outsiders and usually finding this easier to do when confronted by foreign proletarians or by the destitute rather than the majority of miscellaneous fellow citizens who had peopled the novels of Hardy and Bennett.[1] Nowhere is this sense of a special caste of both writers and readers so neatly shown as in the comment of Waugh's biographer, Christopher Sykes, on the reception of his first novel, *Decline and Fall*:

> It would be wrong to say that Evelyn woke up to find
> himself famous, but it is correct to say that he woke up to
> find himself the talk of the town, meaning by 'town' those
> who knew something about public school and university
> life and fashionable society.[2]

Waugh, so his biographer tells us, was always irritated by people who said that *Decline and Fall* was his best novel. It is always annoying for writers to have their later works compared unfavourably with their first, but there is surely a more specific reason here, for, without ever showing signs of wishing to leave the charmed circle of high life which is his chosen sphere, he endeavours in later novels to suggest significances of feeling and depths of belief within it. But his is really an anarchic talent, flourishing in a created world of brilliant lampoons, the willing sacrifice of plausibility for bravura effects, the breaking of taboos and the elegant cultivation of bad taste. These abilities sit uneasily with devotion either to the maintenance of old families with traditional tastes or with the Roman Catholic Church.

The tone which is set at the opening of *Decline and Fall* is one of heartless farce. Paul Pennyfeather, a shy and reclusive young man who is reading for the Church, is debagged by a gang of rampaging undergraduates. The dons, whose main aim is to fine offenders enough to be able to drink Founder's port on the proceeds, realize that he has no money and therefore send him down for indecent behaviour; his guardian takes the opportunity to discontinue his allowance. The college porter has already suggested the course of action which he is expected to follow: 'I expect you'll be becoming a schoolmaster, sir, that's what most of the gentlemen does, sir, that gets sent down for indecent behaviour.' He visits the scholastic agents, Church and Gargoyle, and proceeds into a world of joyfully hailed stereotypes in a plot which is anecdotal, but where Waugh appears to have given the definitive form to what we feel must surely have been pre-existing anecdotes. We follow Paul's progress via Llanabba Castle, the epitome of the appalling prep school, in which he learns how not to teach, to his involvement with the mother of one of his pupils, Margot Best-Chetwynd, which leads to his innocent participation in the white slave traffic and his being hauled off to prison, an experience which, as he reflects, for somebody who has been at an English public school does not seem unduly arduous. He is bought out of prison by Margot's willingness to marry a politician who can arrange for Paul to begin life again under another name. We leave him at the end of the book back at college under his false name, preparing once again to go into the Church.

Virtually all the characters are either venal or deluded and Waugh delights in conspiring with in the breaking of taboos, especially those public taboos which are the province of the well meaning. There was, at the time of the book's publication, a good deal of discussion of prison reform and also of efforts to put down the white slave traffic by agencies of the League of Nations. Predictably in Waugh's world the humane Prison Governor attempts to reform the inmates by finding out what they are interested in and giving them an opportunity to follow up that interest, with the result that one prisoner murders another. But we are not called upon to feel for the victim since he is the comic clergyman with Doubts whom we have previously met as a colleague of Paul at Llanabba Castle. Similarly the dull, pedestrian official of the League of Nations arrests the innocent Paul and we cannot weep for the girls since they are shown as having an enterprising ambition to succeed in their profession.

Decline and Fall may not be the best of Waugh's novels, but it is certainly typical of everything that he wrote before the outbreak of war. Claims have been made for serious moral intentions; Samuel Hynes in *The Auden Generation* (1976), for example, draws parallels between Waugh's second novel, *Vile Bodies* (1930) and Eliot's *The Waste Land* (1922), instancing the emphasis upon the antics of the Bright Young Things under the shadow of war and the prevailing sense of futility. But the energy of the book goes into the concept of Father Rothschild. who 'had a happy knack to remember everything that could possibly be learned, about everyone who could possibly be of any importance' and of Mrs Melrose-Ape, the Evangelist with her singing, dancing, and preaching girls, called Faith, Charity, Fortitude, Chastity (who travels via Buenos Aires to Salisbury Plain to cheer up the soldiers), and Creative Endeavour. In *Black Mischief* (1932), Waugh alternates between farce and the presentation of real fear and pain in his account of civil war in a land approximating to Ethiopia, which he had recently visited. But we feel, in the grimmest section, that what Waugh is really leading up to is the fulfilment of the promise of Prudence to her lover, the worthless but charming Basil Seal. 'You're a grand girl, Prudence, and I'd like to eat you,' he says and she replies: 'So you shall, my sweet, anything you want.' Unwittingly at a ceremonial feast he does precisely what he has wanted and she has promised.

What is potentially serious in these early novels cannot for long engage our attention in competition with the disruptive, the anarchic, and the flippantly cruel. In his later novels, where his intentions are certainly serious, the limitations of his social interests are especially damaging. In so far as affection is ever expressed in his books it seems to be for the high spirits, the frivolity, and frequently the drinking of the Bright Young Things whom, it is sometimes claimed, he was satirizing. He does not seem to me to be satirizing them at all. He loves what he sometimes mocks. Snobbery, the sense that only a few people matter and that the others who are striving for acceptance inevitably bear the marks which exclude them and will have those marks pointed out to them, is central to the society of which he is writing, but it is surely central to Waugh himself. Many of his characters are worthless but they provide the only society in which he can envisage living. When, in *Brideshead Revisited* (1945) the enjoyment of that comforting warmth which comes from the elaboration of rituals and the linguistic usages which are designed to define the exclusion of outsiders is felt in complicity with the Roman Catholic Church (represented by more than Father Rothschild), it appears shoddy.

But the early novels, taken as entertainments and not as satires, will always find readers, not least because of the crisp efficiency of the prose style. Detached, secure, totally unaffected by any of the great stylistic explorations of the early part of the century, the narrative prose makes its point in the traditional manner of farce by keeping a cool head in the midst of chaos.

Anthony Powell, who is chiefly known for his post-war sequence of twelve works, *A Dance to the Music of Time*, prefaced his first novel, *Afternoon Men* (1931), with an epigraph from Burton's *Anatomy of Melancholy*, which might well characterize all his five pre-war novels and, indeed, those of his friend Evelyn Waugh:

> As if they had heard that enchanted horn of Astolpho, that English duke in Ariosto, which never sounded but all his auditors were mad, and for fear ready to make away with themselves . . . they are a company of giddy-heads, afternoon men.

The subject-matter and the choice of clear, elegant, and essentially traditional prose style for the narration are akin to Waugh, but the effect of the books is less savage, though sadder. The world with which Powell deals is one of parties for the young and eccentric hobbies, stamp-collecting, spiritualism, transvestism for the elderly, of seemingly shallow attachments and elaborate cross-purpose conversations. The conclusion of *Afternoon Men* is characteristically inconclusive and muddled.

> Harriet came down the stairs. She was holding the arm of a tall young man whom Atwater had not seen before.
> 'That is a very nice young man,' she said. 'I don't know what his name is, but he says a friend of his is giving a party and we can all come.'

'Yes,' said the young man, rather frightened by his own sudden importance, 'do come, all of you. I don't expect it will be very exciting or anything like that, but all the same we might look in and see what it's like.'

Atwater said: 'How was Susan Nunnery getting on with Verelst?'

Brisket said: 'This is the Freiherr von Waldesch, Harriet. Have you met him?'

Harriet said: 'You'll come to the party, won't you?'

Von Waldesch bowed from the waist.

'Very well,' he said. He looked immensely pleased by the invitation and a little alarmed by Harriet. By way of additional emphasis to his acceptance he said: 'That's right.'

'And you, William?'

'Yes,' said Atwater, 'I'd like to.'

Powell's characters seem to go through life in a dream, clutching at a few fixed ideas, or sometimes, particularly if they are fashionable young women, making a successful social effect by seeming to do so. He is a master at presenting both the comedy, even farce, and also the occasional sense of sad futility of a society in which some questions are never answered or even asked while elsewhere laborious discussion grows pedantic over trifles. It is typical that Atwater's question, in the passage which I have just quoted, is about a girl whom he loves and who has left for America with another man, and it receives no answer. Elsewhere in the same novel, by contrast, four pages are consumed in discussion of what is the right amount to tip a fisherman who has saved one of the characters from drowning after he has repented of an attempt at suicide.

Of all the writers of this period the one who is most specialized and who seems deliberately to have chosen to write perfectly – or as near perfectly as anyone can – in one limited form is Ivy Compton-Burnett. After one false start, *Dolores* (1911), a novel which she later wished ignored, she began with *Pastors and Masters* in 1925 to produce one novel about every two years, all of which have considerable resemblances to one another, all concerned with small groups of people in a closed environment. She is particularly fond of such limited worlds as that of the boarding school and two of her novels deal with such an institution, but she has the ability to make almost any world seem closed, not least the family.

Her view of the family is an exceedingly pessimistic one, logically enough since it is the chief sphere of operation of human behaviour and she is on record as saying on a number of occasions that she takes a very low view of human nature and believes that in family life many horrors are suppressed. In her novels they are not suppressed; jealousy, greed, malice, and deception are given free rein except so far as they are kept in check by hypocrisy.

She makes very few concessions to the normal expectations of fictional form, crowding in a lot of often melodramatic plot with no particular attempt to make it seem convincing and introducing characters with perfunctory factual description. At times she seems to take positive pleasure in emphasizing the wantonness of invention. At the end of *A Family and a Fortune* two brothers remind one another of what has happened in the course of the novel:

> 'How much has happened in the last fourteen months!'
> 'Yes. Matty came to live here. I inherited a fortune. I was engaged to Maria. Blanche fell ill and died. You became engaged in my place. You and Maria were married. Matty's father died. Matty drove her old friend out into the snow. I ran away from my home. I am not quite sure of the order of the last three, but they were all on the same night, and it was really hard on Matty that it happened to be snowing. On a mild night she would not have been blamed half so much. I rescued Miss Griffin and took her into my charge. It was hard on us that it happened to be snowing too. I decided to provide for her for her life. It seemed the only thing in view of the climate. At any time it might snow. I was sick almost to death, and was given back to you all. In more than one sense; I must not forget that. Oh and Clement was gradually becoming a miser all the time. You would have thought he had enough to distract him.'

Her most striking effects are achieved through stylized dialogue which seems intended to be taken in part as what the characters are saying to one another, though with greater coherence, brevity, and wit than most people can command, but in part also as an epigrammatic voicing of what people feel but could never say, though others may deduce their meanings. This surely is the effect achieved in such a passage as that in Chapter 8 of *A House and its Head* (1935), when Alison, Duncan Edgeworth's second wife, first comes down to dinner with him, his nephew and his two daughters:

> Alison came to dinner, radiant and a little strained. She was vivacious in the drawing room, walked to the dining room with head held high, and paused at her place at the bottom of the table.

'Is it my seat all this way from you, Duncan? That is
not a good plan, when you are the only person here who
wants me.'

'That is your place, of course. Whose could it be?'

'Well, I suppose every other belongs to someone else,'
said his wife, sitting down, and then turning to Nance.
'This has been your place until now?'

'It has never really been mine,' said Nance, looking
aside.

'Oh! It is the place occupied by my predecessor! Let me
hasten to another, where it is not sacrilege to sit. I made
sure that one would be sacred and empty, with a halo
round it.'

'That is your place,' said Duncan; 'the place of the
mistresses of the house for generations. You have many
predecessors in it.'

'But I expect most of them corresponded only to one
master.'

Alison is not a monster, as she would surely be if she actually said
these things, for that would imply an intention to shock and hurt by
speaking the unspeakable. If we interpret it as being, in part, what she
thinks and what the others know she is thinking we are presented with
people thinking the unspeakable, and this we can all recognize as not
unusual. But there are plenty of monsters in the novels and it seems
to be central to Ivy Compton-Burnett's way of looking at the world
to believe that there are a goodly number of people in any society who
will never show mercy to those weaker than themselves. She shows
their ruthlessness through various subtle social cruelties and also
through theft and murder but she has a liking for the really tough and
uncompromising and it is notable that her most effective epigrams are
those which exemplify an unflinching recognition of the worst in
people. Nance at the end of *A House and its Head* reflects:

How difficult it would be, if people did not die! Think of
the numbers who die, and all the good that is done! They
never seem to die, without doing something for someone.
No wonder they hate so to do it, and plan to be
immortal.

In *More Women Than Men* (1933), Felix is talking to Josephine, the
headmistress of a school:

'Shall we have a gossip about your staff?'

'No!' said Josephine. 'When you have known me a little

longer, you will know that my mistresses, in their
presence and in their absence, are safe with me. I hope I
could say that of all my friends.'
    'I hoped you could not. But it is interesting that they
would not be safe if we had the gossip. They must have
treated you fully as a friend. I almost feel we have had
it.'   (5)

The characteristics which I have suggested are to be found in
novelists writing after the great period of the earlier part of the century
are, with one exception, very strikingly found in Ivy Compton-
Burnett. She treats of a very limited range of society, she avoids any
public or social issues and sets almost all her novels in the period before
the Great War, she restricts the feelings with which she deals and she
is so far from wishing to go on breaking new ground that she runs
the risk of being repetitious. I do not think that in her work we ever
find an exact repetition, but it is surely significant that many admirers
discuss her works in terms of categories, speaking, for example, of her
'tyrants', her 'fools', and so forth.[3]
    The exception to this generalization is, of course, that she is not
unwilling to make demands upon her readers. Her books need to be
read with care, the more perceptive epigrams frequently lurk in the
middle of apparently quiet dialogue and she normally makes her points
by hints which are given once only. One effect of this is that the reader
who takes the trouble to engage with her claustrophobic, harsh, and
witty view of the world is likely to find it compelling, even if at times
partaking of the nature of a cult.

Ambition was not lacking in Henry Green's choice of theme for his
first novel, *Blindness* (1926), which he started while still at Eton and
which was published when he was twenty-one. Dealing as it does with
a schoolboy who is blinded as the result of an accident it must tackle
extreme feelings of loss and despair in the central character and
complex readjustments in his family and friends. It has the flaws which
one might expect in a youthful work. The schoolboy rivalries, the
sense of being dashing and outspoken and shocking, the juvenile
dandyish aestheticism give the impression of being rather close to
Green's own experience, so that our relationship to them and the
judgements which we are invited to make are not very secure. He has,
also, a certain lack of social awareness; the eccentric daughter of an
alcoholic, dotty, unfrocked parson, with whom the boy falls in love
but whom he never understands, is strikingly well created in her individuality but not very firmly located in any actual social world. But

these are minor flaws in what is a good deal more than an astonishing *tour de force*.

Nothing is more effective than Green's avoidance of anything like a major, set-piece confrontation either between people or issues. Much appears understated, almost desultory, as we realize that what would once have been important is now peripheral to the boy's need to find some way of coming to terms with the loss of the world that he has known. Green is extraordinarily successful in presenting the mental world of someone who is having to relearn in different terms the physicality of life. On the basis of this novel alone Henry Green stands out as potentially a very fine novelist and one hopes that, had one read it at the time, one would have waited expectantly for his next book.

One would not have had to wait long. Nor would one have been disappointed. His next novel, *Living*, was published in 1929, the first of a series of books with present participle titles which imply the capturing of a continuing process. The opening with its strikingly abbreviated form, marked particularly by the omission of articles, suggests an unformed element in the life shown, its immediacy, what might almost be called its gawkiness.

> Bridesley, Birmingham.
> Two o'clock. Thousands came back from dinner along streets.
> 'What we want is go, push,' said works manager to son of Mr. Dupret. 'What I say to them is – let's get on with it, let's get the stuff out.'
> Thousands came back to factories they worked in from their dinners.
> 'I'm always at them but they know me. They know I'm a father and mother to them. If they're in trouble they've but to come to me. And they turn out beautiful work, beautiful work. I'd do anything for 'em and they know it.'
> Noises of lathes working began again in this factory.

The social milieu of *Living* is very different from that of *Blindness*; though the owner of the factory and his family are ultimately responsible for the fate of many of their employees, it is the workmen and their families who take up most of our time and concern. Green certainly provokes reflections about the power of ownership and the powerlessness of labour, but we are more aware of the accidental and the random. Old Mr Dupret is dying and his son takes charge of the family engineering factory, provoked by the sense that the family does not take him seriously as an industrialist and by lack of success in his pursuit of a young woman. His interference sets fears and jealousies going among people who are already worried about the slump. The fragmented structure of the novel, composed of short sections, often of seemingly unedited dialogue, serves well to show the resulting incomprehension, rumour, resentment, and backbiting. Dupret has no conception of the lives of the people whom he employs nor of the managers who intrigue to win favour; the workers are busy with their own concerns and usually misunderstand the causes of what happen to them.

The group upon whom our attention is most fixed consists of Mr Craigan, an old widower who has worked in the factory all his life, and three people who lodge in his house: Lily Gates, to whom he is devoted, her father who sponges on him, and Jim Dale, who wants to marry Lily. She finds Jim dull, falls in love with Bert Jones, who also works at the factory, and plans to run away with him to Canada, where life will be less drab and prospects brighter. The progress of this elopement, which is in fact a slow winding-down, is as close as the book gets to a central, sustained happening. They go first to Liverpool to seek Bert's family; but he has not been in touch with them for a long time and his vague hope of finding them evaporates as it proves that they have moved. The two are left with their plans falling apart, alienated by the strangeness of the city and the people in it (for Liverpool is for them as alien from Birmingham as China would be for the Duprets). Bert is not a villain, no seducer, but he is weak and not very intelligent and he suddenly runs away in the street, feeling that everything has collapsed and he can do no good and that he had better leave Lily to go back home. We realize that this grotesque anticlimax probably is all for the best, Lily does return and the book ends with her keeping house again for Craigan, her spirits lifting.

The elopement section is typical of the whole novel in an apparent arbitrariness which persuades us that people cannot predict what their feelings will be. Each moment is new. We have much less of a sense in Green's novels than elsewhere of a writer constructing a series of happenings which are directed towards some end. There is a great sense of accident, of openness to surprise of mood, with a consequent effect of precariousness. It is for this reason, I think, that we are able to believe in Lily's opening out to happiness at the end of the book, her feeling that life is flowing in her again after the intense shame and depression of her return. We believe in her mood, but we also know that it is the feeling of that moment and it is set against Craigan's realization that he is trapped with Lily's sponging father because he is besotted with paternal love for her and that, sacked because of his age, he will never work again.

>Mr Craigan lay in bed in his house. He thought in
>mind. He thought in mind how he had gone to work
>when he was 8. He had worked on till no-one would give
>him work. He thought what had he got out of 57 years'
>work. Nothing. He thought of Lily. He thought what was
>there now for him? Nothing, nothing. He lay.

None of the characters in this book is in any way out of the ordinary. This is, indeed, true of all Green's novels. Most of them are in
fact ordinary to the point of banality. In *Party Going*, at least, his aim
almost seems to demonstrate the interesting opaqueness of people by
setting up an experiment with the simplest possible organisms, moved
almost entirely by socially conditioned reflexes. They do not normally
reflect upon their lives (Craigan's reflections on old age are unusual),
Green does not draw conclusions or generalize, the books are not
constructed so as to lead to any obvious moment of revelation. What
we are left with is a sense of a number of sharply realized moments
which are none the less significant for being arbitrary. Lily Briscoe in
To the Lighthouse reflects on getting hold of a memory 'that very jar
on the nerves, the thing itself before it has been made anything'.[4]
Green seems to me to succeed remarkably in giving us this sense of
direct uninterpreted experience.

Paradoxically his most artful device – his use of elaborate and
repeated images and apparently symbolic objects – which might seem
to offer an interpretation and connect disparate experiences, in reality
only reinforces the specific and the arbitrary.

We naturally seek to connect episodes in a novel composed of a
large number of short sections and if we cannot connect them in terms
of sequential plot we seek a thematic or symbolic relevance. Green
often tempts us to do this. Craigan's neighbour is Mrs Eames who has
one baby and is pregnant with another; she is frequently playing with
her baby, enjoying the sight of flowers, and looking out of the window
at birds. Early in the novel she frees a bird trapped in a window that
men are unable to rescue. At the very end of the book Lily and Mrs
Eames are seen making a fuss of the new baby while pigeons fly round.
The temptation here is to transform Mrs Eames into a dove-
accompanied mother figure, comforter of Lily. But Green, though he
raises this possibility, makes its achievement impossible. The specific
refuses to be generalized; Mrs Eames remains a woman who loves her
children, likes flowers, likes watching pigeons, gets to know Lily; if
this is to be a mother figure, we feel like saying, then so be it, but it
is not worth saying. The book dismantles the symbol which it may
seem to create.

The pigeons which figure so largely in the book illustrate this unusual trait most thoroughly. Green seems to be fascinated by pigeons and he makes metaphorical use of them on a number of occasions. At the end of Chapter 20 Craigan's love of Lily is related to the bird:

> As pigeon never fly far from house which provides for them (except when they are taken off then they fly back there), as they might be tied by piece of string to that house, so Mr Craigan's eyes did not leave off from Lily where she went.

A little later, as Lily is recovering from the abortive elopement, her feelings, too, are expressed thus:

> Sitting at the window-sill of her grandad's window she overlooked Birmingham and the sky over it. This was filled with pigeon flocks. Thousands of pigeon wavered there in the sky, and that baby's raucous cry would come to her now and again. So day after day and slowly her feelings began to waver too and make expeditions away from herself, though like on a string. And disturbed her hands at sewing.[5]

But the local metaphorical usage does not transform the pigeons into general emblems of human feelings or relationships; if we try to think of them as such the effect would quickly become ludicrous because we have too marked a sense of them as specific birds. The effect is far more to assert that the Birmingham sky of the novel (and doubtless the Birmingham sky of reality) is full of pigeons proclaiming by their circlings and gatherings that whatever the circumstances men and women will have hobbies, including keeping pigeons, that these will from time to time appear beautiful and that sometimes people will look at them and attach feelings to them. Presented as potentially symbolic creatures, they remain real birds, tributes to the tangential.

As, indeed, does the pigeon which appears at the beginning of Green's next novel, *Party Going* (1939). This short novel is an account of how three young men and eight young women, all very rich, very spoilt, and very unaware, are caught by fog on their way to the Continent and take refuge in the station hotel. They have to pass the time and they do it as best as they can. In *Living* Green is fascinated by the minute shifts of position and tactical manœuvres in the conversation of rather simple and inarticulate people; few writers can so well convey the concealed agendas of the banal. In *Party Going* such manœuvring for position plays an even larger part, but whereas the issues of *Living* are often important the characters in *Party Going* are moved entirely by the trivial. They gossip, they flirt, they pretend to know the man who is paying for the trip better than they really do, they recognize this and snub the one who is trying. One of the women in the party sums up her own reflections when confronted by a richer and more dazzling social beauty, and this also sums up, I think, much of what Green wants us to notice:

> If people vary at all then it can only be in the
> impressions they leave on others' minds, and if their turns
> of phrases are similar and if their rooms are done up by
> the same firm and, when they are women, if they go to
> the same shops, what is it makes them different, Evelyna
> asked herself and then gave the answer: money.

Meanwhile, Miss Fellows, the elderly aunt of one of them, who has come to see them off, is startled by the fall of a pigeon, which has collided in the fog with the building. She takes the dead pigeon to the underground cloakroom, washes it, procures brown paper and string, and makes it into a parcel. Then, feeling ill, she drinks a glass of whisky and soon collapses. She is carried to the hotel and lies in one of the rooms, wrongly thought by some to be drunk and by others, perhaps correctly, to be dying. When the message comes that the boring wait is over and the party can go down in the hotel lift and be ushered to their train she has regained consciousness and her niece can, without too much trouble, be persuaded that she need not stay behind to look after her.

As usual in Green's work we can if we wish extract a pattern, construct a symbolic scheme around the pigeon; why else is it there? It is, like Miss Fellows, an embarrassing encumbrance. She has not put away the idea of death as the others strive to. With total lack of consideration they send their servants around the station to do little jobs for them; she washes her own dead pigeon. But here, as in *Living*, the actual effect is to turn any metaphorical system on its head. The pigeon remains irreducibly a dead and washed pigeon in a brown paper parcel, inconvenient and a bit of a puzzle, like Miss Fellows herself.

The novel has a number of hints which provoke wider speculations beyond the claustrophobic world of the little group, but they remain hints. As the crowd on the platforms grows thicker an anonymous voice says 'what targets for a bomb'. It is hard to shrug this off in a novel published in 1939. A somewhat similar menace is created as the party looks down from its privileged rooms high up in the hotel at the packed crowd and one of the girls thinks that they are breaking in. There is plenty of scope for social and political implications but we are more aware, I think, of the girl as only playing at being frightened. That in itself is perhaps a political point but we are not invited to dwell on it. Green gives the impression of great neutrality; his way of relating his characters to their society is to set them apart in their shelter, absorbed in an intensely conscious, if superficial, series of social games, and to set cutting across this arbitrary objects and happenings which they must ignore or evade.[6]

This puzzling effect of extraordinary vividness of presentation combined with an elusiveness which comes from presenting the reader with the possibility of interpretation in terms of symbols and structural metaphors while making him feel that such an interpretation would be crude remained with Green for the rest of his writing. He has been discussed as a fine portrayer of proletarian life in *Living*, of life below stairs in *Loving* (1945), of life in a fire-station in *Caught* (1943), and an equally assured observer of the rich in *Party Going* and his last two novels, *Nothing* (1950) and *Doting* (1952). But, vivid though they are, his books cannot simply be thought of as realistic portrayals of a wide range of milieux. He has been considered as a symbolist and I have suggested why this, though tempting, seems to me almost the opposite of the truth. He has been claimed as a forerunner of such *nouveaux romanciers* as Alain Robbe-Grillet. There have also been attempts to turn him into an auto-destructive fabulator. None of these labels quite fits and it seems arguable that this elusiveness is related to what is perhaps the most important puzzle about his work. Why, though he has written in successive novels about a wide range of social environments and types of personality, has he always chosen in each novel to restrict his range and to produce consciously minor masterpieces. His last two novels, in particular, show most clearly this deliberate restriction. He seems to me to have been the best placed in experience and the most gifted of all the novelists of his generation to produce a major novel to stand beside those of the great fiction writers of the first three decades of this century, but he chose never to attempt to write such a book. It is not to underrate his nine novels to feel that there is more there than ever came out.

Notes

1. There are, of course, other consequences of the educational system. It fixed in the minds of men a sense of the normality of female absence. Waugh's characters may flirt with, seduce, or fall in love with women, but they do not

often make friends with them. One consequence of this abnormal adolescent situation was surely the remarkably high incidence of homosexuality in the literary élite.

2. Christopher Sykes, *Evelyn Waugh* (Harmondsworth, 1975), p. 127.

3. See, for example, Robert Liddell, *The Novels of I. Compton-Burnett* (1955) and Charles Burkhart, *I. Compton-Burnett* (1965).

4. I discuss this in Chapter 8.

5. Mr Craigan is not, in fact, Lily's grandfather, but it is how she thinks of him. Part of the understated complexity of the book is that Joe Gates, her father, has pointed out to Craigan that a widower cannot live with a young woman without scandal, so that he, Joe, can go on sponging on Craigan. Lily has no idea how far the affection which she takes for granted has trapped Craigan.

6. It is very hard to think about these novels without using phrases such as 'Green gives the impression . . .'. The technique of the books is rigorously objective and only occasionally does the author comment, but the frequently puzzling surface provokes speculation about his intention. This is an interesting example of how the reader may be more aware of an ostensibly reticent authorial personal than of an apparently intrusive and commenting one.

CHRONOLOGY

DATE	WORKS OF FICTION	OTHER WORKS	CULTURAL AND SCIENTIFIC EVENTS	HISTORICAL EVENTS
1890	Henry James *The Tragic Muse*	Francis Thompson *The Hound of Heaven* J. G. Frazer *The Golden Bough* (–1915)	Artists at work (with ages) Cézanne (51) Monet (50) Renoir (49) Gauguin (42)	Fall of Parnell Cecil Rhodes becomes President of Cape Colony
1891	Thomas Hardy *Tess of the d'Urbervilles* George Gissing *New Grub Street* Rudyard Kipling *Life's Handicap* Oscar Wilde *The Picture of Dorian Gray*	William Morris *News from Nowhere*	Mahler's first symphony	Renewal of Triple Alliance of Germany, Austria, and Italy Trans-Siberian railway begun
1892	A. Conan Doyle *The Adventures of Sherlock Holmes* James *The Lesson of the Master* Israel Zangwill *Children of the Ghetto*	Kipling *Barrack Room Ballads* W. B. Yeats *The Countess Cathleen*		Gladstone forms government

1893	Kipling *Many Inventions* Gissing *The Odd Women* Mark Rutherford *Catherine Furze*	F. H. Bradley *Appearance and Reality*	Dvořák's symphony 'From the New World'	Franco–Russian Alliance
1894	Conan Doyle *The Memoirs of Sherlock Holmes* Anthony Hope *The Prisoner of Zenda* George Moore *Esther Waters*	G. B. Shaw *Arms and the Man* Kipling *The Jungle Book*	Sibelius: 'Finlandia'	Dreyfus trial
1895	Joseph Conrad *Almayer's Folly* H. G. Wells *The Time Machine*	Yeats *Poems* Lord Acton *A Lecture on the Study of History* A. W. Pinero *The Second Mrs Tanqueray* A. F. Mummery *My Climbs in the Alps and Caucasus*	First Promenade Concert in London Röntgen discovers X-rays Richard Strauss: 'Till Eulenspiegel' Invention of cinematograph	Conservative government under Lord Salisbury Jameson Raid

DATE	WORKS OF FICTION	OTHER WORKS	CULTURAL AND SCIENTIFIC EVENTS	HISTORICAL EVENTS
1896	Hardy *Jude the Obscure* Wells *The Island of Dr Moreau* Conrad *An Outcast of the Islands* Arthur Morrison *A Child of the Jago*	A. E. Housman *A Shropshire Lad* Edward Carpenter *Love's Coming of Age*	Puccini: 'La Bohème'	Gladstone's speech against Turkish massacres of Armenians
1897	James *The Spoils of Poynton* *What Maisie Knew* Kipling *Captains Courageous*	Stanley and Beatrice Webb *Industrial Democracy* Yeats *The Secret Rose*	Tate Gallery opens	Klondike gold rush The Diamond Jubilee
1898	Wells *The War of the Worlds* Kipling *The Day's Work* Conrad *The Nigger of the Narcissus* *Tales of Unrest* Arnold Bennett *A Man from the North*	Hardy *Wessex Poems* Wilde *The Ballad of Reading Gaol* George Saintsbury *A Short History of English Literature*	Curies discover radium	German naval expansion begins US war against Spain

1899	James *The Awkward Age* Kipling *Stalky and Co.* Somerville and Ross *Some Experiences of an Irish RM*	Wilde *The Importance of Being Earnest* Yeats *The Wind Among the Reeds*	Rutherford discovers alpha and beta rays Elgar's 'Enigma Variations'	Dreyfus pardoned Boer War begins
1900	Conrad *Lord Jim* Wells *Love and Mr Lewisham*	Sigmund Freud *The Interpretation of Dreams* Arthur Quiller-Couch (ed.) *The Oxford Book of English Verse*	Planck announces quantum theory Arthur Evans begins his excavations of Minoan civilization Picasso (born 1881) active	Relief of Ladysmith and Mafeking
1901	Kipling *Kim*		Marconi's first transatlantic radio message	Death of Queen Victoria; Edward VII succeeds
1902	Conan Doyle *The Hound of the Baskervilles* Conrad *Youth and other Stories* *Typhoon* James *The Wings of the Dove* Bennett *Anna of the Five Towns* *The Grand Babylon Hotel*	William James *The Varieties of Religious Experience* Hardy *Poems of the Past and Present* Kipling *Just So Stories* J. A. Hobson *Imperialism*	Debussy: 'Pelléas et Mélisande'	End of Boer War

DATE	WORKS OF FICTION	OTHER WORKS	CULTURAL AND SCIENTIFIC EVENTS	HISTORICAL EVENTS
1903	James *The Ambassadors* Samuel Butler *The Way of All Flesh* (posth.) Erskine Childers *The Riddle of the Sands*	G. E. Moore *Principia Ethica* Shaw *Man and Superman* Hardy *The Dynasts* (1903–8) Kipling *The Five Nations*	Wright brothers fly	Bolsheviks under Lenin split from Russian Social Democratic Party
1904	Conrad *Nostromo* James *The Golden Bowl* F. W. Rolfe ('Baron Corvo') *Hadrian the Seventh* Kipling *Traffics and Discoveries* Bennett *Teresa of Watling Street* G. K. Chesterton *The Napoleon of Notting Hill*	J. M. Barrie *Peter Pan* Leslie Stephen *English Literature and Society in the 18th Century* Max Weber *The Protestant Ethic and the Spirit of Capitalism*	Janáček: 'Jenufa'	Russo-Japanese War begins

1905	Conan Doyle *The Return of Sherlock Holmes* Wells *Kipps* Bennett *Tales of the Five Towns* E. M. Forster *Where Angels Fear to Tread*	Havelock Ellis *Studies in the Psychology of Sex* (–1928) J. M. Synge *Riders to the Sea*	Einstein propounds the Special Theory of Relativity	Japanese defeat Russians Revolution in Russia leads to concessions by Tsar Sinn Fein founded
1906	John Galsworthy *The Man of Property* Bennett *Whom God Hath Joined*	Kipling *Puck of Pook's Hill* Conrad *The Mirror of the Sea* C. M. Doughty *The Dawn in Britain*		Liberal government with big majority HMS *Dreadnought* launched San Francisco earthquake
1907	Conrad *The Secret Agent* Bennett *The Grim Smile of the Five Towns* Forster *The Longest Journey*	Synge *The Playboy of the Western World* Edmund Gosse *Father and Son* Joyce *Chamber Music*	Cubist exhibition in Paris	

DATE	WORKS OF FICTION	OTHER WORKS	CULTURAL AND SCIENTIFIC EVENTS	HISTORICAL EVENTS
1908	Bennett *The Old Wives' Tale* Forster *A Room with a View* Conrad *A Set of Six* Henry Handel Richardson *Maurice Guest* G. K. Chesterton *The Man who was Thursday*	James *Views and Reviews* G. Sorel *Reflections on Violence* Kenneth Grahame *The Wind in the Willows*	Ford's Model T motor car	Asquith becomes Prime Minister with Lloyd George as Chancellor of the Exchequer
1909	Kipling *Actions and Reactions* Wells *Tono Bungay*		Vaughan Williams: 'Fantasia on a Theme of Thomas Tallis'	Institution of old age pensions Constitutional crisis over the Lords' powers Austria annexes Bosnia and Herzegovina

1910	Bennett *Helen with the High Hand* *Clayhanger* Forster *Howards End* Kipling *Rewards and Fairies* H. H. Richardson *The Getting of Wisdom*	Bertrand Russell and A. W. Whitehead *Principia Mathematica* Yeats *The Green Helmet*	Stravinsky: 'The Firebird' Post-Impressionist exhibition in London	Death of Edward VII; succeeded by George V
1911	D. H. Lawrence *The White Peacock* Conrad *Under Western Eyes* Bennett *Hilda Lessways* *The Card* Forster *The Celestial Omnibus and Other Stories*	John Masefield *The Everlasting Mercy* Synge *In Wicklow, West Kerry and Connemara*	Amundsen and Scott reach South Pole	Lloyd George's National Health Insurance Bill (one of many pieces of social legislation of this government) Suffragette activity
1912	Lawrence *The Trespasser* Conrad *Twixt Land and Sea* Bennett *The Matador of the Five Towns* Saki *The Chronicles of Clovis*	Conrad *Some Reminiscences*	Loss of *Titanic* Schönberg: 'Pierrot Lunaire'	Strikes by coal-miners, dockers and transport workers

DATE	WORKS OF FICTION	OTHER WORKS	CULTURAL AND SCIENTIFIC EVENTS	HISTORICAL EVENTS
1913	Lawrence *Sons and Lovers*	Freud *Totem and Taboo*		Balkan Wars
	Conrad *Chance*	Lawrence *Love Poems and Others*		
	Bennett *The Regent*	Marcel Proust *Du Côté de chez Swann*		
	Compton Mackenzie *Sinister Street*			
1914	James Joyce *Dubliners*	Lawrence *The Widowing of Mrs Holroyd*	Opening of Panama Canal	Outbreak of Great War Battles of Mons and the Marne
	Lawrence *The Prussian Officer and Other Stories*	Yeats *Responsibilities*		
	Robert Tressell *The Ragged Trousered Philanthropists* (posth.)	Shaw *Pygmalion*		

1915	John Buchan *The 39 Steps* Conrad *Victory* *Within the Tides* Lawrence *The Rainbow* Virginia Woolf *The Voyage Out* Bennett *These Twain* Dorothy Richardson *Pointed Roofs* Ford Madox Ford (Hueffer) *The Good Soldier*	Einstein announces General Theory of Relativity	Gallipoli campaign Submarine warfare
1916	Joyce *A Portrait of the Artist as a Young Man*	A. Quiller-Couch *On the Art of Writing* Lawrence *Twilight in Italy* Isaac Rosenberg *Moses*	Dublin rebellion (Easter) Battle of the Somme First use of tanks
1917	Kipling *A Diversity of Creatures* H. H. Richardson *The Fortunes of Richard Mahony: Australia Felix* Norman Douglas *South Wind*	T. S. Eliot *Prufrock* Lawrence *Look! We Have Come Through* Yeats *The Wild Swans at Coole*	Russian Revolution US enters war Battle of Ypres Balfour Declaration

DATE	WORKS OF FICTION	OTHER WORKS	CULTURAL AND SCIENTIFIC EVENTS	HISTORICAL EVENTS
1918	Bennett *The Pretty Lady* P. Wyndham Lewis *Tarr*	Lawrence *New Poems* Joyce *Exiles* Rupert Brooke *Collected Poems* (posth.) Lytton Strachey *Eminent Victorians*	Mount Wilson telescope finished	Votes for women over 30 Armistice ends Great War Czechoslovakia independent Poland independent Yugoslavia independent Influenza epidemic
1919	Conrad *The Arrow of Gold* Woolf *Night and Day* Ronald Firbank *Valmouth* Somerset Maugham *The Moon and Sixpence*	J. M. Keynes *The Economic Consequences of the Peace*	Rutherford's fundamental research in physics Gropius founds the Bauhaus	Alcock and Brown's transatlantic flight Continuing civil war in Russia with Allied intervention

1920	Galsworthy *In Chancery*	Wells *Outline of History*	End of Russian Civil War Prohibition instituted in USA Government of Ireland Act (separates Ulster from Eire)
	Lawrence *Women in Love* (NY) *The Lost Girl*	C. G. Jung *Psychological Types*	
	Conrad *The Rescue*	Eliot *The Sacred Wood*	
	Katherine Mansfield *Bliss*	Wilfred Owen *Poems* (posth.)	
	Private 19022 (Frederic Manning) *The Middle Parts of Fortune*	Edward Thomas *Collected Poems* (posth.)	Ravel: 'La Valse' Dada exhibition in Cologne
1921	Lawrence *Women in Love* (British publication)	Lytton Strachey *Queen Victoria*	Beginning of inflation in Germany Peace between Ireland and Great Britain
	Aldous Huxley *Crome Yellow*	Conrad *Notes on Life and Letters*	
	Galsworthy *To Let*	Luigi Pirandello *Six Characters in Search of an Author*	BBC founded Nobel Prize for Physics: Einstein Nobel Prize for Chemistry: Soddy
		Ezra Pound *Poems 1918–1921*	
		Lawrence *Sea and Sardinia*	

DATE	WORKS OF FICTION	OTHER WORKS	CULTURAL AND SCIENTIFIC EVENTS	HISTORICAL EVENTS
1922	Buchan *Huntingtower*	Housman *Last Poems*	Nobel Prize for Chemistry: Niels Bohr	Mussolini forms Fascist government in Italy
	Woolf *Jacob's Room*	Lawrence *Fantasia of the Unconscious*	Insulin first used	Gandhi imprisoned
	Bennett *Mr Prohack* *Lilian*	Eliot *The Waste Land*		Irish Civil War
	Joyce *Ulysses*	L. Wittgenstein *Tractatus Logico-Philosophicus*		
	Lawrence *Aaron's Rod* *England, My England*			
	Mansfield *The Garden Party and Other Stories*			
1923	Lawrence *Kangaroo* *The Ladybird*	Lawrence *Studies in Classic American Literature*		End of Irish Civil War
	Bennett *Riceyman Steps*	Shaw *Back to Methuselah*		
	Conrad *The Rover*	Italo Svevo *The Confessions of Zeno*		
	P. G. Wodehouse *The Inimitable Jeeves*			

1924	Forster *A Passage to India*		Foundation of Imperial Airways	Death of Lenin Ramsay MacDonald forms short first (minority) Labour government
	Lawrence *The Boy in the Bush*		
	Ford Madox Ford *Some Do Not*		
	R. H. Mottram *The Spanish Farm*		
	Woolf *Mr Bennett and Mrs Brown*		
	Noël Coward *The Vortex*		
	Thomas Mann *The Magic Mountain*		
	Sean O'Casey *Juno and the Paycock*		
	Shaw *St Joan*		
	I.A. Richards *Principles of Literary Criticism*		
1925	Lawrence *St Mawr*	Woolf *The Common Reader* (first series)	Baird first displays TV Alban Berg: 'Wozzeck'	
	Woolf *Mrs Dalloway*	Eliot *Poems 1909–25*		
	Huxley *Those Barren Leaves*	A. Hitler *Mein Kampf* (vol. 1)		
	Ford *No More Parades*	A. Gide *Les Faux Monnayeurs*		
	Ivy Compton-Burnett *Pastors and Masters*	Kafka *The Trial* (posth.)		
	H. H. Richardson *The Fortunes of Richard Mahony: The Way Home*	E. Hemingway *In Our Time*		

DATE	WORKS OF FICTION	OTHER WORKS	CULTURAL AND SCIENTIFIC EVENTS	HISTORICAL EVENTS
1926	Bennett *Lord Raingo*	Kafka *The Castle* (posth.)	William Walton: 'Façade'	General strike
	Kipling *Debits and Credits*	T. E. Lawrence *The Seven Pillars of Wisdom*		
	Wells *The World of William Clissold*	A. A. Milne *Winnie the Pooh*		
	Lawrence *The Plumed Serpent*	O'Casey *The Plough and the Stars*		
	Henry Green *Blindness*	Hemingway *The Sun Also Rises (Fiesta)*		
	Ford *A Man Could Stand Up*	R. H. Tawney *Religion and the Rise of Capitalism*		
	Ronald Firbank *Concerning the Eccentricities of Cardinal Pirelli*			

1927	Woolf *To the Lighthouse*	Lindbergh flies Atlantic solo Sound films begin to replace silent films	Financial collapse in Germany Trotsky expelled from Communist Party Execution of Sacco and Vanzetti
	Robert Graves *Poems 1914–26*		
	Forster *Aspects of the Novel*		
	R. Bridges *The Testament of Beauty* (vol. 1)		
	Joyce *Pomes Penyeach*		
	Lawrence *Mornings in Mexico*		
1928	Forster *The Eternal Moment*	Lawrence *Collected Poems*	Fleming discovers penicillin Brecht and Weill: 'The Threepenny Opera'	Votes for women from 21
	Woolf *Orlando*	Yeats *The Tower*		
	Joyce *Anna Livia Plurabelle*		
	Lawrence *The Woman Who Rode Away* *Lady Chatterley's Lover*		
	Huxley *Point Counterpoint*		
	Evelyn Waugh *Decline and Fall*		
	T. F. Powys *Mr Weston's Good Wine*		

DATE	WORKS OF FICTION	OTHER WORKS	CULTURAL AND SCIENTIFIC EVENTS	HISTORICAL EVENTS
1929	Graham Greene *The Man Within*	Graves *Goodbye to All That*		Labour government under MacDonald
	Richard Aldington *Death of a Hero*	Woolf *A Room of One's Own*		Collapse of US Stock Exchange
	Elizabeth Bowen *The Last September*	Lawrence *Pornography and Obscenity*		
	Joyce *Tales Told of Shem and Shaun*	W. Faulkner *The Sound and the Fury*		
	Lawrence *The Escaped Cock*	I. A. Richards *Practical Criticism*		
	Henry Green *Living*	Yeats *The Winding Stair*		
	Compton-Burnett *Brothers and Sisters*			
	H. H. Richardson *The Fortunes of Richard Mahony: Ultima Thule*			
	J. B. Priestley *The Good Companions*			

1930	Bennett *Imperial Palace* Joyce *Haveth Childers Everywhere* Wells *The Autocracy of Mr. Parham* Lawrence *The Virgin and the Gypsy* *Love Among the Haystacks* Waugh *Vile Bodies* Somerset Maugham *Cakes and Ale*	Eliot *Ash Wednesday* W. Empson *Seven Types of Ambiguity* F. R. Leavis *Mass Civilization and Minority Culture*	Right-wing government in Poland Rise of Fascism in Austria
1931	Woolf *The Waves* Compton-Burnett *Men and Wives* Anthony Powell *Afternoon Men*	Invention of the cyclotron Walton: 'Belshazzar's Feast' Jacob Epstein: 'Genesis'	Formation of National Government; split in Labour Party Japan invades China

DATE	WORKS OF FICTION	OTHER WORKS	CULTURAL AND SCIENTIFIC EVENTS	HISTORICAL EVENTS
1932	Lawrence *The Lovely Lady* (posth.) Kipling *Limits and Renewals* G. Greene *Stamboul Train* Joyce Cary *Aissa Saved* Bowen *To the North* Huxley *Brave New World* J. C. Powys *A Glastonbury Romance* Waugh *Black Mischief* Lewis Grassic Gibbon *Sunset Song*	Woolf *The Common Reader* (second series) Eliot *Selected Essays* Faulkner *Light in August* *Scrutiny* founded	Nobel Prize for Physics: Heisenberg	Gandhi arrested and Indian National Congress declared illegal F. D. Roosevelt elected President of USA

1933	Cary *An American Visitor* Compton-Burnett *More Women than Men* Anthony Powell *From a View to a Death* L. G. Gibbon *Cloud Howe* Woolf *Flush* Wells *The Shape of Things to Come* Eliot *The Use of Poetry and the Use of Criticism* Orwell *Down and Out in Paris and London*	Nobel Prize for Physics: Dirac and Schrödinger	Hitler becomes Chancellor of Germany and establishes dictatorship
1934	G. Greene *It's a Battlefield* Waugh *A Handful of Dust* George Orwell *Burmese Days* L. G. Gibbon *Grey Granite* W. H. Auden *Poems* R. Carnap *The Logical Syntax of Language* Dylan Thomas *Eighteen Poems*	Hindemith: 'Mathis der Maler'	Beginning of purges in USSR
1935	G. Greene *England Made Me* Bowen *The House in Paris* Buchan *The House of the Four Winds* Compton-Burnett *A House and its Head* Christopher Isherwood *Mr Norris Changes Trains* Orwell *The Clergyman's Daughter* Eliot *Murder in the Cathedral*	Domagk discovers prontosil, the first sulphonamide	Italy invades Abyssinia Saar incorporated into Germany National Government formed under Baldwin

DATE	WORKS OF FICTION	OTHER WORKS	CULTURAL AND SCIENTIFIC EVENTS	HISTORICAL EVENTS
1936	Cary *The African Witch*	Lawrence *Phoenix* (posth.)	Foundation of Penguin Books	Death of George V: accession of Edward VIII, who abdicates later in the year, and is succeeded by George VI
	Huxley *Eyeless in Gaza*	Forster *Abinger Harvest*		Spanish Civil War begins
	Orwell *Keep the Aspidistra Flying*	Eliot *Collected Poems (1909–1935)*		Proclamation of Rome–Berlin Axis
		Auden *Look, Stranger!*		Germany occupies Rhineland
		A. J. Ayer *Language, Truth and Logic*		Defeat of Abyssinia by Italy
		Dylan Thomas *Twenty-five Poems*		
		J. M. Keynes *The General Theory of Unemployment*		
1937	Woolf *The Years*		Construction of first jet engine	Neville Chamberlain succeeds Baldwin
	Wyndham Lewis *The Revenge for Love*		Picasso: 'Guernica'	Moscow show trials
	Compton-Burnett *Daughters and Sons*			Heavy Chinese defeat by Japanese

1938	G. Greene *Brighton Rock*	Woolf *Three Guineas*	Germany annexes Austria Munich conference accepts German annexation of Sudetenland from Czechoslovakia
	Bowen *The Death of the Heart*	Graves *Collected Poems*	
	Isherwood *Goodbye to Berlin*	Orwell *Homage to Catalonia*	
	Waugh *Scoop*		
	Samuel Beckett *Murphy*		
	Dorothy Richardson *Pilgrimage* (12 vols)		
1939	Eric Ambler *The Mask of Dimitrios*	Dylan Thomas *The Map of Love*	End of Spanish Civil War Outbreak of Second World War Germany and Russia divide Poland
	Cary *Mister Johnson*	Eliot *The Family Reunion*	
	Joyce *Finnegans Wake*	Flora Thompson *Lark Rise*	
	Orwell *Coming up for Air*		
	H. Green *Party Going*		
	Compton-Burnett *A Family and a Fortune*		
	Anthony Powell *What's Become of Waring*		

DATE	WORKS OF FICTION	OTHER WORKS	CULTURAL AND SCIENTIFIC EVENTS	HISTORICAL EVENTS
1940	G. Greene *The Power and the Glory* Cary *Charley is my Darling* C. P. Snow *Strangers and Brothers*	Eliot *East Coker*	Development of penicillin by Florey and colleagues Giant cyclotron built at Berkeley	Russia invades Finland Germany invades Norway Churchill forms National Government British troops evacuated from Dunkirk France capitulates Battle of Britain Assassination of Trotsky

General Bibliographies

Note: Each section is arranged alphabetically. Place of publication is London unless otherwise stated.

(i) Historical and political background

Dangerfield, G.   *The Strange Death of Liberal England* (1936). (Elegant account of the period 1910–14.)

Graves, R. and Hodge, A.   *The Long Weekend: A Social History of Great Britain 1918–1935* (1940). (Entertaining. Robert Graves does not know how to be dull.)

Hynes, S.   *The Edwardian Turn of Mind* (1968).

Lewis, J.   *Women in England, 1870–1950: Sexual Divisions and Social Change* (1984).

Marwick, A.   *Britain in the Century of Total War: War, Peace and Change, 1900–1967* (1968). (Lively radical textbook.)

Pugh, M.   *The Making of Modern British Politics, 1867–1939* (Oxford, 1982). (Detailed and sophisticated.)

Shannon, R.   *The Crisis of Imperialism, 1865–1915* (1974). (Readable account of the late Victorian period.)

Stevenson, J.   *British Society, 1914–45* (1984).

Taylor, A. J. P.   *English History, 1914–45* (Oxford, 1965). (Enjoyable, provocative, sometimes debatable.)

Wiener, M. J.   *English Culture and the Decline of the Industrial Spirit, 1850–1980* (Cambridge, 1981).

(ii) Cultural background

Altick, R. D.   *The English Common Reader: A Social History of the Mass Reading Public, 1800–1900* (1957). (Though dealing mostly with an earlier period, it is invaluable in preventing easy generalizations about the twentieth century.)

Bullock, A. and Stallybrass, O., eds	*The Fontana Dictionary of Modern Thought* (1977). (Entries on men, technical terms, catchwords, etc. Comprehensive on the received wisdom of its time.)
Eliot, T. S.	*Notes Towards the Definition of Culture* (1948). (For good and ill an illuminating exposition of Eliot's high conservative line of argument.)
Gross, J.	*The Rise and Fall of the Man of Letters: Aspects of English Literary Life Since 1800* (1969).
Hoggart, R.	*The Uses of Literacy* (1957). (On popular culture and the mass media.)
Leavis, F. R.	*Mass Civilization and Minority Culture* (Cambridge, 1930). (A book whose title sums up an attitude which has been much adopted.)
Leavis, Q. D.	*Fiction and the Reading Public* (1932). (An early discussion of best sellers and their public.)
Moore, G. E.	*Principia Ethica* (1903). (An attempt to propound a rational theory of ethics; the holy book of the Bloomsbury Group.)
Richards, I. A.	*Principles of Literary Criticism* (1924). (This, together with Richards's 1929 *Practical Criticism* and Empson's 1930 *Seven Types of Ambiguity* changed the face of literary criticism in English.)
Williams, R.	*Culture and Society, 1780–1950* (1958). (Discusses the political and social bases for ideas of culture.)
Wintle, J., ed.	*Makers of Modern Culture* (1981). (Excellent biographical entries for over 500 figures in all fields of cultural activity – literary, scientific, musical, sociological, etc.)

(iii) Studies of fiction in general

Allen, W.	*The English Novel* (1954). (A sound and balanced general survey.)
Allott, M.	*Novelists on the Novel* (1959). (A discussion of fictional technique on the basis of extensive comments by novelists.)
Auerbach, E.	*Mimesis* (trans. by Trask, W., Princeton, 1953). (On the concept of 'realism' at different times; better on general ideas than in criticism of individual writers.)
Booth, W. C.	*The Rhetoric of Fiction* (Chicago, 1961). (Important study which, among other things, asserts the right of the author to tell as well as show.)

Culler, J. *Structuralist Poetics* (1975). (Contains a section on fiction.)

Docherty, T. *Reading (Absent) Character: Towards a Theory of Characterization in Fiction* (1983). (Opposes traditional mimetic view of character. More readable than most comparable works.)

Ford, F. M. *The English Novel from the Earliest Days to the Death of Joseph Conrad* (Philadelphia, 1929). (To be read as much for a sense of Ford Madox Ford's enthusiasm as for its informative value.)

Forster, E. M. *Aspects of the Novel* (1927). (Throws light on Forster's own fiction, but contains other shrewd points.)

Friedman, A. J. and Donley, C. C. *Einstein as Myth and Muse* (Cambridge, 1985). (Discusses what influence Einstein may be thought to have on literature. Bibliography.)

Frye, N. *Anatomy of Criticism* (Princeton, 1957). (An exercise in classifying different kinds of fiction; provocative of much debate.)

Halperin, J., ed. *The Theory of the Novel* (1974). (A collection of essays on such issues as realism, point of view, and authorial intention.)

Hardy, B. *The Appropriate Form* (1964). (Emphasizes the variety of narrative forms and argues against a reductively 'Jamesian' view.)

Harvey, W. J. *Character and the Novel* (1965). (Excellent discussion.)

Hazell, S., ed. *The English Novel: Developments in Criticism Since Henry James* (1978). (In the 'Casebook' series; a useful collection of varied essays.)

Hewitt, D. J. *The Approach to Fiction: Good and Bad Readings of Novels* (1972). (Discusses the different kinds of novels and the need for different critical approaches.)

Hirsch, E. D. *Validity in Interpretation* (1967). (Reaffirms the validity of authorial intention.)

Kermode, J. F. *The Sense of an Ending: Studies in the Theory of Fiction* (New York, 1967). (Short, stimulating.)
Essays on Fiction: 1971–82 (1983). (Engages with structuralist criticism, deconstruction, etc.)

Lodge, D. *Language of Fiction: Essays in Criticism and Verbal Analysis of the English Novel* (1966). (An attempt to reconcile modern linguistic theories with traditional criticism.)

Mack, M. and Gregor, I, eds *Imagined Worlds: Essays on some English Novels and Novelists* (1968). (A very varied collection, covering a wide area; useful essays on Conrad, Lawrence, Joyce, and Waugh.)

Mendilow, A. A. *Time and the Novel* (1952). (An excellent and exhaustive study of the novelist's and the reader's dealing with time.)

O'Connor, F.   *The Lonely Voice: A Study of the Short Story* (1964). (By a distinguished practitioner.)

Shaw, V.   *The Short Story: A Critical Introduction* (1983). (Sensible, modest but firm in its claims for the short story as a significant genre. Deals with wide international variety, but sections on James, Lawrence, Kipling, Mansfield.)

Stevick, P., ed.   *The Theory of the Novel* (New York, 1967). (Anthology of statements from critics and novelists on narrative techniques, character, point of view etc.)

Swinden, P.   *Unofficial Selves: Character in the Novel from Dickens to the Present Day* (1973). (Discusses various conventions within which characters can be conceived; sections on Ford, Bennett, and Lawrence.)

Williams, R.   *The English Novel from Dickens to Lawrence* (1970). (Relates the novel to social changes.)

(iv) General studies of literature, 1890–1940

Bergonzi. B.   *Reading the Thirties: Texts and Contexts* (1978). (Discusses the response of the 'Auden generation' to economic and political crises.)

The Myth of Modernism and Twentieth-Century Literature (1985).

Bradbury, M.   *The Social Context of Modern English Literature* (Oxford, 1971). (Discusses the concept of 'Modernism', the relationship between high and low culture, etc.)

Bradbury, M. and Palmer, D., eds   *Contemporary Criticism* (1970). (Anthology of modern critical theories.)

Donoghue, D.   *The Ordinary Universe: Soundings in Modern Literature* (1968). (Tries to redeem the ordinary from the assumptions of the extreme.)

Ellmann, R. and Feidelson, C., eds   *The Modern Tradition: Backgrounds of Modern Literature* (1965). (A thorough study of such issues as realism and symbolism)

Faulkner, P., ed.   *A Modernist Reader, Modernism in England, 1910–1980* (1986). (A useful collection of proclamations and critical statements. Good bibliography.)

Fussell, P.   *The Great War and Modern Memory* (1975). (A study of how the war has entered not only literature but also mythology and everyday speech.)

Gillie, C.   Movements in English Literature, 1900–1940 (Cambridge, 1975). (A general survey which aims to distinguish patterns.)

Hamilton, I.   *The Little Magazines: A Study of Six Editors* (1976). (On *The Little Review, Poetry, Partisan Review, New Verse, Criterion* and *Horizon*.)

Harrison, J. R.   *The Reactionaries* (1966). (A study of the 'anti-democratic intelligentsia', notably Yeats, Pound, Lewis, Eliot, and Lawrence.)

Holland, N.   *The Dynamics of Literary Response* (1969). (Sophisticated Freudian approach.)

Hough, G.   *Image and Experience: Studies in a Literary Revolution* (1960). (A discussion of the literary 'revolution' which Hough locates in the 1920s; emphasis on its international nature.)

Hynes, S.   *Edwardian Occasions: Essays on English Writing in the Early Twentieth Century* (1972). (A bit of a hotchpotch but readable on various issues. Some discussion of minor figures.)

Kumar, K.   *Utopia and Anti-Utopia in Modern Times* (Oxford, 1986).

Lodge, D., ed.   *Twentieth-Century Literary Criticism* (1972). (On fiction contains a number of important essays and extracts. In general provides a good account of critical discussion up to the mid 1960s.)

Lucas, J., ed.   *The 1930s: A Challenge to Orthodoxy* (1978). (Basically Marxist challenge to received wisdom, with emphasis on working-class writers.)

Trilling, L.   *The Liberal Imagination* (1943.) (A wide range of topics; interesting on influence of Freud on critical thinking.)

Wilson, E.   *Axel's Castle: A Study of the Imaginative Literature of 1870–1930* (New York, 1931). (All later writers on this subject must be indebted to this seminal work.)

Wright, A.   *Literature of Crisis, 1910–22* (1984). (Discusses *Howards End, Heartbreak House, The Waste Land,* and *Women in Love*.)

(v) Studies of fiction, 1890–1940

Alcorn, J.   *The Nature Novel from Hardy to Lawrence* (New York, 1977). (Suggests that Hardy places his novel in the context of a natural world and that this liberating force can be distinguished in later writers.)

Batchelor, J.   *The Edwardian Novelists* (1982). (A discussion of what is shared in the outlook of such varied writers as Conrad, Ford, Wells, Bennett, Galsworthy, and Forster.)

Buckley, J. H.   *Season of Youth: The Bildungsroman from Dickens to Golding* (Cambridge, Mass., 1974). (Sensible and lucid; includes sections on Joyce, Lawrence, Wells, and Hardy.)

Coveney, P.   *The Image of Childhood* (1967). (Originally pub. 1957 as *Poor Monkey: The Child in Literature.* Sections on Joyce, Woolf, and Lawrence.)

Daiches, D.   *The Novel and the Modern World* (Chicago, 1939). (Revised edn 1965. Discusses the social implications of a number of writers.)

Edel, L.   *The Modern Psychological Novel* (New York, 1964). (Short introduction.)

Friedman, M. J.   *Stream of Consciousness: A Study in Literary Method* (New Haven, 1955).

Goonetilleke, D. C. R. A.   *Images of the Raj: South Asia in the Literature of Empire* (1986). (A sober account by a critic who takes a hard look at imperialism.)

Gregor, I. and Nicholas, B.   *The Moral and the Story* (1962). (Discussion of narrative, including sections on Lawrence and Greene.)

Hawthorne, J.   *The British Working-Class Novel in the Twentieth Century* (1984). (Sections on Tressell, Lewis Grassic Gibbon, and Lawrence.)

Howe, I.   *Politics and the Novel* (New York, 1957). (Sections on Conrad and Orwell.)

Humphrey, R.   *Stream of Consciousness in the Modern Novel* (Berkeley, 1954). (Short and accessible.)

Isaacs, J.   *The Assessment of Twentieth-Century Literature* (1951). (Popular account of 'Modernism' in the 1920s.)

Josipovici, J., ed.   *The Modern English Novel: The Reader, The Writer, and the Work* (1976). (Miscellaneous essays, mostly emphasizing novels considered as constructions rather than mimetically.)

Kettle, A.   *An Introduction to the English Novel; vol.II: Henry James to the Present Day* (1953). (Intelligent Marxist interpretations.)

Leavis, F. R. .   *The Great Tradition: George Eliot, Henry James, Joseph Conrad* (1948). (Better on Eliot and James than on Conrad.)

McCormick, J.   *Catastrophe and Imagination: An Interpretation of the Recent English and American Novel* (1957).

Meyers, J.   *Homosexuality and Literature, 1890–1930* (1977). (A study of the prevalence of homosexuality in the writers of this period. Some interesting points, but rather too pedestrian.)

Miller, J. H.   *Fiction and Repetition* (1982). (Wrestles with deconstruction in a discussion of Conrad, Hardy, and Woolf.)

O'Connor, F.   *The Mirror in the Roadway* (1957). (A shrewd study of modern fiction by a practitioner.)

O'Connor, W. V., ed.   *Forms of Modern Fiction* (Minneapolis, 1948). (Includes sections on Joyce, Lawrence, Conrad, and Huxley and Mark Schorer's celebrated essay 'Technique as Discovery'.)

O'Faolain, S.   *The Vanishing Hero* (1956). (Comments by a short-story writer on this topic from Joyce to Waugh.)

Sandison, A.   *The Wheel of Empire* (1967). (Subtitled: 'A study of the imperial idea in some late nineteenth- and early twentieth-century fiction', it deals with Kipling, Conrad, Rider Haggard, and Buchan.)

Savage, D. S.   *The Withered Branch: Six Studies in the Modern Novel* (1950). (An interesting attack by an opponent of the orthodoxy of 'Modernism'.)

Stewart, J. I. M.   *Eight Modern Writers* (1963). (The novelists are Hardy, James, Conrad, Kipling, Joyce, and Lawrence.)

Street, B. V.   *The Savage in Literature: Representations of 'Primitive' Society in English Fiction, 1858–1920* (1975). (A meeting between literary criticism and social anthropology. Most enlightening on the bad writers.)

Stubbs, P.   *Women and Fiction: Feminism and the Novel 1880–1920* (1979). (Discusses the relationship between social reality and the fictional presentation of women.)

Turner, E. S.   *Boys Will Be Boys* (1953). (On penny dreadfuls, comics, etc.)

Usborne, R.   *Clubland Heroes* (1953). On the heroes of the thrillers of the 1930s.)

Van Ghent, D.   *The English Novel: Form and Function* (New York, 1953). (Discusses Conrad, Lawrence, and Joyce.)

Williams, R.   *The Country and the City* (1973). (Dissects the myth of the golden age. Useful on Hardy and Lawrence.)

Winks, R. W., ed.   *Detective Fiction in English, 1840–1979* (1980). (Miscellaneous essays in the series 'Twentieth-Century Views'.)

(vi) Bibliographies

Bateson, F. W. and Meserole, H. T., eds   *A Guide to English and American Literature* (1965; various editions thereafter). (Packed with information about general criticism, author bibliographies, editions, and critical studies. Lively judgements. The concentration obliges the contributors often to mention a critic's name but not the title of his/her book, so that it should be used in parallel with such a volume as the *New Cambridge Bibliography of English Literature*.)

Blamires, H. and others — *A Guide to Twentieth-Century Literature in English* (1983). (Reliable and readable entries on authors and main texts.)

Watson, G., ed. — *The Concise Cambridge Bibliography of English Literature, 600–1950* (Cambridge, 1958; revised 1965). (Too concise to be more than a quick way of checking dates of main works, etc. but useful for that.)

Watson, G., ed. — *The New Cambridge Bibliography of English Literature;* vol. III: *1800–1900* (Cambridge, 1969).

Willison, I. R., ed. — *The New Cambridge Bibliography of English Literature;* vol. IV: *1900–1950* (Cambridge, 1972). (The most complete bibliography covering all aspects of literature, including minor ones. It can be confusingly comprehensive but is indispensable.)

Individual Authors

Notes on biography, major works, and criticism

Each entry is divided into three sections:
(a) *Outline of author's life and literary career.* Dates of novels are normally those of first English volumes.
(b) *Selected biographies, memories and letters.* Place of publication is London unless otherwise stated.
(c) *Selected critical works.* Listed chronologically; place of publication is London unless otherwise stated.

The main works of the important authors in this period are all available in reliable paperback editions – Penguin, Fontana, World's Classics, Everyman, Norton (US), etc. Scholarly editions exist for some works (e.g. the 'Abinger' edition of E. M. Forster, ed. by O. Stallybrass, the Clarendon *Tess of the d'Urbervilles*, ed. by J. Grindle and S. Gatrell) and others are planned. Details of collected editions and, where they existed at the time of publication, scholarly editions can be found in the *New Cambridge Bibliography of English Literature* and the Bateson and Meserole *Guide* (see (vi) on p. 243). The *Cambridge Edition of the Letters and Works of D. H. Lawrence* (general editors J. T. Boulton and Warren Roberts), of which the first volume appeared in 1979, is a rather special case. The editors claim that earlier editions are so corrupt that the new edition is the only authentic text and hence establishes a claim to copyright. The correctness of this may be disputed; in this book I quote from earlier editions.

A series of studies which can be thoroughly recommended is the Critical Heritage, volumes of which deal with most of the writers whom I discuss. These reprint a large selection of contemporary reviews and also summarize the development of the critical debate up to the present. The volumes are, inevitably, of unequal value (in this period the *Conrad* volume by Norman Sherry is very good and the *Kipling* by Roger Lancelyn Green a good deal less satisfactory) but the general level is high and most of the editors are scrupulously fair in their summaries of critical opinions.

BENNETT, (Enoch) Arnold (1867–1931), son of a solicitor, was born at Hanley in the Potteries, one of the Five Towns of his fiction. He left Newcastle under Lyme Middle School at sixteen to work in his father's office, but went to work for a firm of solicitors in London in 1888. In 1893 he became assistant editor of *Woman* and was its editor from 1896 to 1900. His first novel was *A Man from the North* (1898) and in the same year he published *Journalism for Women: A Practical Guide*. Thereafter he produced over forty novels and volumes of stories, some pot-boilers and some masterpieces, an immense amount of journalism and criticism of equally varying quality, and a considerable number of plays. *The Grand Babylon Hotel* (1902), one of the pot-boilers, was followed by his first serious treatment of the inhabitants of the Potteries, *Anna of the Five Towns* (1902). In 1903 he moved to France where he lived in Paris and later in Fontainebleau until 1912. In 1907 he married Marguerite Soulié. During this period he produced a great deal of fiction, including *Teresa of Watling Street* (1904), *Sacred and Profane Love* (1905), *Whom God Hath Joined* (1906), *Buried Alive* (1908), *Helen with the High Hand* (1910), and *The Card* (1911), three significant volumes of short stories, *Tales of the Five Towns* (1905), *The Grim Smile of the Five Towns* (1907), and *The Matador of the Five Towns* (1912), and two of his masterpieces, *The Old Wives' Tale* (1908) and *Clayhanger* (1910). The latter, which contains a good deal of autobiographical material, especially about his relationship with his father, forms part of the trilogy which was completed by *Hilda Lessways* (1911) and *These Twain* (1915). He had a very wide circle of friends both in France and England and generously encouraged many young writers. His literary journalism, unabashedly popular in form – *Literary Taste: How to Form it* (1909) is a typical title – is often shrewd and perceptive. During the Great War he served on various official bodies concerned with propaganda; his non-fictional work of the time reflects this: *Liberty! A Statement of the British Case* (1914) and *Over There: War Scenes on the Western Front* (1915); a novel, *The Pretty Lady* (1918) also draws on his wartime work and experiences. He separated from his wife in 1921 and in 1922 formed an attachment with Dorothy Cheston, by whom he had a daughter in 1926. The novels of the last decade of his life include *Mr Prohack* (1922), *Lord Raingo* (1926), and *Imperial Palace* (1930), in which he gives free rein to his fascination with the organization of large hotels; but by general consent the best work of this period is his study of a miser, *Riceyman Steps* (1923).

Pound, R., *Bennett, A Biography* (1952). (Pound acknowledges much help from Bennett's friends and family, including Dorothy Cheston Bennett. Contains many good photographs.)

Drabble, M., *Bennett* (1974). (Good on the early life.)

Hepburn, J. G., ed., *Letters of Arnold Bennett* (vol. I 1966, vol. II 1968).

Flower, N., ed., *Journals: 1896–1928* (3 vols 1932–33).

Swinnerton, F., ed., *Arnold Bennett: The Journals* (1954). (A selection from the Journals edited by Flower, plus the Journal of 1929. A later edition, 1971, also includes the Florentine Journal from 1910.)

See: Allen, W., *Bennett* (1948).

Hepburn, J. G., *The Art of Arnold Bennett* (Bloomington, Indiana, 1963).

Wain, J., *Bennett* (New York, 1967).

Lucas, J., *Arnold Bennett: A Study of his Fiction* (1974). (A very good general account; it is interesting that as late as 1974 Lucas still sees the need to emphasize that Bennett is a major novelist.)

BOWEN, Elizabeth (1899–1973), born in Dublin of a landowning Irish family; *Bowen's Court* (1942) is a history of her family and of the house which she inherited. She moved to England in 1918 and in 1923 married Alan Charles Cameron and lived thereafter in Oxford and, later, Thame. Her earlier – and by general consent best – novels are usually concerned with the plights of children or young women in complex emotional situations which are not of their own making: *The Hotel* (1927), *The Last September* (1929), *Friends and Relations* (1931), *To the North* (1932), *The House in Paris* (1935), and *The Death of the Heart* (1938). The novelists with whom she has most often been compared are Jane Austen and Henry James. During the Second World War she worked in London for the Ministry of Information and *The Heat of the Day* (1949) is set in wartime London and, dealing with treason, is notably more dramatic than her previous work. Her later novels are *A World of Love* (1955), *The Little Girls* (1964), and *Eva Trout* (1968). She also wrote many short stories, including some on the supernatural; she collected them in several volumes, including *Joining Charles* (1929), *Look at all those Roses* (1941), *The Demon Lover* (1945). These have been gathered together as *The Collected Short Stories of Elizabeth Bowen* (1981).

Glendinning, V., *Elizabeth Bowen: Portrait of a Writer* (1977). (A biography; draws largely on reminiscences of friends and colleagues and on papers.)

See: Heath, W., *Elizabeth Bowen: An Introduction to her Novels* (Madison, 1961).

Austin, A. E., *Elizabeth Bowen* (New York, 1971). (A sound, if unexciting, survey of the novels.)

Lee, H., *Elizabeth Bowen: An Estimation* (1981). (An intelligent discussion of all the fiction.)

BUCHAN, John (1875–1940), the son of a Free Kirk minister, was born at Peebles and educated at Hutcheson's Grammar School, Glasgow, the University of Glasgow, and Brasenose College, Oxford. Studied law, acted as Lord Milner's secretary in South Africa 1901–3, returned to the law but left it to enter publishing. In 1906 married Susan Grosvenor. Published volumes of essays and sundry historical and romantic novels but achieved his first major success with *The Thirty-Nine Steps* (1915), a thriller which was followed by a succession of others, including *Greenmantle* (1916), *Mr Standfast* (1919), *Huntingtower* (1922), *The Three Hostages* (1924), *John Macnab* (1925), and *The Courts of the Morning* (1929) as well as historical novels, *Midwinter* (1923), *Witch Wood* (1927), *The Blanket of the Dark* (1931), biographies, *Montrose* (1928; a revision of an earlier version of 1913), *Sir Walter Scott* (1932), *Oliver Cromwell* (1934), and an autobiography, *Memory Hold-the-Door* (1940). He worked in intelligence and propaganda during the Great War, was elected as Conservative MP for the Scottish Universities in 1927 and was appointed Governor-General of Canada in 1935, becoming Lord Tweedsmuir.

Smith, J. A., *John Buchan: A Biography* (1965). (Sympathetic but sometimes critical. Of particular interest not only about Buchan himself but about the political context of a thoughtful and conscientious imperialist.)

See: Usborne, R., *Clubland Heroes: A Nostalgic Study of Some Recurrent Characters in the Romantic Fiction of Dornford Yates, Buchan and Sapper* (1953). (Entertaining; Buchan suffers somewhat from his companions.)

Himmelfarb, G., 'Buchan: An Untimely Appreciation', *Encounter*, 84 (1960, pp. 46–53). (Shrewd criticism.)

Daniell, D., *The Interpreter's House: A Critical Assessment of the Works of John Buchan* (1975). (Takes his novels very seriously. Not very critical.)

CARY, (Arthur) Joyce (1888–1957), of Anglo-Irish extraction, was educated at Clifton and – after a time studying art in Paris and Edinburgh – Oxford. In 1912 he fought for the Montenegrins against the Turks in the Balkans, an experience described in *Memoir of the Bobotes* (1964 posth.) He joined the Nigerian Political Service in 1913, fought in the Cameroon campaign from 1915 to 1916, was wounded and, while on leave in England married Gertrude Ogilvie, by whom he had four sons. He returned to Nigeria but retired in 1916 and devoted himself thereafter to writing. His first books deal with West Africa: *Aissa Saved* (1932), *An American Visitor* (1933), *The African Witch* (1936), and *Mister Johnson* (1939). As well as several single novels he wrote two trilogies: the first, *Herself Surprised* (1941), *To Be a Pilgrim* (1942), and *The Horse's Mouth* (1944) is concerned largely with art and the nature of the artist; the second, *Prisoner of Grace* (1952), *Except the Lord* (1953) and *Not Honour More* (1955) is centred on politics and religion.

Foster, M., *Cary: A Biography* (1968). (Sound and straightforward; makes use of Cary papers.)

See: Wright, A., *Cary: A Preface to his Novels* (1958). (Useful critical survey.)

Bloom, R., *The Indeterminate World: A Study of the Novels of Cary* (Philadelphia, 1962).

Wolkenfeld, J., *Joyce Cary: The Developing Style* (New York, 1968). (Discusses his differences from other modern novelists and relates technique to subject-matter.)

Echeruo, M., *Cary and the Novel of Africa* (1973). (Discusses the European representation of Africa; of interest far beyond Cary.)

Cook, C., *Joyce Cary: Liberal Principles* (1981). (Claims that his passionate liberalism determines the freedom of his form.)

Adams, H., *Joyce Cary's Trilogies: Pursuit of the Particular Ideal* (1983). (Discusses technique of narration in detail.)

COMPTON-BURNETT, Ivy (1892–1969), was born at Pinner, Middlesex, one of twelve children (by two wives) of a doctor. She was educated at Royal Holloway College and took a degree in classics. Her first novel, *Dolores* (1911), was later regretted by her. In 1919 she began sharing a flat in London with Margaret Jourdain with whom she continued to live until the latter's death in 1951. *Pastors and Masters* (1925) was the first novel in her intensely idiosyncratic style, and this was followed by seventeen others, including *Men and Wives* (1931), *More Women than Men* (1933), *A Family and a Fortune* (1939), *Parents and Children* (1941), *Manservant and Maidservant* (1947), *Mother and Son* (1944), and – her last – *A God and his Gifts* (1963).

She was created a Dame Commander of the Order of the British Empire in 1967.

Sprigge, E., *The Life of Compton-Burnett* (1973). (Shortish and rather desultory.)

Spurling, H., *Ivy When Young: The Early Life of Compton-Burnett* (1974). *Secrets of a Woman's Heart: The Later Life* (1984). (Very full and thoroughly documented; a great deal about her family background.)

  See: Liddell, R., *The Novels of I. Compton-Burnett* (1955). (An early attempt to make clear her particular qualities.)

Baldanza, F., *Ivy Compton-Burnett* (New York, 1964). (A straightforward introduction.)

Burkhart, C., *I. Compton-Burnett* (1965). (Comments on her technique and on her repeated character types.)

Burkhart, C., ed., *The Art of I. Compton-Burnett* (1972). (A miscellaneous collection of essays of varying quality.)

CONRAD, Joseph (1857–1924) born as Józef Teodor Konrad Korzeniowski at Berdiczew in the Polish Ukraine, at that time part of Russia, the son of Apollo and Ewa (née Bobrowska), members of the minor Polish nobility. His father took part in a conspiracy against the Russian rulers and he and his wife were exiled to northern Russia in 1862. Ewa died in 1865 and Apollo was reprieved in 1868, but died in 1869. Thereafter Joseph Conrad was in the charge of his uncle, Tadeusz Bobrowski. He went to Marseilles in 1874 and served in the French merchant marine, but, after a bungled attempt at suicide, shipped in a British vessel and first set foot in England in 1878. In 1886 he acquired his certificate as a master mariner and in the same year took British nationality. During his years at sea, which lasted until 1894, he sailed mostly in Eastern waters, though in 1890 he served in a river steamer on the Congo. His first two novels, *Almayer's Folly* (1895) and *An Outcast of the Islands* (1896), drew on his experience in Eastern seas. He married Jessie George, by whom he had two sons, in 1896. In 1898 he published *The Nigger of the 'Narcissus' – a Tale of the Sea* and a collection of stories mostly about the East, *Tales of Unrest*. In 1899 he wrote 'Heart of Darkness' (published in a volume, *Youth and Other Stories* in 1902, the title story dealing with one of his early voyages) and this was followed by *Lord Jim* (1900). At this time he was seeing a good deal of Ford Madox Ford, with whom he collaborated in *The Inheritors* (1901) and *Romance* (1903). *Nostromo – a Tale of the Seaboard*, a story of revolution in South America, for some details of which he was indebted to another friend, R. B. Cunninghame Graham, appeared in 1904 and this was followed by two other political novels, *The Secret Agent* (1907) and *Under Western Eyes* (1911). At this period of his life he also collected two volumes of short stories, *A Set of Six* (1908) and *'Twixt Land and Sea'* (1912), which contains the highly regarded 'The Secret Sharer', and two volumes of reminiscences, *The Mirror of the Sea* (1906) and *Some Reminiscences* – later retitled *A Personal Record* – (1912). He achieved his first popular success with *Chance* (1913). He visited Poland with his family in 1914 and was caught there by the outbreak of the Great War, but made his way back to England by November 1914. *Within the Tides – Tales* and *Victory* appeared in 1915 and *The Shadow Line*, in which he reverts once more to his early days as ship's captain, in 1917. Throughout this period he was often nearly crippled with rheumatism and his wife, also, suffered badly from a series of operations on her hip. He was also the victim throughout most of his life of depressive states. *The Arrow of Gold* (1919) draws on a highly romanticized version of his time in Marseilles, *The Rescue* (1920) is a novel which he had started in 1896 and abandoned, and *The Rover* (1923) was the last novel. The unfinished *Suspense* came out after his death in 1924.

Baines, J., *Joseph Conrad, a Critical Biography* (1960).
Najder, Z., *Joseph Conrad, A Chronicle* (1983). (This is particularly informative about Conrad's Polish connections.)
Conrad, B., *My Father: Joseph Conrad* (1970).
Conrad, J., *Joseph Conrad: Times Remembered* (1981).
Several miscellaneous volumes of letters have appeared, and the complete letters, ed. by Karl, F. and Davies, L., are being published, the first volume in 1983.

See: Gordan, J. D., *Conrad: The Making of a Novelist* (Cambridge, Mass., 1940). (Includes a detailed study of Conrad's method of writing and revising from the manuscripts, especially of *Lord Jim*.)
Hewitt, D., *Conrad: A Reassessment* (1952). (Shortish general study.)
Moser, T. C., *Conrad: Achievement and Decline* (Cambridge, Mass., 1957). (Discusses the inferiority of later works and relates this to Conrad's inability to deal with sex.)
Guerard, A. J., *Conrad the Novelist* (Cambridge, Mass., 1958). (A lengthy and influential study, influenced by Jungian interpretation.)
Stallman, R. W., ed, *The Art of Joseph Conrad: A Critical Symposium* (East Lansing, 1960).
Hay, E. K., *The Political Novels of Conrad* (Chicago, 1963). (Excellent discussion.)
Sherry, N., *Conrad's Eastern World* (1966). (Relates the works to his early experiences.)
Sherry, N., *Conrad's Western World* (1971). (Deals with the background to his political novels.)
Watt, I., *Conrad in the Nineteenth Century* (1980). (An exhaustive treatment of the early works which relates them to contemporary influences and beliefs.)
O'Hanlon, R., *Joseph Conrad and Charles Darwin: The Influence of Scientific Thought on Conrad's Fiction* (Edinburgh, 1984).

FIRBANK, (Arthur Annesley) Ronald (1886–1926), educated at Uppingham School, by a private tutor, and at Trinity Hall, Cambridge, where he took no degree but was received into the Roman Catholic Church. He was of a delicate constitution, travelled widely, and early acquired a reputation as an aesthete. His highly mannered novels include *Valmouth* (1919), *The Flower Beneath the Foot* (1923), *Prancing Nigger* (1924), and *Concerning the Eccentricities of Cardinal Pirelli* (1926).

Benkovitz, M. J., *Ronald Firbank: A Biography* (1969). (Makes use of family papers and sundry reminiscences.)

See: Brophy, B., *Prancing Novelist* (1973). (Subtitled: 'A Defence of Fiction in the Form of a Critical Biography in Praise of Ronald Firbank'.)
Horder, M., ed., *Ronald Firbank, Memoirs and Critiques* (1977). (Includes personal reminiscences by Wyndham Lewis, Osbert Sitwell, and others.)

FORD, Ford Madox (1873–1939); works before 1923 were signed Ford Madox Hueffer; his full name was Joseph Leopold Ford Hermann Madox Hueffer. His first published work was a fairy story, *The Brown Owl* (1892), illustrated by his grandfather, the pre-Raphaelite painter Ford Madox Brown. He became a Roman Catholic in 1892 and married Elsie Martindale in 1894 (they separated in 1909). He collaborated with Conrad in *The Inheritors* (1901) and *Romance* (1903). He produced a great deal of literary journalism, criticism, memoirs, and over thirty works of fiction; his reputation as a novelist rests upon *The Good Soldier* (1915) and a tetralogy *Parade's End* centring on the Great War (in which he served in the trenches and was gassed) and the break-up of society: *Some Do Not* (1924), *No More Parades* (1925), *A Man Could Stand Up* (1926), and *Last Post* (1928). He founded and edited *The English Review* for fifteen months from December 1908, where he was the first to publish work by D. H. Lawrence, Ezra Pound, and Wyndham Lewis as well as contributions from James, Bennett, Hardy, and Yeats; after the war he lived in France and America where he edited *The Transatlantic Review* in 1924. His last book was *The March of Literature from Confucius to Modern Times* (1938).

MacShane, F., *The Life and Work of Ford Madox Ford* (1965). (Balanced account of his life and career; good on his editorships.)
Mizener, A., *The Saddest Story* (1971). (Lengthy biography, well documented.)
Ludwig, R. M., ed., *Letters* (1965).

See: Cassell, R. A., *Ford Madox Ford: A Study of his Novels* (Baltimore, 1961).
Meixner, J. A., *Ford's Novels* (Minneapolis, 1962). (High claims, but balanced.)
Lid, R. W., *Ford Madox Ford: The Essence of his Art* (Berkeley, 1964).
Green, R., *Ford Madox Ford: Prose and Politics* (1981).
Stang, S. J., ed., *The Presence of Ford Madox Ford* (1981). (A selection of critical comments and also some memoirs.)

FORSTER, Edward Morgan (1879–1970), the son of an architect who died when his son was a few months old, leaving him to be brought up by his mother. He suffered a good deal when he left this sheltered environment first for a prep school and then for Tonbridge School. He went up to King's College, Cambridge in 1897 and the sense of liberation there is reflected in *The Longest Journey* (1907) which also gives an unflattering picture of a public school based on Tonbridge. A legacy from his aunt allowed him to travel in Greece and Italy. He commemorated her and her membership of the evangelical Clapham Sect in *Marianne Thornton 1797–1887* (1956). His first novel, *Where Angels Fear to Tread* (1905), contrasts the narrow snobbery of middle-class England with the liberation of Italy, as does *A Room with a View* (1908). *Howards End* (1910) is a more ambitious novel and he published a volume of short, often fanciful stories *The Celestial Omnibus* (1911). In 1913 and 1914 he wrote *Maurice*, a homosexual love story, which was published posthumously in 1971 and began writing overtly erotic homosexual stories, some of which, together with some later ones, were also published posthumously as *The Life to Come and Other Stories* (1972). From 1915 to 1919 he lived in Alexandria, working for the Red Cross, an experience which found expression in *Alexandria: A History and a Guide* (1922) and a volume of essays, *Pharos and*

Pharillon (1923). He was for a short time literary editor of the Labour newspaper, the *Daily Herald*, and in 1921 he went to India, which he had visited in 1912, as secretary to the Maharajah of the small State of Dewas Senior; his account of this is given in *The Hill of Devi* (1953), but the most important outcome of his Indian experience was the novel, *A Passage to India* (1924). This, apart from a collection of stories, *The Eternal Moment* (1928), was the last fiction published in his lifetime. His Clark lectures at Cambridge were published as *Aspects of the Novel* (1927) and he wrote a biography, *Goldsworthy Lowes Dickinson* (1934), of the don whom he had known at King's, and a very large number of essays, collected in *Abinger Harvest* (1936) and *Two Cheers for Democracy* (1951). In the latter part of his life he worked for many liberal causes. He was President of the Council for Civil Liberties, President of the Humanist Society, witness for the defence in the *Lady Chatterley* trial. He refused a knighthood, was made a Companion of Honour in 1953 and was awarded the OM on his ninetieth birthday. In 1946 he was elected to an Honorary Fellowship at King's College and spent most of his time thereafter in Cambridge, very accessible and very revered.

Furbank, P. N., *E. M. Forster: A Life: The Growth of the Novelist 1879–1914* (1977); *E. M. Forster: A Life: Polycrates' Ring 1914–1970* (1978).

Lago, M. and Furbank, P. N., eds, *Selected Letters, vol. 1 1879–1920* (1983).

See: Macaulay, R., *The Writings of Forster* (1938).

Trilling, L., *Forster, A Study* (Norfolk, Connecticut, 1943, revised ed. 1967). (Perhaps the best general introduction.)

Johnstone, J. K., *The Bloomsbury Group: A Study of Forster, Strachey, Virginia Woolf and their Circle* (1954). (Somewhat pedestrian but informative.)

Beer, J. B., *The Achievement of Forster* (1962). (A sound general account of the works.)

Crews, F. C., *Forster: The Perils of Humanism* (Princeton, 1962). (Emphasizes the Victorian liberal elements in the works and Forster's awareness of their limitations.)

Stone, W., *The Cave and the Mountain: A Study of E. M. Forster* (Stanford, 1966). (Makes claims for Forster as a quasi-mystical writer with a private myth.)

Cavaliero, G., *A Reading of E. M. Forster* (1979). (A sensitively firm account; as good as anything on Forster.)

Das, G. K. and Beer, J., eds, *E. M. Forster: A Human Exploration* (1979). (A collection of centenary essays; varied in quality but worth attention for the sake of May Buckingham's moving account of her and her husband's relationship with Forster.)

GALSWORTHY, John (1897–1933), educated at Harrow and New College, Oxford, called to the Bar in 1890 but practised very little. He published a number of early novels under the pseudonym 'John Sinjohn'. Married Ada, wife of his cousin, in 1905, having been her lover since 1895. *The Man of Property* (1906) was the first novel in the series of novels about the Forsyte family, which finally grew to three trilogies, of which the first, *The Forsyte Saga* (*The Man of Property, In Chancery* (1920), *To Let* (1921) plus two interludes) established his reputation. He was also a prolific dramatist (*The Silver Box* (1906), *Strife* (1909), *The Skin Game* (1920), and

Loyalties (1922) are probably the best known). Nobel Prize for Literature 1932.

> Dupré, C., *John Galsworthy* (1976). (Relates his love-affair with Ada and their marriage to the works, exploring the stresses and strains and the accommodations with convention.)
>
> Marrot, H. V., *The Life and Letters of Galsworthy* (1935).

See: Lawrence, D. H., *Phoenix* (1936). (Lawrence's essay on *The Forsyte Saga* is perhaps as damaging as any criticism can be.)

> Mottram, R. H., *John Galsworthy* (1953). (Introductory pamphlet.)
>
> Holloway, D., *John Galsworthy* (1968).
>
> Fréchet, A. (trans. D. Mahaffey), *John Galsworthy: A Reassessment* (1982). (Claims that his work, determined by his background, has been vastly underrated.)

GIBBON, Lewis Grassic (pseudonym of James Leslie Mitchell, 1901–35), born in Aberdeenshire and brought up on farms in that region. Worked as a local journalist and then as clerk in the Army, 1918–22, and the Royal Air Force, 1923–29. Thereafter he devoted himself to writing, publishing many works on archaeology and exploration and a biography, *Spartacus* (1933) under his own name. His reputation rests on the trilogy *A Scots Quair*, published under his pseudonym – *Sunset Song* (1932), *Cloud Howe* (1933), and *Grey Granite* (1934) in which, with a highly original use of the Scots language of his birthplace, he follows the life of a crofter's daughter from childhood to old age and the impact of war, poverty, and political beliefs.

> Munro, I. S., *Leslie Mitchell: Lewis Grassic Gibbon* (Edinburgh, 1966). (A critical biography which makes use of information from Gibbon's widow and others.)

See: Young, D. F., *Beyond the Sunset: A Study of Gibbon* (1973). (A general study which emphasizes the unity of all his work, fiction and non-fiction. Pays great attention to his quasi-anarchist political views.)

> Campbell, I., *Lewis Grassic Gibbon* (Edinburgh, 1985). (Short introduction in the 'Scottish Writers' Series. Appropriate emphasis on Scottish background.)

GREEN, Henry (pseudonym of Henry Yorke: 1905–73), began his first novel, *Blindness* (1926), while still at school at Eton; it was published when he was at Oxford. He worked in the family business in Birmingham, the scene of *Living* (1929). He married the Hon. Mary Adelaide Biddulph in 1929. In 1939 he published *Party Going* and an interim autobiography, *Pack My Bag*, in 1940. By this time he was a fireman in the Auxiliary Fire Service in London, an organization which figures in *Caught* (1943). After the war he continued his career in industry, becoming the managing director of the family business, while writing *Loving* (1945), *Back* (1946), *Concluding* (1948), *Nothing* (1950), and *Doting* (1952). The last two consist almost·entirely of dialogue, a subject about which he spoke in two broadcast talks in 1950 and 1951, two of the rare occasions when he gave any clues to his enigmatic novels. His description of his favourite activity was 'romancing over a bottle to a good band'.

See: Melchiori, G., *The Tightrope Walkers* (1956). (Chapter on 'The Abstract Art of Henry Green'.)

Hall, J., 'The Fiction of Henry Green: Paradoxes of Pleasure-and-Pain', *Kenyon Review* (Winter 1957).

Stokes, E., *The Novels of Henry Green* (1959). (Emphasizes the representational quality of the works.)

Ryf, R., *Henry Green* (Columbia, 1967). (A pamphlet which pays great attention to symbolic effects but is weakened by unfamiliarity with the English scene.)

Mengham, R., *The Idiom of the Time: The Writings of Henry Green* (1982). (Discusses, in terms of modern critical theory, Green's linguistic devices and makes use of manuscripts and typescripts.)

Swinden, P., *The English Novel of History and Society, 1940–80* (1984). (An excellent account which pays rewarding attention to the effects of Green's stylistic oddities.)

GREENE, Graham (born 1904) was educated at Berkhamstead School, of which his father was headmaster, and Balliol College, Oxford. He worked for *The Times* and as a film critic. In 1926 he entered the Roman Catholic Church and in 1927 married Vivien Dayrell-Browning, by whom he had one son and one daughter. His first novel was *The Man Within* (1929) and this was followed by *The Name of Action* (1930), *Rumour at Nightfall* (1931), and his first success, *Stamboul Train* (1932), which is described on the title page as 'an entertainment'. A number of his succeeding works are so characterized, though the distinction between novel and entertainment is not always clear: *It's a Battlefield* (1934), *England Made Me* (1935), *A Gun for Sale* (1936), *Brighton Rock* (1938). He travelled widely and wrote *Journey Without Maps* (1936) about Liberia and *The Lawless Roads* (1939) about Mexico. *The Power and the Glory* (1940) draws in part on his experiences in Mexico. He served, mostly in West Africa, in the Foreign Office 1941–44. His later novels include *The Ministry of Fear* (1943), *The Heart of the Matter* (1948), *The End of the Affair* (1966), *The Honorary Consul* (1973), and *The Human Factor* (1978). He has also written a number of plays, short stories, essays, and autobiographical works.

See: Allott, K. and Farris, M., *The Art of Graham Greene* (1951). (A discussion of the earlier works which concentrates attention on his reigning idea.)

'O'Donnell, D.' (C. C. O'Brien), *Maria Cross: Imaginative Patterns in a Group of Modern Catholic Writers* (New York, 1952).

Atkins, J. A., *Graham Greene* (1957, revised edn, 1966). (Deals, not sympathetically, with the evidences of his Catholicism.)

Hynes, S., ed., *Greene: A Collection of Critical Essays* (1973). (A very varied collection, including essays by Waugh, Auden, Orwell, Kermode, and Hoggart.)

Kurismootil, K. C. J., *Heaven and Hell on Earth: An Appreciation of Five Novels of Graham Greene* (Chicago, 1982). (A discussion by a Jesuit of the religious nature of the novels.)

HARDY, Thomas (1840–1928), the son of a stonemason, was born near Dorchester and was educated at the school there. Articled, 1856–62, to John Hicks, a Dorchester architect. Worked 1826–67 in London for Arthur Blomfield on church design and restoration. At this time he read widely, began to write poetry, and published a sketch 'How I Built Myself a House' in 1865 in *Chamber's Journal*. He returned to work with Hicks in Dorchester. In 1868 he unsuccessfully submitted a first novel *The Poor Man and the Lady*, but the publisher's reader, Meredith, encouraged him to continue writing. His first published novel, *Desperate Remedies* (1871), was followed by the first 'Wessex' novel, *Under the Greenwood Tree* (1872). With *A Pair of Blue Eyes* (1873) he began for financial reasons the practice of serial publication (often making changes for volume publication), and he continued so with the very successful *Far From the Madding Crowd* (1874). By this time he had abandoned architecture for a career as a novelist; he married Emma Lavinia Gifford in 1874. For the next two decades he produced a succession of novels and volumes of short stories centring on Wessex, including *The Hand of Ethelberta* (1876), *The Return of the Native* (1878), *The Trumpet Major* (1880), *Two on a Tower* (1882), *The Mayor of Casterbridge* (1886), *The Woodlanders* (1887), *Wessex Tales* (1888), *Tess of the d'Urbervilles* (1891), and *Jude the Obscure* (1896). Thereafter, moved partly by hostile reviews and partly perhaps by a sense of having written himself out as a novelist, he devoted himself to writing poetry, though a few stories and a novel written earlier, *The Well-Beloved* (1897), appeared after this decision. He had lived in London from 1878 to 1882 and moved in literary circles, but returned to Dorset and made his last move in 1885 into Max Gate, a house in Dorchester which he designed himself. His first volume of poems was *Wessex Poems and Other Verses* (1898) and this was followed by nine other volumes which include nearly one thousand poems, as well as a vast poetic drama, *The Dynasts: A Drama of the Napoleonic Wars* (3 vols 1903–8). His wife died in 1912 and his mingled grief and guilt for unkindness are superbly displayed in the twenty-one 'Poems of 1912–13' which appeared in the volume *Satires of Circumstance* (1914). He married his secretary, Florence Emily Dugdale, in 1914. He was the recipient of many honours, including the OM in 1910, though he refused a knighthood.

Hardy, F., *The Early Years of Thomas Hardy, 1840–1891* (1928). *The Later Years of Thomas Hardy, 1892–1928* (1930). (Though ostensibly by his second wife these are in fact a selective autobiography dictated to her by Hardy himself.)

Stewart, J. I. M., *Thomas Hardy: A Critical Biography* (1971). (Very much a study of the novelist.)

Gittings, R., *Young Thomas Hardy* (1974). *The Older Hardy* (1978). (Pays particular attention to those aspects of his life which the autobiography omits, especially various love-affairs and Hardy's evasive attitude towards his relatively humble origins.)

Millgate, M., *Thomas Hardy: A Biography* (Oxford, 1982). (Sound and well documented. Recommended.)

Purdy, R. L. and Millgate, M., eds, *The Collected Letters of Thomas Hardy* (Oxford, 1978–). (It is planned to produce seven volumes of the letters.)

See: Brown, D., *Thomas Hardy* (1954). (Short sensible introduction.)

Morrell, R., *Thomas Hardy: The Will and the Way* (Singapore, 1965). (Lively attack on received wisdom of the time; emphasizes Hardy's feeling for freedom and humane affections.)

Millgate, M., *Thomas Hardy: His Career as a Novelist* (1971). (Substantial study with details of publications, etc.)

Williams, M., *Thomas Hardy and Rural England* (1972). (Relates Hardy to the social situation.)

Davie, D., *Thomas Hardy and British Poetry* (1973). (Contrasts Hardy's work with the international Modernist tradition.)

Laird, J. T., *The Shaping of Tess of the d'Urbervilles* (Oxford, 1975). (Study of the evolution of the novel through its various versions.)

Butler, L. St J., ed., *Thomas Hardy After Fifty Years* (1977). (Miscellaneous essays of varying value.)

Sumner, R., *Thomas Hardy: Psychological Novelist* (1981). (Discusses the deep and complex forces at work behind the stories. Interesting and controversial.)

Brady, K., *The Short Stories of Thomas Hardy* (1982). (Considers the unity of the volumes of stories.)

HUXLEY, Aldous Leonard (1894–1963), was the grandson of the great biologist T. H. Huxley and his mother was Matthew Arnold's niece. Educated at Eton and Balliol; an eye disorder made him give up medical studies and he took a degree in English. He married Maria Nys in 1919. After four volumes of verse he published a volume of short stories, *Limbo* (1920), and his first novel *Crome Yellow* (1921) which established his reputation as a witty novelist of ideas. There followed further volumes of stories, *Mortal Coils* (1922), *Little Mexican and other Stories* (1924), *Two or Three Graces* (1926), *Brief Candles* (1930) and novels, *Antic Hay* (1923), *Those Barren Leaves* (1925), *Point Counterpoint* (1928), the dystopia, *Brave New World* (1932), and *Eyeless in Gaza* (1936). He produced further volumes of poetry and collections of essays of which the most notable is *Ends and Means* (1937). In his early work he combined wit with increasingly serious concern for moral and political issues and was prominent as a pacifist. In 1937 he moved to California. His later novels are more obviously sombre, *After Many a Summer* (1939), *Time Must Have a Stop* (1944), *Ape and Essence* (1948), and he became increasingly interested in mystical and quasi-mystical experiences; *The Doors of Perception* (1954) and *Heaven and Hell* (1956) deal with psychedelic experiences caused by hallucinatory drugs. After the death of his wife in 1955 he married Laura Archera in 1956. His *Collected Short Stories* appeared in 1957 and in *Island* (1962) he produced a Utopia of a rather different kind from *Brave New World*.

Bedford, S., *Aldous Huxley* (1974). (A biography in two volumes.)

Smith, G., ed., *Letters of Aldous Huxley* (1969).

Huxley, L. A., *The Timeless Moment* (New York, 1968). (An account of his last years by his second wife).

See: Huxley, J., ed., *Aldous Huxley, 1894–1963: A Memorial Volume* (1965). (A tribute by his brother.)

Watts, H. H., *Aldous Huxley*. (New York, 1969). (A straightforward account of the works.)

Bowering, P., *Aldous Huxley: A Study of the Major Novels* (1969).

Woodcock, G., *Dawn and the Darkest Hour: A Study of Huxley* (1972). (A very engaged study; Woodcock argues that Huxley follows the wrong path in his later works.)

May, K. M., *Aldous Huxley* (1972). (A claim that the novels are more concerned with feeling than is often thought and that Huxley's quest is religious.)

Baker, R. S., *The Dark Historic Page: Social Satire and Historicism in the Novels of Aldous Huxley, 1921–1939* (1982).

JAMES, Henry (1843–1916) was born in New York City, son of Henry James Sr, a Swedenborgian who arranged unconventional educations for his children, and brother of the philosopher William James. He travelled a great deal in Europe as a boy. Studied briefly at Harvard Law School before devoting himself for life to the profession of writing. He lived mostly in Europe from 1872 to 1876 and met many of the leading writers, including Zola, Flaubert, Maupassant, and Turgenev; he settled in London in 1876 where he was an insatiable diner out. In 1896 he moved to Rye, where one of his neighbours was Conrad. He was an immensely productive writer and produced over one hundred short stories and more than thirty novels (of which some might be classified as *contes* while others are very long), several plays (whose lack of success was a grief to him), many essays, books of travel, and reviews. The first novel of note was *Roderick Hudson* (1875), the first volume of short stories, *A Passionate Pilgrim*, appeared in the same year, and they were followed by *The American* (1877) and *The Europeans* (1878). *Daisy Miller* (1879), a short 'Study', established his reputation. Notable among his early novels are *Washington Square* (1881), *The Portrait of a Lady* (1881), *The Bostonians* (1886), and *The Princess Casamassima* (1886). During this period he was writing a very large number of short stories, a fine critical study, *Hawthorne* (1879), *Portraits of Places* (1883) and *A Little Tour of France* (1884) and *The Art of Fiction* (1885). His middle period, in which he turns away from the theme of the conflict between the values of America and those of England which dominate the earlier work, is marked by *The Spoils of Poynton* (1897), *What Maisie Knew* (1897), and *The Awkward Age* (1899). His last three completed novels, *The Wings of the Dove* (1902), *The Ambassadors* (1903), and *The Golden Bowl* (1904), represent for many of his admirers his 'major phase' and certainly show many of the characteristic features of his fiction in their most developed form. He revised his novels between 1907 and 1909 for the collected 'New York' edition, making substantial alterations to some of the earlier ones, and wrote prefaces to them which have been collected as *The Art of the Novel* (edited by R. P. Blackmur, 1935). This, together with his other critical studies, have been extremely influential for later critical thinking. He became a naturalized British subject in 1915 and was awarded the OM one month before his death.

Edel, L., *Henry James: A Biography: The Untried Years 1843–1870* (1953); *The Conquest of London 1870–1883* (1926); *The Middle Years 1884–1894* (1963); *The Treacherous Years 1895–1901* (1969); *The Master 1901–1916* (1972).

Matthiessen, F. O. and Murdock, K. B., eds, *The Notebooks of Henry James* (New York, 1947).

Edel, L., *Henry James: Letters* (There are to be four volumes. So far three have appeared, the first in 1974.)

Lubbock, P., ed., *The Letters of Henry James* (2 vols 1920). (A selection only.)

See: Matthiessen, F. O., *Henry James: The Major Phase* (1944). (Influential study of the last novels.)

Cargill, O., *The Novels of James* (1961). (A general study which makes good use of James's own comments on the works.)

Krook, D., *The Ordeal of Consciousness in Henry James* (Cambridge, 1963). (A detailed study of a number of the major novels.)

Geismar, M., *Henry James and his Cult* (1964). (A polemic against James's restrictions of sensibility and a claim that he converted his weaknesses into assertions of strength.)

Tanner, T., ed., *Henry James: Modern Judgements* (1969). (Miscellaneous essays of varying value.)

Grover, P., *Henry James and the French Novel (A Study in Inspiration* (1973). (A discussion of the influence especially of Flaubert.)
Bradbury, N., *Henry James: The Later Novels* (1979). (Claims *The Golden Bowl* as the culmination of his craft.)
Kappeler, S., *Writing and Reading in Henry James* (1980). (Takes as starting-point the axiom of Barthes that the reader is the proper writer of the text.)

JOYCE, James Augustine Aloysius (1882–1941), born in Dublin, the son of an eloquent and convivial failure and his long-suffering wife. He was educated at Clongowes Wood College, the Jesuit Belvedere College, and University College, Dublin. His first publication was 'Ibsen's New Drama' in *The Fortnightly Review* (1900). He rejected the idea of entering the priesthood and, becoming progressively alienated from Roman Catholicism and nationalist ideas, went to Paris to study medicine. He returned to Ireland when his mother became fatally ill in 1903. In 1904 he published poems in *The Saturday Review* and stories (which later appeared in revised form in *Dubliners*) in *The Irish Homestead*, lived briefly in a Martello tower at Sandycove with Oliver St John Gogarty while teaching at Dalkey, had some success as a singer, and began work on a novel, *Stephen Hero*, which was to be transformed into *A Portrait of the Artist as a Young Man* and of which a surviving fragment was published in 1944. In October 1904 he went abroad with Nora Barnacle, with whom he lived for the rest of his life and whom he married in 1931, and settled in Trieste where he earned his living teaching English. *Chamber Music*, a volume of poems, was published in 1907 and a satirical broadside poem, *Gas from a Burner*, in 1912. *Dubliners* (1914) was only published after great problems with publishers, *A Portrait of the Artist as a Young Man* appeared serially in *The Egoist* in 1914–15 and in volume form in 1916; a play, *Exiles*, was published in 1918 and was first performed in a German translation in Munich in 1919. During the Great War Joyce and his wife with their children, Giorgio and Lucia, were in Zurich; after the war they returned to Trieste but moved in 1920 to Paris. *Ulysses*, on which Joyce had been working since 1914, began to be published serially from 1918 in the American *Little Review* but was halted in the middle of the fourteenth section as the result of a prosecution for obscenity. It appeared in full in Paris in 1922. An unauthorized and mutilated version was published in New York in 1929; since the book had been banned in the USA Joyce had no copyright. A protest was signed by a dazzling collection of writers as varied as Bennett, Eliot, Forster, Lawrence, Mann, Pirandello, Woolf, and Yeats. In 1933 the ban was lifted in the USA and *Ulysses* was published there in 1934. An English edition followed in 1936. A thoroughly revised edition, taking account of scholarly work by H. W. Gabler and others, appeared in 1986. There was a further volume of poems, *Pomes penyeach* (1927), but the main work of the remainder of Joyce's life was *Finnegans Wake* (1939). Sections of this appeared at various times over a decade: *Work in Progress; volume 1*, (1928), *Anna Livia Plurabelle* (1928), *Tales Told of Shem and Shaun* (1929), *Haveth Childers Everywhere* (1930) and *Storiella as she is syung* (1937). Throughout the writing of *Ulysses* and *Finnegans Wake* Joyce suffered from an extremely painful disease of the eye which necessitated a number of operations and he was also distressed by the increasing mental illness of his daughter. Soon after the outbreak of the Second World War he moved with his family to Zurich where he died.

Ellmann, R., *James Joyce* (1959). (A critical biography; a revised edition appeared in 1982.)

Letters of Joyce, vol. I, ed. by S. Gilbert (1957); vols II and III, ed. by R. Ellmann (1966).

Joyce, S., *My Brother's Keeper* (1958). (Joyce's brother Stanislaus is interesting on the early life and relationship with his father.)

See: Gilbert, S., *Joyce's Ulysses* (1930). (Joyce assisted Gilbert in this early work of explanation; it is still one of the best guides.)

Budgen, F., *James Joyce and the Making of Ulysses* (1934; enlarged edn 1972). (Lively and anecdotal account by a friend of Joyce.)

Levin, H., *James Joyce: A Critical Introduction* (1941; revised edn 1960). (Short and persuasive.)

Campbell, J. and Robinson, H. M., *A Skeleton Key to Finnegans Wake* (New York, 1944). (An early exegetical study.)

Kenner, H., *Dublin's Joyce* (1955). (Idiosyncratic discussion of some key issues, especially in *Ulysses*; one of the best critical studies.)

Atherton, J. S., *The Books at the Wake* (1960). (An account of the intertextuality of the novel.)

Goldberg, S., *The Classical Temper: A Study of Joyce's Ulysses* (1961). (A balanced assessment, constantly rising above exegesis to criticism.)

Adams, R. M., *Surface and Symbol: The Consistency of Joyce's Ulysses* (New York, 1962). (Highly entertaining exploration of the implications of some of the puzzles in the novel.)

Goldberg, S. J., *James Joyce* (Edinburgh, 1962). (A good introduction.)

Hart, C., *Structure and Motif in Finnegans Wake* (1962). (An intelligent guide.)

Blamires, H., *The Bloomsday Book* (1966). (An unpretentious but informative introductory guide.)

Tindall, W. Y., *Reader's Guide to Finnegans Wake* (1969). (Like Tindall's 1959 *Reader's Guide to James Joyce* this is stronger on exegesis than criticism.)

Ellmann, R., *Ulysses on the Liffey* (1972). (Reproduces and makes use of the schema which Joyce gave to Linati, which differs in some details from that provided for Gilbert.)

McHugh, R., *The Sigla of Finnegans Wake* (1976). (A discussion of the structure of the novel, making use of Joyce's notebooks.)

Groden, M., *Ulysses in Progress* (Princeton, 1977). (A very important account of the various stages of the writings and rewritings and the critical implications of them.)

Hodgart, M., *James Joyce: A Student's Guide* (1978). (Sound and readable; good on the Irish background.)

MacCabe, C., *James Joyce and the Revolution of the Word* (1979). (A theoretical approach in terms of semiotics, psychoanalysis, and the politics of language.)

Benstock, S. and Benstock, B., *Who's He When He's at Home: A James Joyce Directory* (Urbana, 1980). (Just what it says and very full for the works up to *Ulysses*).

Gabler, H. W., *Ulysses: A Critical and Synoptic Edition* (New York, 1986). (The result of immense labour on editions, manuscripts, etc.)

KIPLING, Rudyard (1865–1936), born in Bombay, son of Lockwood Kipling who was professor in a school of art there. After five happy years he was sent to England where he was made intensely miserable by the couple who looked after him. He deals with this experience in the story 'Baa, Baa, Black Sheep' (1888) and later in his autobiography *Something of Myself* (published posthumously, 1937). Educated at the United Services College, Westward Ho!, about which he wrote in *Stalky and Co.* (1899). In 1882 he returned to India and worked as a journalist first in Lahore on the *Civil and Military Gazette* and then in Allahabad on the *Pioneer*. Most of the poems collected in *Departmental Ditties* (1886) and the short stories in *Plain Tales from the Hills* (1888) were first published in these newspapers. When he came to England in 1889 he was already known as a writer on exotic and imperial themes. His first novel, *The Light That Failed*, appeared in 1890, but his talents were more strikingly displayed in short stories: *Soldiers Three* (1890), *Wee Willie Winkie* (1890), and *Life's Handicap* (1891). In 1892 he married Caroline Balestier, an American from Vermont, and he moved to Brattleboro, Vermont, in 1892 and planned to settle there. To this period belong a volume of stories, *Many Inventions* (1893), *The Jungle Book* (1894), and *The Second Jungle Book* (1895). His life in Vermont was disrupted by a quarrel with his brother-in-law and he returned to England. He had published *Barrack-Room Ballads* in 1892 and a volume of poems, *The Seven Seas*, followed in 1896; there was some talk on the death of Tennyson of making him Poet Laureate but he would probably have refused; later in life he certainly refused offers of titles and the OM. The year 1898 saw the publication of *The Day's Work*, the last volume of stories largely about India. The culmination of his writing about India is marked by *Kim* (1901). A close association with Cecil Rhodes confirmed his belief in the British Empire and in the Boer War he played a public role as propagandist, as can clearly be seen in the stories in *Traffics and Discoveries* (1904). In 1902 he moved to 'Bateman's' in Sussex and that county came to have a particular importance for him as a representation of a continuity with the past. He was awarded the Nobel Prize in 1907. His son was killed in the battle of Loos in 1915. Many of the stories in *A Diversity of Creatures* (1917), *Debits and Credits* (1926), and *Limits and Renewals* (1932) deal with grief, shell-shock and depressive states and suggest little comfort but comradeship and endurance. Kipling died in 1936 and was buried in Westminster Abbey. His pall-bearers included the Prime Minister, an admiral, a general and the Master of a Cambridge College, though by this time he had come in literary circles to seem a representative of an age that was past.

Carrington, Charles, *Rudyard Kipling: His Life and Work* (1955). (The authorized biography and somewhat uncritical.)
Wilson, A., *The Strange Ride of Rudyard Kipling* (1977).
Birkenhead, Earl, *Rudyard Kipling* (1978).

See: Escarpit, R., *Kipling: Servitudes et Grandeurs Impériales* (Paris, 1955).
Tompkins, J. M. S., *The Art of Kipling* (1959).
Rutherford, A., ed., *Kipling's Mind and Art* (1964). (This includes valuable essays by Edmund Wilson, George Orwell, and Lionel Trilling.)
Stewart, J. I. M., *Rudyard Kipling* (1966).
Gross, J., *Rudyard Kipling: The Man, his Work and his World* (1972).
Mason, P., *Kipling: The Glass, the Shadow and the Fire* (1975). (An

interesting account by a writer with an Indian Civil Service background.)

LAWRENCE, David Herbert (1885–1930), was born at Eastwood, Nottinghamshire, the son of a coal-miner. Educated at Nottingham High School; worked briefly as a clerk and then as a pupil teacher in Eastwood and Ilkeston. Two-year teacher training course at University College, Nottingham, 1906–8, followed by schoolteaching in Croydon until 1912. During this period he ended his long love-affair with Jessie Chambers, his mother died, and he had poems and short stories published in the *English Review*; his first novel, *The White Peacock*, appeared in 1911. In 1912 he met Frieda (née von Richthofen), wife of Professor Ernest Weekley, and eloped with her (they married after her divorce in 1914); by this time he had finished writing *The Trespasser* (1912) and *Sons and Lovers* (1913). Thereafter, except for a period during and immediately after the war (when he met and argued with members of the Bloomsbury Group and other intellectual luminaries) he lived abroad. Despite poor health (he suffered for many years from the tuberculosis which eventually killed him) he was immensely energetic, producing many volumes of poetry: *Collected Poems* (2 vols, 1928), *Pansies* (1929); short stories: *The Prussian Officer* (1914), *England, My England* (1922), *The Woman Who Rode Away* (1928); books of travel: *Sea and Sardinia* (1921), *Mornings in Mexico* (1927); plays: *The Widowing of Mrs. Holroyd* (1914), *Touch and Go* (1920); critical and polemical studies: *Fantasia of the Unconscious* (1922), *Studies in Classic American Literature* (1923); and translations: *Mastro-Don Gesualdo* by Giovanni Verga (1923), *The Story of Doctor Manente* by A. F. Grazzini (1929), as well as ten novels. *The Rainbow* (1915) produced his first brush with censorship; it was suppressed after two months and only issued in an unexpurgated form in America in 1924 and in England in 1926; its sequel, *Women in Love*, was privately printed in New York in 1920 (English edition 1921). After the war he lived in Italy where he wrote *The Lost Girl* (1920) and *Aaron's Rod* (1922). A short stay in Australia produced *Kangaroo* (1923). From 1922 to 1925 he lived mainly in New Mexico and *The Plumed Serpent* (1926) is concerned with the revival of the old Mexican religion. *Lady Chatterley's Lover* was published in Florence in 1928; imported copies were seized by the police along with copies of a volume of poems, *Pansies* (1929), and later in the year an exhibition of his paintings was also raided. Though dying, he continued writing energetic polemic, especially concerned with the moral dishonesty of censorship: *Pornography and Obscenity* (1929). A good deal of his work was collected and published posthumously: *Phoenix I* (1936) and *Phoenix II* (1968) and most recently a novel, *Mr. Noon* (1984), an amalgam of two stories, one of which is an autobiographical account of Lawrence's elopement with Frieda.

Moore, H. T., *The Intelligent Heart: The Story of Lawrence* (New York, 1954), revised and enlarged as *The Priest of Love: A Life of D. H. Lawrence* (1976).

Nehls, E., ed., *D. H. Lawrence: A Composite Biography* (3 vols, Madison, 1957–59). (Uses Lawrence's own writings, memoirs of friends, letters, etc.)

E. T. (Jessie Chambers), *Lawrence: A Personal Record* (1935). (An indispensable account of his youth; particularly interesting on his reading. An enlarged version of 1965, edited by J. D. Chambers, contains recollections by other old friends.)

Neville, G. H., *A Memoir of D. H. Lawrence: The Betrayal* (1981). (A record by his closest school friend.)

Boulton, J. T. and others, eds, *The Letters of D. H. Lawrence*. There are to be seven volumes; the first appeared in 1978. (Thorough, scrupulously edited and annotated.)

See: William Tiverton (M. R. Jarrett-Kerr), *Lawrence and Human Existence* (1951). (Tendentious but interesting Catholic interpretation.)

Leavis, F. R., *D. H. Lawrence, Novelist* (1955). (Passionate advocacy of Lawrence as a great life-enhancing novelist.)

Hough, G., *The Dark Sun: A Study of D. H. Lawrence* (1956). (Detailed and balanced discussion of major works and ideas.)

Moynahan, J., *The Deed of Life: The Novels and Tales of D. H. Lawrence* (Princeton, 1963). (Good on themes and patterns of major novels.)

Lerner, L., *The Truth Tellers* (1967). (A very good section on Lawrence which contrasts his best and his worst.)

Clarke, C., *River of Dissolution: D. H. Lawrence and English Romanticism* (1969). (A counterblast to the 'life enhancing' view.)

Niven, A., *D. H. Lawrence: The Novels* (Cambridge, 1978). (A lively general study.)

Worthen, J., *D. H. Lawrence and the Idea of the Novel* (1979). (Interesting on the process of composition of the works.)

MacLeod, S., *Lawrence's Men and Women* (1985). (An intelligent application of psychosexual concepts.)

Black, M., *D. H. Lawrence: The Early Fiction* (1986). (A detailed discussion of the works up to *Sons and Lovers*, paying particular attention to their imagery.)

LEWIS, (Percy) Wyndham (1884–1957) was born on his father's yacht off the coast of the USA, educated at Rugby School and the Slade School of Art. He was a painter, critic, and propagandist for his ideas about art as well as a novelist. For much of his life was at the centre of artistic warfare; with Ezra Pound he edited *Blast*, two numbers of which appeared in 1914 and 1915, and he describes his many battles in his autobiography *Blasting and Bombardiering* (1937). His first novel, *Tarr*, appeared in 1918. *The Lion and the Fox: The Role of the Hero in the Plays of Shakespeare* (1927), *Time and Western Man* (1927), and *Men without Art* (1934) fling out ideas in all directions to more use than some of his other critical works. In 1928 he published the first volume, *The Childermass*, of a proposed sequence, *The Human Age*, and this was continued with *Monstre Gai* and *Malign Fiesta* in 1955. A fourth section of this apocalyptic fantasy was never written. His other novels include *The Apes of God* (1930), *The Revenge for Love* (1937), and *Self Condemned* (1954), which deals in part autobiographically with his time as a lecturer in Canada during the Second World War.

Meyers, J., *The Enemy: A Biography of Wyndham Lewis* (1980). (Informative but uncritical.)

See: Grigson, G., *A Master of Our Time: A Study of Wyndham Lewis* (1951). (A committed defence.)

Kenner, H., *Wyndham Lewis* (1954). (A claim for his central importance.)

Pritchard, W. H., *Wyndham Lewis* (New York, 1968). (A general survey.)

Bridson, D. G., *The Filibuster: A Study of the Political Ideas of Wyndham Lewis* (1972). (Defends, against charges of Fascism, the ideas which caused Lewis to call himself 'a Tory Bolshevik'.)

Meyers, J., *Wyndham Lewis: A Revaluation* (1980). (A collection of essays on widely varied topics.)

MANSFIELD, Katherine (pseudonym of Kathleen Mansfield Beauchamp: 1888–1923), was born in Wellington, New Zealand, and educated there and in London. She settled in London in 1908. She married George Bowden in 1909 but separated from him the same year and lived with John Middleton Murry from 1912 and married him on her divorce in 1918. Her early stories were published in *The New Age* and collected in *In a German Pension* (1911). She began writing stories of New Zealand and this movement was confirmed when her younger brother came to England to enlist in the Army and was killed in an accident in 1915. *Bliss and Other Stories* (1920) and *The Garden Party and Other Stories* (1922) contain the best of her work. She developed tuberculosis and spent her winters in the South of France and Switzerland. After her death Murry collected two volumes of stories, some unfinished: *The Dove's Nest and Other Stories* (1923) and *Something Childish and Other Stories* (1924).

Mantz, R. E. and Murry, J. M., *The Life of Katherine Mansfield* (1933). (The official life by her husband.)

Alpers, A., *Katherine Mansfield: A Biography* (New York, 1953). (Makes a point of dealing with areas of the life which Murry had omitted.)

Murry, J. M., ed., *The Journal of Katherine Mansfield* (1927; enlarged edn. 1954).

Murry, J. M., ed., *The Letters of Katherine Mansfield* (1928; enlarged edn. 1951).

See: Gordon, I. A., *Katherine Mansfield* (1954). (Brief introduction.)

Hormasji, N., *Katherine Mansfield: An Appraisal* (Auckland, 1967).

Hanson, C. and Gurr, A., eds, *Katherine Mansfield* (1981). (Straightforward, fairly elementary introduction.)

Hankin, C. A., *Katherine Mansfield and her Confessional Stories* (1983). (Claims that her stories are in the tradition of the confession and pays attention to unconscious as well as conscious forces.)

Fullbrook, K., *Katherine Mansfield* (Brighton, 1986).

MAUGHAM, William Somerset (1874–1965), born in France, educated King's School, Canterbury, Heidelberg University, and St Thomas's Hospital, London, where he qualified in medicine, though he never practised. *Of Human Bondage* (1915) draws on his early experiences. *Liza of Lambeth* (1897) was his first novel; he gained success as a comic dramatist before the war. He married Syrie Wellcome in 1915 (divorced 1927); during the war he was in Intelligence, which gave him material for the short stories in *Ashenden* (1928). He travelled widely and settled in the South of France. Among his novels are: *The Moon and Sixpence* (1919), *Cakes and Ale* (1930), *The Narrow Corner* (1932), and *The Razor's Edge* (1944).

Cordell, R. A., *Maugham: A Biographical and Critical Study* (Indiana, 1937; revised edn. 1969). (Fairly short and rather pedestrian.)

Morgan, T., *Somerset Maugham* (1980). (Lengthy, readable, does not shrink from the scandalous.)

See: Brophy, J., *Somerset Maugham* (1958). (Introductory pamphlet.)
Brander, L., *Maugham: A Guide* (Edinburgh, 1963).
Raphael, F., *Maugham and his World* (1976). (One of the series which combines a brief biography and commentary on works with a large number of illustrations. Here there are scenes from plays and films as well as background photographs.)

ORWELL, George (pseudonym of Eric Blair, 1903–50), was born in India, the son of an Indian Civil Servant. After school at Eton he joined the Indian Imperial Police in 1922 and served in Burma. He grew to hate imperialism and resigned in 1927. *Down and Out in Paris and London* (1933) is based on his experiences (undertaken to see how the poor live) as a tramp in England and a period of poverty in France. *Burmese Days* (1934), a didactic novel, was followed by *The Clergyman's Daughter* (1935) and *Keep the Aspidistra Flying* (1936) which deals with physically and emotionally impoverished lives. In 1936 he went to the depressed areas of the North of England on behalf of the Left Book Club and recorded his experiences in *The Road to Wigan Pier* (1937), married Eileen O'Shaughnessy on his return to London, and, at the very end of the year, went to Spain and joined the POUM (basically Trotskyist) militia. He was wounded in the throat and was invalided home in 1937 but not before being involved in the struggle between the POUM and the Stalinist Communist forces. *Homage to Catalonia* (1938) deals with his time in Spain and caused great dissension in left-wing circles. He joined the Independent Labour Party in 1938. *Coming Up for Air* (1939) was his last novel before the outbreak of war, in which he worked for the BBC and wrote a great deal of political journalism, notably in *Tribune*, of which he was for some time the literary editor. His critical and political essays have been gathered together in *The Collected Essays, Journalism and Letters* (4 vols, ed. by S. Orwell and I. Angus, 1968). *Animal Farm* (1945) was a great success but by this time the tuberculosis from which he had long suffered made him a very sick man. His wife died in 1945. By the time he finished *Nineteen Eighty-Four* (1949) he was dying. He married Sonia Brownell in hospital three months before his death.

Crick, B., *George Orwell: A Life* (1980).(The authorized biography, drawing on a wide range of documents and recollections.)

See: Atkins, J. A., *Orwell: A Literary Study* (1954).
Lee, R. A., *Orwell's Fiction* (Notre Dame, 1969). (A straightforward study of all the novels.)
Williams, R., *Orwell* (1971). (Short; good discussion of the politics and the internal contradictions.)
Zwerdling, A., *Orwell and the Left* (New Haven, 1974). (Discusses the development of his socialism; emphasizes the continuity of his work.)
Hammond, J. R., *A George Orwell Companion* (1982). (Critically rather elementary but good on the social and political background.)

POWELL, Anthony (b. 1905), of a military family, was educated at Eton and Balliol College, Oxford and before the Second World War worked for a publisher and as a film scriptwriter. In 1934 he married Lady Violet

Pakenham, by whom he had two sons. He published five novels before the war, in which he served first in his father's regiment and then in the Intelligence Corps: *Afternoon Men* (1931), *Venusberg* (1932), *From a View to a Death* (1933), *Agents and Patients* (1936), and *What's Become of Waring* (1939). After the war he edited Aubrey's *Brief Lives* (1949) and published *John Aubrey and His Friends* (1948) and then began a sequence of twelve novels, *A Dance to the Music of Time*, of which the first volume, *A Question of Upbringing*, appeared in 1951 and the last, *Hearing Secret Harmonies*, in 1975. He has also produced a series of four memoirs and further novels.

See: Bergonzi, B., *Anthony Powell* (1962). (Introductory pamphlet.)
        Tucker, J., *The Novels of Powell* (1976). (Contains a section on the early novels.)

POWYS, John Cowper (1872–1963), son of a clergyman and brother of the writers Llewelyn and T. F. Powys, was educated at Sherborne School and Corpus Christi College, Cambridge. He taught in girls' schools and became a free-lance lecturer, having great success in the USA, where he lived for part of each year from 1910 to 1928 and for the whole of the period 1928–1934. He married Margaret Lyon in 1896 and had one son. He first published poetry: *Odes and Other Poems* (1896), *Poems* (1899), and followed these with novels, including *Wood and Stone: A Romance* (1915) and *Ducdame* (1925). He produced numerous volumes of poems, the last being *Lucifer* (1956), many critical and polemical works, including *In Defence of Sensuality* (1930), an *Autobiography* (1934) and some fifteen novels. His reputation rests on three of these: *Wolf Solent* (1929), *A Glastonbury Romance* (1932), and *Weymouth Sands* (New York, 1934; published as *Jobber Skald* in London in 1934).

        Collins, H. P., *John Cowper Powys: Old Earth-Man* (1966).

See: Humfrey, B., ed., *Essays on John Cowper Powys* (Cardiff, 1972).
        Brebner, J. A., *The Demon within: A Study of John Cowper Powys's Novels* (1973).
        Cavaliero, G., *John Cowper Powys: Novelist* (1973). (Enthusiastic but balanced.)

RICHARDSON, Henry Handel (pseudonym of Ethel Florence Richardson 1870–1946) was born, the daughter of a doctor, in Melbourne, Australia. She was educated at the Melbourne Presbyterian Ladies' College, which is the setting of the largely autobiographical *The Getting of Wisdom* (1910). In 1889 she went to Leipzig to study the piano but decided against attempting a career as a concert pianist. She married J. G. Robertson, then a free-lance teacher, in 1895. They lived in Strasbourg, until Robertson's appointment in 1903 to the Professorship of German at London University. Thereafter she lived in England. *Maurice Guest* (1908) is set among music students in Leipzig and her major work, the trilogy *The Fortunes of Richard Mahony* (*Australia Felix*, 1917; *The Way Home*, 1925; *Ultima Thule* 1929) is the tragic story of a doctor and his family in Australia. *The Young Cosima* appeared in 1939 and the autobiographical *Myself When Young* posthumously in 1948.

        Purdie, E. and Roncoroni, O., eds, *Henry Handel Richardson: Some Personal Impressions* (Sydney, 1957). (Contributions from those who knew her from her days in Leipzig until her death.)

See: Palmer, N., *Henry Handel Richardson: A Study* (Sydney, 1950). (A pioneering study by an enthusiastic personal supporter.)

Green, D., *Ulysses Bound* (Canberra, 1973). (A comprehensive study which gives a good deal of biographical information.)

McLeod, K., *Henry Handel Richardson: A Critical Study* (Cambridge, 1985). (Through a discussion of all the works argues convincingly that she should be regarded as a major English novelist.)

RICHARDSON, Dorothy (1873–1957), born at Abingdon, Oxforshire, she became a teacher first in Hanover, an experience on which she drew for her first novel, *Pointed Roofs* (1915), and then in London; she later became secretary to a dentist. She moved in feminist and socialist circles in London, undertook a number of translations and had a love affair with H. G. Wells which is reflected in one of her novels. She married Alan Odle in 1917. Her life's work was a series of thirteen linked novels centred on a character who has many resemblances to the author, in which she makes use of a form of internal monologue. The first twelve novels were collected in 1938 as *Pilgrimage* and the last was added for an edition in 1967. Interest in her work has always centred on the technical method which she developed in isolation from other practitioners of the 'stream of consciousness'.

Rosenberg, J., *Richardson: The Genius They Forgot* (1973). (A critical biography which makes use of letters, recollections, etc. and deals straightforwardly with the novels.)

Fromm, G. G., *Richardson: A Biography* (Urbana, 1977). (Longer and more detailed and making use of more documents.)

See: Friedman, M. J., *Stream of Consciousness: A Study in Literary Method* (New Haven, 1955). (Discusses Richardson's technique by comparison with Virginia Woolf.)

Edel, L., *The Modern Psychological Novel* (New York, 1964). (Interesting on her technical method.)

Staley, T. F., *Richardson* (Boston, 1976). (A sound discussion of the novels.)

SAKI (pseudonym of H. H. Munro, 1870–1916), born in Burma, the son of an officer in the military police; his mother died when he was aged two and he was brought up by maiden aunts in Devonshire and took his revenge on them in many of his witty and cruel stories. After a short period in the Burma Police he became a journalist, acting as foreign correspondent in the Balkans and St Petersburg, and began writing short stories. These were collected in a number of volumes, including *Reginald* (1904), *Reginald in Russia* (1910), *The Chronicles of Clovis* (1912), and *Beasts and Super-Beasts* (1914). *The Unbearable Bassington* (1912) is a novel of the same feline type and *When William Came* (1913) is a story of Britain under German occupation intended as a warning. He joined up in 1914, refused a commission and was killed on the Western Front.

Langguth, A. J., *Saki: A Life of Hector Hugh Munro* (1981). (Informative, not least on those aspects of his life – notably his homosexuality – which his family endeavoured to conceal. Contains six previously uncollected short stories.)

See: Gillen, C. H., *H. H. Munro – Saki* (New York, 1969). (A general study in the Twayne English Authors series.)

WAUGH, Evelyn Arthur St John (1903–66), son of a publisher, was educated at Lancing College and Hertford College, Oxford, and thereafter briefly at Heatherley's Art School. He taught for a short time at two private schools, and in 1928 published *Rossetti: His Life and Works* and his first novel, *Decline and Fall*, and married the Hon. Evelyn Gardner (from whom he was divorced in 1929). A series of novels established his reputation as a comic writer: *Vile Bodies* (1930), *Black Mischief* (1932), *A Handful of Dust* (1934), *Scoop* (1938), *Put Out More Flags* (1942). He became a Roman Catholic in 1930 and in 1936 his first marriage was annulled and in 1937 he married Laura Herbert, by whom he had three sons and three daughters. At this period he also produced a biography, *Edmund Campion* (1935), and a number of travel books from which selections were included in *When the Going Was Good* (1946). He served in the Royal Marines during the Second World War and on a military mission to Yugoslavia. *Brideshead Revisited* (1945) was very successful and was followed by *Scott King's Modern Europe* (1947). *The Loved One* (1948) a satire on American funeral practices, a historical novel about St Helena, the Mother of Constantine the Great, *Helena* (1950), and a remarkably frank fictional account of delusions from which he suffered as a consequence of mixing too much drink and drugs, *The Ordeal of Gilbert Pinfold* (1957). The most substantial works of the latter part of his life are three novels concerned with the war: *Men at Arms* (1952), *Officers and Gentlemen* (1955), and *Unconditional Surrender* (1961), which were revised as a trilogy, *Sword of Honour* (1965).

> Sykes, C., *Evelyn Waugh: A Biography* (1975). (This memoir by a friend is interesting as illustrating the assumptions and prejudices of the circle to which Waugh belonged.)
> Stannard, M., *Evelyn Waugh: The Early Years, 1903–39* (1986). (Makes use of various sources unavailable to Sykes.)

See: Hollis, C., *Waugh* (1954). (An introductory pamphlet.)
Stopp, F. J., *Waugh: Portrait of an Artist* (1958). (Emphasizes the craftsmanship as against the ideas and convictions.)
Bradbury, M., *Evelyn Waugh* (Edinburgh, 1964) (In the Writers and Critics series.)
Davis, R. M., *Evelyn Waugh. Writer* (Norman, Oklahoma, 1981).
Littlewood, I., *The Writings of Evelyn Waugh* (Oxford, 1983). (Discusses the blending of comic and serious in the novels and sees Waugh as in constant battle against modern corruption.)

WELLS, Herbert George (1866–1946), was the son of a shopkeeper who had previously been a gardener and professional cricketer, and a former lady's maid. When his father was injured in 1877 his mother went to work as a housekeeper and young Wells was apprenticed first to a draper, then to a chemist, and then to another draper in Southsea – an experience on which he drew for *Kipps* (1905). He then went to Midhurst Grammar School (whose headmaster had met him earlier and been impressed) from which he won a scholarship to the Normal School of Science (now Imperial College). After a spell of teaching in North Wales he returned to London and took a first-class London external degree in biology. He supported himself by teaching but began scientific journalism. In 1891 he married his cousin Isabel Wells but was soon attracted by one of his students, Amy Catherine Robbins (always known as Jane), and left his wife for her in 1894. He was divorced in 1895, married Jane and started his serious career as a writer (a textbook of biology in 1893 may be passed by) with the publication of *The Time Machine* (1895). This was followed by a succession of works of science fiction, including *The Island of Dr Moreau* (1896), *The Invisible Man* (1897), *The War of the Worlds* (1898), and *The First Men on the Moon* (1901) as well as many short stories. He became friendly with many other writers, Conrad, James, Stephen Crane, and especially Bennett; he began writing novels (as distinct from science fiction) – *Love and Mr Lewisham* (1900), *Kipps* (1905), and also political pamphlets and tracts provoked by the arguments within the Fabian Society, of which he was a member from 1903 to 1908 and where he and Bernard Shaw were frequently opponents. With some exceptions (such as *The History of Mr Polly* (1910)) his novels tend,to become increasingly concerned, frequently didactically, with social problems: *Tono Bungay* (1909), *Ann Veronica* (1909) – the product of one of his frequent love-affairs of which the most significant was with Rebecca West by whom he had a son – *The New Machiavelli* (1911). A lengthy dispute with Henry James about how far fiction can be a pure art and how far it should include 'journalistic' elements culminated in his parody of James in *Boon* (1915) which led to a breach between them. Wells's desire to teach became stronger and stronger and found expression not only in novels – *Mr Britling Sees It Through* (1916), *The World of William Clissold* (1926), *The Bulpington of Blup* (1932) – and the science fiction *The Shape of Things to Come* (1933), but also in *The Outline of History* (1920), *The Work, Wealth and Happiness of Mankind* (1931), and *The Open Conspiracy* (1928) in which he puts forward the idea of a declared conspiracy of superior men and women who alone can put the world right. His productivity remained extraordinary (altogether he published nearly one hundred books) but most of the later works are pamphlets or didactic novels which corresponded to his mixture of optimism that a reasonable mankind could manage things better and pessimism that observed that mankind was not reasonable. He died in 1946.

Brome, V., *H. G. Wells: A Biography* (1951).
Mackenzie, N. and J., *The Time Traveller: The Life of H. G. Wells* (1973).

See: Bergonzi, B., *The Early H. G. Wells: A Study of the Scientific Romances* (1961).
Bloom, R., *Anatomies of Egotism: A Reading of the Last Novels of H. G. Wells* (Lincoln, Nebraska, 1977). (Detailed discussion of some of the last novels which, unlike most critics, Bloom praises highly.)
Haynes, R. D., *H. G. Wells: Discoverer of the Future* (1980). (Discusses the influence on him of science and argues that aesthetic terms are not the only ones in which his books should be discussed.)
Kemp, P., *H. G. Wells and the Culminating Ape: Biological Themes and Imaginative Obsessions* (1982).
Batchelor, J., *H. G. Wells* (1985). (An introductory survey.)

WOOLF, Virginia (1882–1941), daughter of Sir Leslie Stephen, critic, mountaineer, and editor of the *Dictionary of National Biography*, and his second wife, Julia. She was educated at home. Her mother's death in 1895 was followed by the first of the periods of mental disorder which recurred throughout her life. After her father's death in 1904 she moved with her two brothers and her sister Vanessa to a house in Bloomsbury; here, and in another house nearby to which she moved after the death of her brother Toby and the marriage of Vanessa, she was a member of a group of friends, commonly known as the Bloomsbury Group, who met to talk and argue about politics, the arts, philosophy, and morals. The group included, at different times, Lytton Strachey, Clive Bell (her sister's husband), J. M. Keynes, Duncan Grant, and Leonard Woolf, whom she married in 1912. *The Voyage Out* (1915) was published in the middle of one of her attacks of insanity (which usually followed the effort of working on a novel and did not accompany it). In 1917 she and Leonard founded the Hogarth Press, which published, besides other work of distinction, almost all her subsequent books. Her second novel, *Night and Day* (1919), was followed by *Jacob's Room* (1922) in which she first developed her individual narrative technique. She reviewed regularly for the *Times Literary Supplement* and other journals and collected her essays in two volumes of *The Common Reader* (1925 and 1932); other essays, including the well-known *Mr Bennett and Mrs Brown* (1924), appeared as Hogarth Press pamphlets. *Mrs Dalloway* (1925) and *To the Lighthouse* (1927) develop with great success the method first used in *Jacob's Room*, and *The Waves* (1931) takes the dematerialization of plot and character to its furthest development. Her last two novels are *The Years* (1937) and *Between the Acts* (1941, posth.). She also wrote a number of short stories, collected in *Monday or Tuesday* (1921) and (with some omissions and additions) in *A Haunted House* (1943). *Orlando* (1928), a historical fantasy about androgyny, sprang from her love-affair with Vita Sackville-West, *Flush* (1933) is the biography of Elizabeth Barrett Browning's spaniel, *Roger Fry* (1940) is a biography of an old friend. *A Room of One's Own* (1929) reprints two lectures about the position of women in a masculine literary world and *Three Guineas* (1938) deals with women and war. In 1941, having just completed *Between the Acts* and depressed by bombing and fears for her own sanity, she drowned herself.

Bell, Q., *Virginia Woolf, vol. I*: Virginia Stephen (1882–1912; vol. II: Mrs Woolf (1912–41) (1972). (A detailed biography by her nephew, making great use of family recollections and papers.) (In one volume 1982.)

Gordon, L., *Virginia Woolf: A Writer's Life* (1984). (Pays a great deal of attention to the 'hidden' life of the mind and feelings.)

Nicolson, N. and Trautmann, J., eds, *The Flight of the Mind: The Letters of Virginia Woolf* (1975–8).

Bell, A. O., ed., *The Diary of Virginia Woolf* (1977–82).

Woolf, L., ed., *A Writer's Diary* (1953). (A selection from the Diary.)

See: Bennett, J., *Virginia Woolf: Her Art as a Novelist* (1945). (A short, sensible account.)

Johnstone, J. K., *The Bloomsbury Group* (1954).

Brewster, D., *Virginia Woolf* (1963).

McLaurin, A., *Virginia Woolf: The Echoes Enslaved* (1973). (Relates her work to the aesthetics of the Bloomsbury Group and especially to Roger Fry.)

Lee, H., *The Novels of Virginia Woolf* (1977). (A clear and perceptive critical study.)

DiBattista, M., *Virginia Woolf's Major Novels; The Fables of Anon* (Yale, 1980). (A discussion of the implications of her language and narrative method.)

Clements, P. and Grundy, I., eds, *Virginia Woolf: New Critical Essays* (1983).

Zwerdling, A., *Virginia Woolf and the Real World* (Berkeley, 1986). (Emphasizes her response to the social conditions and changes of her time. Closely argued.)

Index

Note: bracketed page-numbers refer to bibliographical entries.